Defy Definitions

Celebrating Extraordinary Journeys of Underrepresented Lives

Defy Definitions

Celebrating Extraordinary Journeys of Underrepresented Lives

Edited by

Dr. Khusi Pattanayak

&

Candice L. Daquin

BLACK EAGLE BOOKS

Dublin, USA | Bhubaneswar, India

 Black Eagle Books
USA address:
7464 Wisdom Lane
Dublin, OH 43016

India address:
E/312, Trident Galaxy, Kalinga Nagar,
Bhubaneswar-751003, Odisha, India

E-mail: info@blackeaglebooks.org
Website: www.blackeaglebooks.org

First International Edition Published by
Black Eagle Books, 2024

DEFY DEFINITIONS
Celebrating Extraordinary Journeys of Underrepresented Lives
Edited by **Dr. Khusi Pattanayak & Candice L. Daquin**

Cover: **Aakriti Kuntal**
Interior Design: Ezy's Publication

ISBN- 978-1-64560-544-7 (Paperback)
Library of Congress Control Number: 2024907650

Printed in the United States of America

Dedicated
to the
Indomitable Spirit

CONTENTS

Prologue

Candice Louisa Daquin

Many of us, including myself, are the epitome of ordinary in so many ways and yet have had some extraordinary experiences based upon being underestimated. Sometimes our lives turn out differently because of underrepresentation or circumstance, far more than we could have even anticipated and that journey is memorable. It helps to see the positive, even in the struggle. Underrepresented lives may not be the staple of our society, but their value is enduring and their legacy impossible to erase.

The first time I acknowledged inequality and cruelty which is often linked to defying anything, I saw kids at school bullied for being a certain ethnicity or skin color, a gypsy, having an accent, wearing an eye patch for a lazy eye, having freckles, glasses, a withered arm, being on the spectrum, a limp, anything. It seemed even from childhood, humans were prone to judgment.

A kid in my class called Patience, came from Africa and was thrown in the deep end without being taught her new language. She was ridiculed for her accent, being tall, dark skinned, and having a lazy eye. She and I were friends because I also wore a patch over my eye and I also was an immigrant and my mother was from Africa. It was much harder for her and I became hyper aware of these inequities from an early age. I didn't like when someone was mistreated, there is never a justifiable reason yet it's so commonplace. Much like bullying. Kids shouldn't grow up in terror because of other kids. Then those kids become adults who bully adults. Think of how many children give up because someone said they couldn't do it? That's a terrible thing to do to a child.

Some people may complain and condemn people of color for demanding equality and say stupid things like "they haven't been in slavery for years so why don't they let it go?" They do the same with other 'minorities' and this is because they cannot put themselves in the position of someone different. When you put yourself in the position of someone else you can empathize with why that person isn't happy with the situation and see from their perspective. Without that we fall into judging others, and defining others when we don't properly understand. Sometimes prejudice is just out of spite, even people who were once immigrants, may not have empathy for new immigrants, because they've forgotten their own struggles.

I am mixed-race (my mother African, my father French), a lesbian and an only-child. I feel I have been different since birth because I always seemed so disparate to my peers. They had mothers at home, I lived with my father. I wore what I wanted to school, which was often a dragon outfit. I don't look mixed-race, I look anglo. I know I have 'white privilege' but in my lifetime I have actually been ostracized from groups that were brown, because I was not visibly brown despite my genes and I have seen a lot of racism towards my mother and cousins with brown skin. I often think the labels we put on each other are the hardest things to live with and if we could stop condemning and pigeon-holing each other we'd do much better. Those labels are how others define us but they are often very wrong.

Those who think racism is easily overcome need to consider the legacy of racism, which includes those of privilege and their access to inherited generational-wealth. Someone who immigrated to a country cannot always provide their kids the same access to equality as someone of privilege and that can make it hard for those kids to succeed. Indirectly this is the result of racism and economic inequity. The same is true for any prejudiced group. In little ways they can be undermined or not given access to the same privilege and this can have a very deleterious impact on their future. Despite this, many people work incredibly hard and overcome immense obstacles to become successful in countries they were not born in. That's without talking about the legacy of worldwide colonization, slavery and controlling populations deemed 'less than.'

For many it is not easy and they are held back by the racist, prejudiced system or from lack of support, and lose many of the opportunities others get. If you do not have economic stability, it is incredibly hard to live a full life, when you are worrying about whether you can pay the bills. If you are judged for the color of your skin or your culture, the cost can be felt throughout generations. It's something so many people experience but we white-wash this reality and focus on those who are 'successful' and judge those who are not. Perhaps we should see that many people who are not conventionally successful have legitimate reasons and not judge them as failures or condemn them for needing support.

Hate toward minorities will never go away. Even the term minority is offensive. Most of us have some minority status and it is not fair to point to one group and assume they have ultimate privilege because they may not. What you see isn't always what is and we should go beneath the surface and not judge based on stereotypes or as a means of controlling another. Someone who is black may genetically be less black than the white person standing next to them. There are many nuances and if we just look at the obvious, we miss a lot so we should be more probing and subtle before jumping to any conclusion. By attempting to define others, we limit their potentiality and our own.

Can we change the way society at large values others? Does it help anyone that we put value on the wrong things? We pay athletes a fortune and many in the media for doing what is relatively not-valuable work, whereas we don't pay nurses, teachers and others who do such valuable work, near enough. Our priorities are misguided and we define success wrongly too. It's all part of being judging and as humans we're really prone to comparison, exclusion and cultural-insensitivity. All judgment does is pigeon-hole people and reduce them. Society judges all of us for something and it's such a waste of time because ultimately why does it matter if we are female, or the color of our skin or whom we love? Why is that even relative or necessary of judgment? How does it help anything or anyone? It doesn't. Because labeling and judging has no value.

For example; the media regularly highlights childless couples fight to conceive. We hear about 'miracle' babies being born to 50+ women and the wonders of science seem ever-progressing to find ways to conceive. What we hear less often, are those women in society who elect to remain childfree. We're more familiar with the moniker, *'childless'* implying a loss in its use of *'less.'* And certainly, such women are perceived as *'less than.'* But a woman who chooses to be childfree; remains an enigma at best. Our society is unaccepting of 'difference' including the decisions we do-or-don't-make. But diversity of all kinds is rampant and it's what leads to innovation and new ways of challenging old norms that no longer work.

Tying a woman's worth to her ability to procreate is at the heart of a patriarchal system that historically controlled women. Just as taking children away from Indigenous populations 'for their own good' was akin to terrorism. Things haven't changed as much as they should. Girls in Iran are currently being poisoned by extremists who do not want them to get an education. Imagine if they said they didn't want to marry and/or have children? For those *'progressive'* cultures, such thinking also exists but not as overtly. Women without children are isolated, asked repeatedly, *'what do you do?'* Considered selfish for putting their needs first, made to work holidays, *'because you don't have a family'* and still considered *'less than,'* including by potential mates.

Do we really respect individual choice? With abortion access dwindling, the move from the 1970s onward to give women choice over their reproductive rights, is closely linked with the subsequent choice to have children. If you are raped and have no abortion access, a child is forced upon you. When working in rape crisis centers I was often told how selfish the women were who elected to abort, *'after all'* others said; *'they could have adopted them out.'* What kind of society thinks forcing a woman to be an incubator for her rapist's child is okay? Economically many women remain in poverty, unable to afford access to healthcare, contraception, terminations or basic childcare. What of their children's futures?

A new generation has decided such inequality will not be their future and fortunately from this advancement in societal equity, immigration, education, LGBTQ, employment-law, women's-rights and disability/ableism rights have become catalysts to engender fairness in how we're all treated. The crux is choice. Choice to be who you are, if you are not hurting anyone else. Choice means autonomy and not needing to apologize for not doing what your parents did. These relative experiences vary greatly from country-to-country: Growing up in India versus France you're going to see a significant difference. Let's not divide ourselves further out of outrage but come together more and halt our human tendency to divide and conquer.

We began this anthology with one idea (examining how child-free women defy definition) and it naturally expanded to inclusiveness, considering the question on a world stage; how do you defy definition in your life? What have you done that you are proud of that defies the ordinary labels you'd usually be given? Aside from stories of women defying the traditional role of being a mother, we've included stories of individuals who are testament to change, acceptance, and overcoming barriers, in a celebration of these extraordinary lives of underrepresented people. Furthermore, the stories we present here are varied, a rich tapestry of experiences and overcoming obstacles or expectations. They teach us much about the diversity of the world, its nuances and differences, which we embrace and learn from. We are more for knowing more not just about our own culture(s) but others, of whom we are unfamiliar. It is not possible to grow unless you consider outside of yourself. You can only do this if you are willing to hear what others have to say and lay aside any preconceptions.

This collection of writing attests to the strength of individuals to speak their truth, to defy definition through overcoming racism, prejudice, stereotypes, condemnation, and hardship, to be themselves. To be valuable in a world that may judge them for being different or daring not to fit in with the norm. The sooner we realize 'norm' is just a label to control us, and let go of the urge to define people based upon certain criteria, the sooner we'll be free to be the rainbow of diversity and difference we actually are.

A note of thanks to all the contributors of *Defy Definitions* who have written their raw truth. It is only with truth we can be truly free. Reading your submissions has enriched me as a person and I am humbled and incredibly grateful for that opportunity. Many times reading this I broke down, but that is a very good thing because we NEED to see this and not look away.

Thank you to Black Eagle Books for your support and generous belief in this collection. Thank you to Dr. Khusi for this marvelous idea, and the sustained passion behind it. You are an inspiration to me as well as a dear friend and I value you deeply. Dearest Aakriti Kuntal, I have known you for years, and still I am staggered at your endless talent and humility. Long may we be friends. Thank you so much for your stunning artwork for *Defy Definitions*.

I find hopefulness in knowing of people like these brave writers, who possess a third-eye to the truth of the world. Let us all defy definition.

Ann Doyon

*Ann Doyon is a
writer from Regina,
Saskatchewan. She is an accomplished
multi-media artist with a career that has
spanned decades garnering national and
international attention for her powerful
design and intense performing style. Her
design and artwork is in various private
and public collections across Turtle Island.
She lives in a heavily fortified compound
in the wilds of British Columbia where she
works on decolonizing her diet. See her at
anndoyon.com*

How Do You Kill a Culture?

I am the product of the government of Canada's first eugenics experiment which was in place from 1898 to 1954 where generations of Indigenous children were bred from the residential schools in the area to become "good Indians".

The File Hill's colony was developed in 1898 on the

Peepeekisis Reserve by Indian Affairs inspector Graham William Morris. Graham, with Kate Gillespie at the File Hills boarding school and Father Joseph Hugonard at the Qu'Appelle industrial school, they selected the students based on skin tones, intelligence, and adaptability. The colony members were married to others chosen and moved onto the reserve without a thought of the displacement of the original members much less the land base they were dividing up and giving to colony members.

For the Canadian government, the colony was a source of pride to show off how they could tame and train the 'savages.' British royalty and U.S. government officials visited to witness the results of KKKanada's first eugenics program. Newspapers regaled at how Graham could civilize even the most formidable Cree nation.

How do you kill a culture?

Rip it out from the root and make sure it is continuously beaten down for generations. If you teach them to hate themselves, it makes it easier to erase the things that keep them alive.

Let me tell you about my roots. My Mother was Beatrice Keewatin a Cree Matriarch from Peepeekisis First Nation 81, and my father was Melvin Hanson a third generation Canadian Norwegian from Kelvington Saskatchewan. My Mother lost status when she married my father under the 1985 Bill C-31 amendments. In 1985 we became Status again. In this process, two broad categories of Federal Indian Status were created – sections 6(1) and 6(2). I am a 6(1). My children are 6(2). As such, entitlement is cut-off for their children unless they marry a full status Indian, then their children would continue to be Indigenous. I am now the last of my line.

Back to my mother's family; for four generations the Keewatin's were forced to attend residential schools. The File Hills Residential school was in operation from 1889 to 1949 and was run by the Presbyterian Church until the United Church of Canada took over its operations in 1925. The children were forced to attend and faced severe abuse and despite the name of school it was more known as a workhouse. The children were being used as slave labor and the elders complained their children were there to learn the white world and not just to be slaves. In 1922, H.P. Bryce reported in The Story of a National Crime: Being an Appeal for Justice to the Indians of Canada, that at the File Hills school, "75 percent were dead at the end of the 16 years since the school opened." Those who survived were bred with other graduates to hopefully stop them from returning to their old ways.

The elders of Peepeekisis said Graham was a dictator in the community. He controlled every aspect of life. My own elders told me of a rough year when crops were failing, and they looked at the cattle they tended knowing they could not slaughter it and feed their kids or serious repercussions like jail or beatings lay in their future. They slaved and could not eat what they had grown or tended. They could not sell or make anything without permission from Graham. He ruled over generations of our people with an iron fist.

One of my old uncles was 8 years old when he ran away from the school during winter following the train tracks to go home. Instead, he was caught by another Indian agent and sent to Graham's office. There he was fitted with a ball and chain he wore for the next 10 years. My uncle lifted his pant leg up and there you could see a deep circle indentation around his ankle two inches deep. They never took it off for the entirety of his time there and it had grown into a permanent reminder of what happened when you tried to leave.

I remember going to my uncle's funeral. When our spiritual helpers started the ceremony in Cree, moms back stiffened and she hung her head down while she clasped her hands in her lap like a child would. After the ceremony I asked her why she never taught us Cree. She told me what she had always hidden from us in our childhood. My Mom was 6 years old when the Indian agent came to take her away from my Kokum Maggie. Mom's Father had died at Fort San after contracting Tuberculosis in the war and having no male around caused great interest in the community. The RCMP came as well and told her how she would be thrown into jail if she tried to keep them at home. She relented and they were given only moments to say their goodbyes. She hugged my mom and my Auntie Cindy giving them the sock dolls she had made for them for Christmas. They gathered their few belongings and were driven to the city where they were piled into a cattle truck and driven away to Manitoba.

She told me about the first day there. The Grey Nuns had all the little people lined up by age. Then by sex with all the boys being taken away to the back of the school. They gathered all the girls and made them strip naked in front of each other as their clothing was thrown into burning barrels. The sock doll was ripped from her arms as she clung to it. She ran after it and tried to pull it from the fire resulting in one of many scars she carried from that place. She told me how they pulled her by her ear to the chair where one of the Nuns was shaving the girls' heads before rubbing a white powder all over her bleeding head. It was DDT. The rates of Cancer amongst survivors have never been investigated but that's true of many things. Then after she was clothed in itchy sackcloth clothing she was dragged into the church.

The Nuns made them bow before their god Jesus and when they tried to stand to go to the bathroom it was example time. They smacked her face with a ruler every time she spoke Cree. They continued to beat her around her face until she fell to the floor. Being the select of God they revelled in their divine mission as they threw a bucket of cold water on her tiny six-year-old body before locking her in a special room where the priests waited for the new children. She was told she was not to speak to her sisters or any family in Cree or she would be beaten. Some cherry-picked line about sparing the rod to spoil the child. I only know half the stories, the rest she kept to herself. I would break down into tears and feel the rage of a thousand children as she told me the truth. The truth was they tried everything to make her ashamed of herself, her people, and her culture. There she remained for 10 years before ever seeing her mom again. But by this time my grandmother's heart was broken and she had fallen into the depths of alcoholism after having all her children taken from her. What was she supposed to do?

Mom went home and found this new woman where her mother once stood. Now a once proud woman her own mother was a mere shell of herself and upon her return it was like they were strangers. Every time she tried to talk to her in Cree, she would ask to speak English instead. No one spoke Cree anymore and the old ways fell to the side for another couple decades as slowly as our family began to unshackle our addictions and started ceremonies and singing again.

These were led by my older uncles and they created lodges and vowed we would rise again stronger. Each one of us had a duty to learn and share in maintaining the knowledge.

My uncle Richard told us of how my mother's family had to preserve our cultural traditions and traditional knowledge in secret. I was told of midnight ceremonies and gatherings in the middle of fields where my family would sing the old songs and tell the old stories. They would rotate between cousins' homes and ride through blizzards just to hear the stories of dreamers, healers, dancers, and the unseen worlds beyond our own versions of reality. These are the stories that were told repeatedly feeding our minds and spirits of our people to be able to stand strong in the face of genocide. He told me of how when he was young the Indian agents would kick in doors and pull elders out of sweat lodges before arresting all helpers. They would pay the 15 bucks bail each and learn how to create underground societies of knowledge keepers. The eldest from each family would be given duties to carry forward what came so close to being erased. We carried our own way of stories. Our own ways of understanding. Our own ways of sharing the knowledge of the elders with the children.

I can say that no amount of money will heal the pain that echoes in our blood. How do you reconcile inner generational poverty, addictions, and traumas? How do you quantify the damages done to generations? Leave it to the KKKanadian government to try. In 2004, the Indian Claims Commission (ICC) released its report on the Peepeekisis First Nation's File Hills Colony claim inquiry, which found that Canada had breached its lawful obligation to the reserve. The Commission recommended that the Peepeekisis claim be accepted for negotiation under Canada's Specific Claims Policy. As of this writing the chief and council of Peepeekisis has decided to move forward in accepting the claim only having 974 voting Yes. With 25 voting No and 9 rejected ballots out of its 3100 members. Of which only 635 of its membership are living on the reserve with the majority being off reserve. So, for 125 years of poverty and degradation we shall receive $30,000 per member. Working out to $1.85 cents per year of intergenerational trauma and abuse.

The Honourable Marc Miller the then Minister of Crown–Indigenous Relations said this upon the offer of claim. "On behalf of the Government of Canada, I am truly sorry for the harm, trauma, and significant loss in agricultural land the community of Peepeekisis Cree Nation has experienced due to Canada's role in the File Hills Colony Scheme. Acknowledging our past wrongs and addressing them is critical to building trust and renewing and improving our relationship with Indigenous Peoples."

Now that sneaky old friend intergenerational effect, reared its ugly head again, as the Indigenous people whom he speaks of must now face the repercussions of settlement. This claim should be a boon to membership, but it might not be. The health of the Nation is in great peril still. Membership in urban settings face a perfect storm that no one is really prepared for. The sudden influx of money on a population that has grown up in poverty and addiction, should be researched to determine the possible and expected outcomes. My generation has become adept at funeral arranging and catering wakes. We have had to learn to walk without our elders as they die young of cancer, diabetes, and alcoholism.

Another gift of the residential schools that haunts us

all today. We have family members on the street homeless who we fear for in the coming months. We pray they are strong enough to survive. My Mother is gone now; she died young leaving five children and many great grandchildren behind to mourn her loss. Now, I am the only one in my family left alive to remember the stories of the old people. Without learning about what happened to her I would have not learned to forgive, how to heal and grow. Our past must be remembered, the truth can not and will not be forgotten.

The removal of our families' languages and culture under the school and church influence has done untold damage to our families to this day. We are collectively working through our inner generational traumas and working towards relearning our languages and traditional knowledge from the Elders who remain. Elders who endured physical, mental, and sexual abuse by adults entrusted to care for them.

We remain as witnesses to the tyrannical and vulgar displays of power exercised over our people by church and state working hand in hand in genocide. As long as we live, we are dealing with the true history of KKKanada. As we all begin healing as much as we can, so that future generations can go forward without having to deal with the continuous effects of this failed experiment.

We are known as the artists and dreamers that the elders dreamed of. We remain and carry our own bundles to share our gifts and heal and repair the damages done. The very act of existence as a nêhiyaw is an act of resistance and remembrance.

I defy the definition of being a "good Indian" as my family was bred to be.

Didi Artier

*Didi Artier writes for
fun and elucidation and
has been published in
a few anthologies. She
believes in speaking out
in defense of causes that matter and need
highlighting. Didi works in a career she loves
and still finds time to read plenty of books.
Didi supports equal rights for women and
doesn't believe that makes her a man-hater;
she thinks her male friends would agree, it's
about damn time women were given equality
throughout the world.*

Why I'm Childfree at 53

I'm relatively lucky. I grew up in France, one of the Western countries where birth rates are declining, and many women elect not to have children. Nevertheless, I have been made to feel like a pariah and outcast. I can't imagine what it is like in other countries where the entire social structure expects motherhood from women. I ask myself, if it's hard for me, how is it for those women living in countries like Mexico and India, where motherhood is expected and not having children is seen as a tragedy or nullifies the worth of a woman.

Just because I lived in a country where that's not supposed to happen, a country that claims to be more progressive when it comes to how they perceive women, don't kid yourselves. France, like most if not all 'Western' nations, has its own set of expectations and judgements. They're just less overt.

Whilst we're told we can have full lives without children, without motherhood, the truth is other people and organizations remind us daily we're the minority. I don't fit in as easily because I am not a mother, I don't have children, I'm not a grandparent, I haven't given birth etc. On top of this I am a lesbian so that just doubles the ostracization that may not be as overt as the past, but still exists.

I was told when I was young that because I was beautiful, I should have children. It seemed incredibly stupid to me. I was told because I didn't have a close loving family I would 'make my own' as I got older and had children and married. Nobody ever told me I might grow up to be a gay woman and not want to marry anyone. Nobody ever gave me the option of not having children. It was something I had to claim as part of an identity that isn't the 'norm.'

My friends have all had children, barring two who were unable to. They are viewed with pity. I don't know any woman who didn't want children. Some of my female friends have punishing, demanding careers but they still 'made time to have kids' as they say. I am seen by some, as selfish, lazy, self-interested, and just plain strange for not having children.

When I moved to another city, I found it hard to make friends because I didn't attend church and I didn't have children. Those seemed to be the most common ways women could make friends. Men would feel it was okay to say 'you'd be a lovely mother' as if by saying that, I would shed any reserves I had, and dutifully get pregnant. Just like I was perceived to have 'wasted' my good looks on being a lesbian, the same judgement was levied upon my lack of motherhood. Especially in my late 20's through 30's and early 40's all my 'friends' were in the throes of motherhood and I couldn't relate to them anymore than they could relate to me. I was often called 'aunty' which seemed a bit like a desperate prize for a childless woman.

But the truth is I didn't want children and it wasn't a tragedy. Yes at 53 I do wonder who will take care of me if I ever need it when I'm older. But I see the same with friends with children, who live abroad or simply aren't close. Having a child doesn't ensure you'll be looked after, and it's a terrible reason for having children. Aside from that understandable concern, which many of us have regardless of our child status, I haven't regretted not having children.

What I do regret is that I have had to explain my decision as if it demands explanation. I'm loathe to do that because it's a bit like being a lesbian, I just am. Why do I need to explain it? Isn't that suggesting it's a pathological condition rather than an alternative natural condition? I was told once I shouldn't have children because I'm a lesbian and for a second, I wanted to just to spite them but again, not a reason to have kids.

Why didn't I have kids? There's rarely one reason. Mine were: I was deathly afraid of childbirth, I mean deathly afraid. I was deathly afraid of not wanting to be a mom once I became one and not doing a good job. This was based upon my mother's and her mother's experience of childbirth. They both had one child, they swore they'd never have another. They found childbirth the most traumatic experience of their life. They didn't bond with their child. They experienced postpartum depression, they didn't want their child, they became estranged from their child.

I'm the third possibly fourth generation of women in my family who didn't want children. They didn't have choices. They got pregnant and there were no options. But I recall asking my grandmother and her saying she wished she hadn't had children. It didn't hurt me, because I knew she didn't mean she wished I wasn't alive, or my mother, but she was being honest about her experience as a mother. She also told me her mother hadn't wanted her.

I believe pragmatically that bringing children into the world who are not wanted or won't be treated right, isn't a good idea. I believe in choice, so if a woman gets pregnant under any circumstances, she should have the choice over what she does with that pregnancy. I have long felt we are going backwards in terms of equality over the rights of a woman's body. As a feminist I don't hate men at all but I demand women have equality. Being able to choose if she becomes a woman is at the foundation of that equality.

Aside from my terrors of pregnancy and motherhood, I disliked babies and children. You really are seen as a bad person if you don't like children, it's like not liking puppies (I don't like them either). But I find babies ugly, demanding and irritating. If I say that out loud how many people will think I'm a terrible person? Quite a few. But I'm sure I'm not alone. When my friends had children, I would leave my visiting them with relief thinking 'I'm so glad I don't get stuck like that.' Is that selfish or just honest? The world would have me believe I'm unnatural and selfish but not all of us are made to be carers of babies.

Ironically, I care for quite a few people, and always have, but I like adults. I can deal with adults. I'm terrible with babies, toddlers and children (and even teens). It's just not natural to me. In addition, when I was younger, I didn't have much money and I had zero family support, so I worried about bringing a child into the world under those circumstances. Fair enough if you have nothing but you still want children, that's your choice. But isn't it my choice not to?

Every time I go to the doctors, they ask me why I didn't have children. Every time I meet a new person they ask if I have children. And then ask why I didn't have children or worse, say 'there's still time' and when I patiently explain there isn't because I'm 53 and they finish complimenting me and saying I don't look my age, they say 'have you thought of adoption?' They never assume or consider; I might not have ever wanted children. And if I tell them that's it, they look at me silently, because they don't know what to say and they begin to feel a divide between us.

I don't feel a divide if I talk to someone of a different culture, race, background etc. but if you are a childless/ childfree woman then you are definitely treated like you are a pariah or unnatural. My friends LOVE children and even those who aren't big baby fans, will go along with it. As if it's expected of us women. Maybe once we had no choice but we do now, so why are we still persecuted and judged?

Finally, the biggest reason I didn't have children was I believe the planet is really full. I don't think humans are far off being parasites. I know many of us are good people who help others, but there are too many of us. Some countries literally don't have the resources. Our planet is being slowly destroyed by an infestation of humans. Maybe once it was okay to have 6 kids but now, I think it's selfish. As I'm called selfish, I think of what is really selfish. Taking up precious resources, having too many children to add to a burgeoning world population. That seems far more selfish than a woman who doesn't want children.

The fact of my being a lesbian was also a consideration. It's hard enough for kids, kids who grow up with two mothers, that's not easy. Where I lived I could imagine it and I decided that would be selfish of me too. So those were my reasons. And whilst I don't judge anyone for choosing to have children, I do wonder why I'm perpetually judged in small micro aggressive ways, or through gas lighting means, for my decision? Just like women who have abortions are guilted by 'why didn't you adopt the baby out? There are many childless couples who would have loved to have your baby!' Should a woman ever be an incubator? Does her choice to abort make her selfish? It scares me how many people think it does.

If I'm selfish then why aren't men held to the same standard? A man who doesn't have kids doesn't get judged as much. Men who have multiple children and leave them don't get judged as much. Men who rape a woman can claim paternity. I find those things far more reprehensible than my choice not to have children. I know if I had got pregnant, I probably would have had an abortion and then I'd be judged for that as well. Most of the time those women who do get pregnant don't do so deliberately. So why should they be deliberately forced to go through with the pregnancy? The two subjects are interwoven in my mind and relate to fundamental equal choice and freedom.

True, once in a while I wonder if I have made the right decision, because I get lonely in a world that promotes motherhood and heterosexuality, but is that really surprising? Women shouldn't be forced to be mothers, yet this roll back of abortion access forces women into struggling with unwanted pregnancies. I know so many women who are doomed to extreme poverty because they had children and were left by their partners. It's not always possible to get them to pay. I also know many women who had abortions because they had children and couldn't cope with any more. If they talked publicly about this they would be condemned, it's such a double standard because if men got pregnant, I think the way we talk about it and handle it would be completely different.

I am a godmother and I have nieces and nephews. It makes me happy but it's not the same as being an elective mother, nor does it mean I wish I were. I don't live a life of freedom which entails being selfish and thinking only of my own pleasures. I volunteer. I do charitable work aside from my career and I give to others. I shouldn't have to say that but I am, because the perception of childfree women is we're pleasure seekers. At the same time, I admit I am better off financially for not having had children, I have traveled a lot and I found it easier to build my career than if I were juggling babies.

The modern idea of a woman having 'it all' is a fallacy. Few women have it all. They may try and be pressured by the counterintuitive demands of society that tells them they're equal. But as child bearers they will never be equal biologically. They are more likely to be raped and impregnated, they are at the mercy of that pregnancy especially if termination is outlawed or socially condemned. They are dependent upon others helping them in most circumstances. And if any of those areas are lost, they can be quickly fragile economically and emotionally.

Women who have children later in life have to contend with higher risks of breast cancer than even childless women. Women who have IVF to conceive, also run higher risks. Mothers are expected to: Bring up multiple children and be the primary carer, whilst running a household, keeping their husband happy, being eternally youthful and competitive and making time to work out and stay slim. It's an absurdity few of us can meet. Not to mention the pressure and lack of support in many countries for women with sick kids, or who get sick themselves.

I'm lucky because in France we have great maternity and paternity leave. But other countries have next to none. Putting your child in childcare when they are a baby seems counterintuitive, and the rates of autism are going through the roof. Having a child can be scary when you have no idea of the issues that will exist down the road. I have friends with autistic children or down syndrome whose lives are hijacked 24/7 to their conditions. It's nobody's fault and some of those friends are glad for it, but many are stretched to breaking point with few resources to help them. In some ways it's ironic that France had to improve its social infrastructure to promote more French women having children. Whilst it worked, it didn't consider that some modern women are opting out, it only considered how to improve the lot of those pregnant and with children. I'm glad this happened because it's hard being a mom and society can't demand motherhood and then not give that mother support and financial assistance if she needs it.

Coming from a line of women who didn't want children, I found it hurtful and shocking when my mother expressed regret, I hadn't had children. Sometimes there's no pleasing anyone. But I had to do what was right for me, and I'm so grateful I had that choice, especially as a woman who is aware of the historical lack of choice women had endured, and continue to endure. I have had friends who were married off very young and had 6 kids by the time they were 30. When I ask them, some of them admit they never wanted children, but in their culture, they had zero choice. I feel lucky I did but angry that this isn't universal. As long as some women have no choice, we must fight for their right to have a choice. It scares me to consider how many women throughout the world are forced into motherhood repeatedly. Nothing justifies that, not religion, not doctrine or men, nothing.

Friends of mine in other countries and cultures, have literally been forced into motherhood and many times this causes tremendous upset and pain. The mental health of a woman matters and we should do more as a culture to support her right to equity and freedom. No woman is free if we're still being told our value depends upon our status as a mother. Many of my heterosexual friends say they feel their male partner would leave them if they didn't have children. How many women have children to please others? Why should her giving birth be a factor in a relationship? Yet so often it is.

True, a world without children doesn't work either. But there will always be plenty of women who want to be moms and be great moms. If some of us don't fit into that category isn't that okay? Why then are we marginalized, judged, and condemned almost unconsciously, by society at large? What has to happen to change that? Like any minority, I understand that 'being different' is looked at suspiciously. But if you think about it, we're all different in some way. Not being allowed to be different, that doesn't seem healthy. I also think females are held to higher standards than men and the expectations levied at them are both unrealistic and unyielding.

Many of my friends are grandparents now. I feel a whole new phase of exclusion. But rather than feeling sorry for myself, which I really don't, I carved out my own life. I have a career I love. I have a partner I love. I have a lovely home and we travel and have many friends. That's my life. I don't need children to complete that and I don't feel a loss in not having children. But how many childfree women are depicted in literature, TV, the media? Why do we exclude other choices and continue to push the idea a woman is only complete if she's a mom? If I'm able to not judge others, then I think they should be able to not judge me. I'm not a deviant, I'm just a woman who chose to be childfree. If we don't have a choice, we have nothing. Being childfree doesn't mean you're selfish, it means you chose not to have children. That simple.

Devereaux Frazier

*Devereaux Frazier is
a published poet and
writer, contributor to
Blood Into Ink, Guest
Barista for Go Dog Go
Cafe. His work has also
been featured on SpillWords.com, where he
was nominated for the May Publication of
the Month in 2017. You can also find him
published in Literary Arts Review and Teen
Ink, the latter of which published his work
in their monthly magazine in 2016. You
can read more of Devereaux's writing on
Instagram: @dfrazier_0.*

I Could Tell a Lie

I could tell you about the top of the mountain and the tranquility of freedom. I could tell you how perseverance and resilience will get you anywhere in this world. I could reminisce about the good times, the laughs, and the joy in discovering purpose. I could tell you that I don't remember anything about the bad times; that they did the best they could.

I could tell a lie.

Instead, I'll dial back the clock to a time when I wasn't so sure I'd make it to twelve, much less twenty-four. The brain is a powerful tool, and I thought if you tell it to forget, eventually it will comply. The scars embedded in my skin remain, but a quick trip to the local tattoo parlor remedies some of those. The mental and emotional lashes, however, aren't easily dispatched. I took to the bottle rather easily, as you will see why rather soon. When I got my second job at a furniture store, the peace it brought me to furnish my dwelling was a drug unlike any other. The ability to wield control is a high that you just don't come down from. The closets designed for clothing became a menagerie for the wicked. Adult magazines, prescriptions, and empty Hennessy bottles screamed of anxiety, confusion, and regret.

Untold days of my life have been lost from late night binges and subsequent passing out.

The vicious underbelly of childhood trauma and abuse was fed by my ability to self-medicate. Every two weeks I could go to the liquor store and wash away my sins for an hour. If only I had chosen better methods, or what if it had never happened in the first place? I hated myself for living, for surviving.

I could tell a lie.

No, really. I was the quintessential weird kid. I loved trains, hated being in public places, and suffered from asthma. Hell, I even had a sports coat phase. At twelve years old. I also gave myself haircuts far too often, so baseball caps became a staple of my youth. I'm sure everyone has a part of their life when they feel like they don't fit in, but that's the thing: it's just a part. I felt that way all the time. I could be at home, at school, or out with the family having dinner. Nothing ever changed. It didn't help that they didn't exactly make me feel better about my mental health. Of all the things I told myself to forget, I readily recall the social outings where I'd be ridiculed for not being "friendly" enough. I would even be punished for it; sometimes I couldn't eat dinner, other times I wouldn't be allowed on the next outing. Surely, this wasn't the most sane or sensible decision to levy against a child, but I'm not the parent. How would I know? The constant ridicule and harassment mixed with a rapidly failing self-esteem was the runway needed towards a destination of addiction, depression, and suicide. That was only the potential energy, though. The kinetic energy would come later.

I could tell a lie.

Autism, much less Aspergers, was not on the single imaginable horizon of explanation for my behavior. I had never even heard of the latter, until a life altering visit to the Kennedy Krieger Institute. After several tests, some of which were mildly intrusive, their doctors had come to the conclusion that I had displayed all the "interesting" traits of someone with Aspergers Syndrome: the oddball mannerisms, poor eye contact, reclusiveness, and general social awkwardness. As I would come to learn, fitting in socially and understanding nonverbal cues would always be a struggle. Making and having relationships would be a bumpy road, too. Despite having what appeared to be answers, I still had so many more questions. I was just fifteen. My family was just grateful to be able to give my oddities a name, though that hardly made my life more palatable. Mostly, because giving something a name doesn't exactly eradicate the need for understanding, but also because there wasn't much interest in helping me navigate this newfound knowledge.

Books were bought and websites explored. I became acquainted with the work of John Elder Robinson, who wrote with an insightful and hopeful perspective into living with my condition. However, I struggled to find my own identity in the midst of the confusion, impatience, and a certain degree of shame. Was something wrong with me? Why was I made this way? Sure, my dad was an alcoholic and drug addict. Did he fuck my genes up that badly? For the next five years I would embark on a painful journey of self-harming, drinking, and ill-advised relationships. All in the name of proving to the world that I wasn't what it said I was.

I could tell a lie.

Remember when I told you the bottle came easy? There's a reason for that. My father was a narcissist through and through, and he didn't take to disagreement too well. On one occasion, he even beat me to the point of needing surgery. He gave me a hernia. My family told the doctors it was from moving furniture, but I knew the truth. Fast forward a few years to the day I turn twenty-one. I must've drank two or three bottles of Jack Daniels that night, but my tolerance was too high. It wasn't my first drink, not by a long shot. Cutting yourself is one form of release, but there's something sensual about drinking to the point of collapse. I couldn't just make marks every time I succumbed to the pain of memory, I needed to forget.

By this time, I had made a few friends so I can always get a drink or two when we hang out. The sneaking out was great, but the raucous backseat flings that the alcohol led to were even better. I was working a good job and had even started my own business selling collectibles, so I had the money to travel and meet people. The adventures even led me to my first girlfriend, though we weren't very compatible in the least. She was lonely and I was caught in an ugly spiral of perpetual self-numbing. Being with her intimately was the best feeling I'd ever had, but truthfully it only pushed me further down the dark road that I was all too eager to remain on. I was the fool, and too desperate to notice or even care.

I don't care. About being black, especially in a society so convoluted and hellbent on squashing anything and anyone that does not conform. I could remain stuck inside my head and choose to ignore what the world thought. Surely, someone with my skin color and the sickness in my mind could only produce negative results. An overlooked aspect of being male these days, is this societal expectation of having unfulfilled, pent-up anger. The way people would walk on eggshells around me is certainly comical now, but then it was a crippling blow to my self-esteem.

So much is made of a man's ability to stand firm, be strong, and exude this sort of masculinity that is often bastardized by western society. A black kid with anxiety and depression can't possibly be the alpha male you hear about on podcasts or a certain Twitter account, so what does this mean for my place in the world? Yes, I was undeniably angry, but not in a theatrical, raging sense. Rather, it was the smoldering, self-reflective kind that stirred thought and provoked desires to be better.

The suffering from stigma and the fear of being lost to time if never understood had created in me, this need to be heard. What started out as a school project became a profession, and a quest to overcome the hand I was dealt at birth. More than just a way to vent, writing became the way I reversed everything said and done against me for good. Simply put, writing saved my life. Black men are always looked upon as being angry or aggressive, but when you consider what so many of us are going through, it's not hard to see why. More importantly, it is having the courage and self-awareness to use that energy to create awareness and a better understanding of the issues facing our men today.

So much of our present society is hilariously superficial, from our movies and entertainment to the money in our bank accounts or the rights we think we own. Government leaders misuse power, police officers harass at every corner, and so-called "friends" disown at the first sign of reflection. It is tribalistic in nature to do things that your "culture" suggests you do, even if they are detrimental to your health, wellbeing, and success. Whether it be monetary, spiritual, or some other accomplishment that you seek, simply acting in a certain way that pleases or admonishes the group for the sake of said group, drastically diminishes the individual. Relegated to a position of uselessness, that individual becomes self-absorbed in finding identity or lets the outside world decide instead. The mental health crises we are seeing in the western culture is a direct result of this stifling of behavior, and until we are able to speak truthfully and outwardly about it, we will continue to see more and more people succumb to drugs, alcoholism, depression, sickness, and death.

I could tell you that my girlfriend and I are still together, or that I don't drink too much anymore. I could say I've arrived at a place of mental and emotional stability and peace. My scars healed, my oddities faded away, and my outlook on life less pessimistic. But, like so much of the life that I've lived so far, that would be a lie. I am not conventionally strong, attractive, or desired. I fly in the face of societal expectation and demand. I will never do, say, or think the way I'm supposed to. I will always stand on the outside of their inside, and that's the truth.

The fact of the matter is, everyone doesn't always get a happy story with a happy ending. We've allowed ourselves to believe that things always work out for the better, in the sort of fantastical and predictable way that movies and TV have made us believe they do. Nothing could be further from the truth. Maybe there is light at the end of the tunnel, or maybe the road eventually stops winding, but it's hardly ever the same for anyone. I wish I had the normal, fun-filled childhood that some of my peers did. I wish the rash and violent actions taken against me didn't happen, and I wasn't so easily pushed into a spiral of self-harming. Maybe I'd have more friends, or even a wife. Maybe I'd be on one of those "30 under 30" lists. Or maybe, it would've been the same. The best part of life is also the most defeating, and that is sometimes you just don't know. The doors you open could lead to lifelong success and fame, or your very first brothel.

So where does this leave me?

I could tell a lie and say I've completely overcome my failures, weaknesses, and a past that probably should've buried me. That no part of me wishes I could go back and do it again, because of course I could do it better this time. I could lie and say every day is spent dreadfully inside a masterclass of persistent reminiscence. That I can't sleep, socialize like a regular adult, or go two days without a drink. The truth however, lies somewhere in the middle, and since we've already been over the beginning story, continuity dictates there must be an ending, right?

Well, I don't know. Unlike a fictional story, mine is far from finished. I started this piece talking my way down from the mountain. Now, I have to climb back up. Everything that's ever happened, and everything that's going to happen, is carried on my shoulders. Society doesn't understand, and even the people that shared my name couldn't ease those burdens. Each day is a chance for something new to be learned, about myself or the world that I'm in. Some days are better, others are worse, but no matter the situation I've learned that I have to keep moving forward. Higher. Further. Equally, if I don't see my life through, did I prove everyone wrong? Would I instead have proved them right? My story isn't over and it is far from perfect, but it's mine to live and share.

So that's what I'll do, because I won't lie anymore.

Rebecca Huston

*Rebecca Huston spent
her formative years with
her grandparents, avid
photographers, who
informed her love for visual images and
cinema. At the age of 18, she interned with
NBC News, and subsequently produced her
first independent documentary. Ms. Huston
has worked for ABC, CNN, Dreamworks
Television and Women in Film.*

Freak

Returning to school after the Christmas holiday, my fourth-grade teacher, Mrs. Becker, asked us to share with the class something we had done over the vacation break. When my turn came to speak, I explained I had made a list of my favorite things. She asked, such as? I pulled out a small notebook in which I had written "Five Favorite Movies" and read aloud: Number Five, *Bambi*; Number Four, *Dumbo*; Number Three, *The Aristocats*; Number Two, *Lady and the Tramp*. Then I announced: Number One, Francois Truffaut's *Fahrenheit 451*, starring Oskar Werner and Julie Christie! I beamed knowing I had perfectly pronounced the name of the French director as I had heard it on television. Mrs. Becker hissed, you're a freak!

Perhaps.

It is true I had watched *Fahrenheit 451* only the night before on a portable television in the third floor attic of a farmhouse where I lived with my mother and stepfather. I was fascinated by the scene of policemen searching a baby carriage, rummaging under a crying baby to find a book banned by the government. On the black and white screen, the triumphant policeman vigorously shook the book in the mother's face: AHA! We got you! I wondered why it was so important that the police confiscate books? Were books really THAT dangerous? What might happen if we read the books the authorities did not want us to possess?

I am still asking those questions.

What is not true is that I had seen *Bambi, Dumbo* or *The Aristocats.* I was trying to imagine what a girl my age was supposed to have seen at the movies. I was trying to fit in. I had watched only *Fahrenheit 451* and *Lady and the Tramp* but had written the header "Five Favorite Movies" in my palm-sized notebook and was determined to fill in the list. Perhaps Mrs. Becker was right.

Was I a freak in a rural town watching a foreign film, late at night, after I was supposed to be asleep? Perhaps I wasn't supposed to wonder about banned books and authoritarian regimes, but I did. Who knows, really, what a nine year old should wonder about, or anyone at any age? Is it really up to anyone else to determine how we think? Isn't it the point that we think as we individually do, so we might be who we really are? Apparently, Mrs. Becker did not want me to so freely contribute what I thought as she never again called upon me for the duration of the school year despite my oft-raised hand.

Being weird is its own birthright.

At first it hurt: not fitting in, not understanding, not knowing how to gain the nod and grin of peers. Parents didn't count. As long as I did not embarrass them in public, my mother and stepfather could skate by with their odd child in tow. Around this same period, my mother was driving a panel van as part of her job refilling Tom's Candy vending machines at gas stations and markets. I accompanied her as she drove a weekly route. Propped up on a telephone book in the passenger seat of the van, I wedged my small feet around a box between my knees chock full of cellophane bags filled with Boston Baked Beans, Candy Corn, Licorice, and striped Peanut Butter Bars.

One sweltering afternoon, while making the vending machine rounds, a station wagon crossed over into our lane and hit the Tom's van head on. I was thrown into the windshield, and cratered the glass with my skull. My mother sheared her front teeth on the steering wheel. While a man from the gas station tended to my mother, I took out the same notebook in which I had written my list of favorite movies and approached the distraught driver of the station wagon. I asked politely to see his car registration and insurance papers. I faithfully wrote down the information and returned to my mother. I asked her for a quarter. My mother shook her head, why do you need a quarter? It was obvious to me. I explained so I could use the pay phone to call in the accident to the insurance company. My mother glared.

Freak. Part Deux.

In junior high school, I joined the Speech Club. Because nobody else on my team volunteered to compete for the school in the category of Expository Speaking, I did. Uff, why? I did not know what Expository Speaking meant or even how to write such a speech. The day before the first tournament, having not written my speech, much less practiced it, I heard in my mind's ear a Simon and Garfunkel song, *The Sound of Silence*. I asked my mother if we could go to a music store in town. For $1.99 we bought a folder of sheet music for *The Sound of Silence*. I read the lyrics 50 times before going to bed sick to my stomach, still with no idea of what to do next.

The next morning, I arrived at the speech tournament carrying only *The Sound of Silence* sheet music. In the classroom where the Expository Speaking category was to be judged, I hoped I would be called last to perform. The judge had us write our names on slips of paper; she dropped them in a hat. My name was drawn first. I closed my eyes and thought of my grandfather, a minister, and the sermons he delivered, full of faith and love. I silently prayed, raised slowly from my chair and approached the front of the room. There, I rested the folder of sheet music on the lectern's tilted ledge and turned to the audience, utterly void of a plan.

The Sound of Silence, I asked, what does that mean? Blank stares, a ho hum or two. I read the first line of the lyrics: "Hello darkness, my old friend, I've come to talk to you again." Then, akin to jumping on a toboggan at the top of a mountain where you cannot see the slopes, I slid skittering around mounds of meaning I did not understand. Somewhere in the mist, feeling more like a floating observer than driver, I heard myself ask a koan: what is the sound of one hand clapping? I wondered, where did that come from? —I've never said those words before. A philosophical answer wafted out of my mouth and I watched the judge's eyes widen and widen again, until I summed up the oration and sat down, utterly in a daze.

After the six other students completed their speeches, the judge thanked us all. As I was leaving, the judge asked if she could have a copy of the speech I had given. I handed her the folded sheet music. No, she said, I want a copy of your speech. That's all I have, I explained. This? Yes. I made it up. I tried to explain my grandfather was a minister in Arizona and I felt what it felt like to sit in his church. She stared at me, then *The Sound of Silence* sheet music, puzzled.

I fled the tournament and hid in the school library, convinced the very next day I would drop out of Speech Club. AHA! There you are! My speech coach found me and dragged me by the proverbial ear to the awards ceremony. Quite unexpectedly, the judge for Expository Speaking had given that dizzy stream of (un)consciousness the highest points in the tournament; I took home a funky plastic trophy for something the "I" who I knew, did not do.

In high school, I was improbably both athletic and clumsy. Playing Varsity Volleyball, I jumped to block the ball at the net with such poor timing I would hang in mid-air so long that my teammates had a derisive nickname for me: "Hang Ten." Not particularly popular with my volleyball colleagues, I talked too much and played too weirdly. When all the rage in service sports like tennis or volleyball was an overhand smash, I served old-school underhand with a side-to-side motion like mopping the floor, and the slow floater moved like a drunken moth just over the net. So disjointed was my serve that players on the opposing team collided trying to just pitch it up in the air. Worse, when opposing players saw the odd ball coming, they ran to reach it like a dink then stopped mid-track, wondering which one should take it; the ball plummeted untouched between them and we won the point. A dink-ace what?

Twenty years later, I visited my high school. Standing in the gymnasium that still smelled the same, I looked up at the banners and jerseys hung in honor of the school's championship teams. There in the middle of the display was the only California Interscholastic Federation pennant won for Girls Volleyball. Oh yeah, I remembered, I served that final game, 21 to 0. I closed my eyes and recalled the lackluster hugs and half-hearted high-fives of my teammates. Yes, we had won the state championship but on a dorky serve no one could believe made it over the net.

Freak. Part Trois.

It mattered not to me, my obvious clumsiness in sports or inability to think up a topic good enough to compete upon. My only intention after the head-on collision was to help my mom, and, certainly, I was enthralled discussing *Fahrenheit 451*. Even to this day, I delight in pronouncing Truffaut correctly—then again it makes me grin to say *Pepe Le Pew* with flourish.

So, who decides who the freaks are? Is it an outside job or an inside one? Is it all right to just be me? What choice do we really have? Honestly, no matter how hard you or I try, we could never be anyone else. As such, could we be gentler with ourselves—forgoing the definitions applied by others or our own internal critique in an attempt to (impossibly) fit in? Maybe there is no place to fit in. Maybe if we had to reduce our full selves to squeeze into that space, we wouldn't want to be there. Maybe it's the freaks who show us how to get out of the box. Maybe there is no box.

My mother is about to be admitted into hospice. There are phone calls I need to make even as I type this sentence. I am not happy with the way the Alzheimer's facility has handled her recent care. I hear my mother's voice in my mind's ear: there are no mistakes, only teachable moments. A college instructor for 25 years, I know if my mother understood her words still make an impact even now, after she has lost the faculty of cognitive speech, she would be pleased. I feel she has been right all along: we are more than the circumstances of our lives and more than we know. Maybe it was my grandfather's spirit guiding me when I knew not what to say. Maybe it will be my mother's spirit smiling when the arrangements have been made. Maybe there is no place to get to at all. Maybe there is just now.

My mother and I shared an odd sense of humor. Once she laughed so hard at a quip I made, that she had to run outside into the backyard; there wasn't time enough to reach the bathroom. I, of course, having no remorse, grabbed my camera and took a picture of her holding up her fuzzy red plaid bathrobe, laughing and urinating— the stream illuminated by the midday sun while our black poodle nearby sniffed. A doggie version of, what the heck? These are the memories, mom, memories I will hold dear while you go. Thank you for reminding me to let my wierdo light shine so the other weirdos can find me. I am sure you will be shining a spotlight from wherever you are: there she is, my precious little freak.

Yep, mom, I'm yours.

Nimisha Bowry Dhawan

I enjoy writing blogs, short articles and have my opinion shared sans the judgement aspect of it, but more from a point of view, that things may be different for different people, and that relativity is a reality that we all need to embrace if we truly want to live in a peaceful world.

Childfree by Choice

As a girl born in the 80s, one grows up in the lap of nurturing. You play with dolls that are role-play defined and designed—mothers and their babies, sisters, best friends. Many roles, many stereotypical characteristics. Not judging the scenarios of our adolescent minds but just going by what our social programming has led us to. The dolls are at tea parties or bubble baths, oftentimes though doctors or nurses or teachers too. Also characteristic of nurturing. Again, not judging, just me reflecting upon what I grew up with—a fairly sincere, simple and straightforward world.

Cut to the current world we live in. It's been fast paced for the last 2 decades. The concept of parenting has changed. Children and their DNA have changed. Emotions have changed. Times have changed. The dolls have changed too! Somehow the disparity just didn't feel conducive to parenting. I'd like to believe it was largely due to this change that I, single then, wondered if this was making any sense. The innocence of childhood had long slipped the next generation and it was only going to get shorter with every xennial, GenZ, Gen Alpha. My mother always said 'child is the father of man' and while we all unanimously agreed upon evolution, this pace was all too overwhelming. It was reason enough for me to doubt my own ability to keep up.

So many theories form our subconscious over such topics. At college is when I first heard the concept of DINKS—double income, no kids—and it sounded like so much fun! All the financial freedom in the world! Why is it stuck? Because the world got so expensive, that if you wanted to do this the way you had imagined it, it was not going to be as much fun! Did we buckle under conformist parenting? Yes! Because they say, if you tweak your imagination a bit, anything's possible, provided you still want to go ahead with the plan! Were we selfish? Not just cautionary of a very big responsibility.

It's not a decision you come to overnight, neither over the initial few years of being married. The usual picture in one's mind, is at an inherent level, rooted to that picture perfect family photo, but somewhere along the way, it starts to dwindle. Why? There are no definitive answers. It's like a good day versus a not so good one.

Did we put too much thought into it? But should you not?

I'll go back to the word 'doubt'. Should you accept that you are 'doubting' your parental instincts and outcomes? Yes, you can! After all, this is the future you're about to raise.

The world needs this future to be a happy, healthy, content one. Can 'doubt' raise that?

Or are your mind's most inner thoughts being harsh on you?

I married early, 25, and I was very sincere about my role as wife and enjoyed the 'adult' companionship of my husband. Did I imagine us with children? Yes! Two! One of each! We even had names! Why did my sincerity give way over the years? He loves children, me, not as much! I would have been happy playing bad cop to our kids, he, the doting dad! Yes, the times changed, but they weren't reason enough for me to be an influencer to my husband about the concerns of parenting well. I had to be sure that I was not imposing my viewpoints on him. We both genuinely felt it was a tougher society, with so much more to be careful of and for. We'd grown up care-free and cute! Was this the playground or the lack of it that we wanted for our children? No! How can you be so sure of this imaginary world that you've assumed for your children? You can't be. But you go with the majority gut feeling...

Doubts were then heavily imposed with a decade that brought in the highest levels of human crime, climate change, communal disharmony, global market instabilities, addictions—not limited to substance abuse, but addictions like consumerism, financial greed, digital overload, social manias and phobias, the inability to hear no—and so much more, all of which are so influencing for a growing society. Did I want to take on such a prime responsibility in such challenging times? Were the challenges real or just excuses of a lazy mind? I was all for the internal debate at a healthy level. Who draws the healthy level limits? All this confusion just led me to believe that there was no way I wanted to pass this cynicism on. Why had I become such a cynic? The undiluted exposure we got to the vastness of the world we lived in?

Speaking of vastness, our current world is such a melange of possibilities. I'd like to believe we the 'non-contributors' of the world generate a high level of otherwise not so easily accessible possibilities. We tend to put our minds and actions to sometimes even higher levels of responsibility like the planet, nature, hobbies, passions, pets, a cause close to our hearts and so much more. I'm an eco-warrior of sorts, and I feel like somewhere I'm contributing to the theory of reduction! Are we all going to turn a blind eye to the issue of population? Or are we going to let this satisfy our own needs? To be parents, to have lineage, to leave behind an apparent legacy? I'd like to believe in my husband and me as two free, unique individuals. We can be remembered irrespective, no? I often read the term pet parent or plant parent these days, and it also does feel all warm and fuzzy!

And we're happy doing this for the other children of the world! We are loved as much—yes, we know it's different with your own—as aunts and uncles, and are all too happy to be the cool ones, and letting the actual parents do all the hard work. We've been told we're being short sighted, and that every child comes with its own destiny path and that we should go with the natural flow of society. Is it really that important? And if that were truly the case, then we would have been parents by now?

Kind people say "You'd both make great parents!" to urge and encourage you. The one's judging you actually don't say a word. Not to your face. At least from where I come. Often, you hear about your non-existent physiological shortcomings from a gossipy community. Can you explain a valid, very thought-through practical analysis to this community? Can you not make this decision without there being any suggestive implications?

And then there are some who advocate pets. But no, we're ok being the both of us, independent and secure. A rescue pet, ok! But a really expensive high pedigree one, now how do you get down to that in a world that's got humans in such extreme conditions?

This one's been the toughest for us—seeing babies and children in abject poverty. We've both had tears in our eyes, and a throat full of lumps when you see that. We're hoping that we can get ourselves to be more worthwhile in the future and aid this space.

Today, we are married 14 years with umpteen instances of being for and against this big life changing, often enough life stimulating and life enhancing phase. I still ask my husband if we lost out, and so far his answer is always, "No, we 'loved' out". Him supporting our cause has and will always be a decision sticker. I feel sorry where the opinions conflict for other couples. But I also feel braved by those who stuck it out in more testing, stigmatic times. From that point of view, an urban, independent lifestyle allows us so much more freedom to choose beyond the obvious. A choice that is not aligned to expectation or conformism.

We don't advocate our stand to others, then why should people impose theirs on us? There's a common phrase that states "mind your own womb", which I think should be accepted as a kind, caring acceptance rather than a reactional retort.

Like life, this one's a short, simple point of view on being Child-free. A decision made by my consenting husband and me, and quite honestly, there needn't be a third angle to the triangle. We've been lucky sans the pressures. The strongest pressures are imposed by us on ourselves. It's time that changed.

Dr. Belinda Román

Dr. Belinda Román is Associate Professor at St. Mary's University, San Antonio, Texas. Prior to that position, she was Professor of Economics at Palo Alto College, San Antonio. She's a member of the American Economic Association and member of the Committee on the status of minority groups in the Economic profession. She's a member of the American Society of Hispanic Economists (ASHE) and the International Federation for Feminist Economics. She's recently been awarded a National Science Foundation Grant and is taking a Fellowship at the University of Surrey, UK, in 2024. She has lived in Bolivia, Canada, England and America and credits travel as one of the best means of learning as well as developing a passion for Vindaloo chicken and KitKats. www.romaneconomics.com

Breaking Borders

Growing up in El Paso, a Bordertown between Mexico and America, the middle-child of 6, I recall my father always emphasizing education. This is because both he and my mother, first generation immigrants to America from Mexico, grew up being labeled 'black' in the census and having to go to 'black only' toilets, as part of the segregated society of the 1920's/30's. My father felt education was the only way to free yourself of the assumptions, biases and bigotry of main-stream-America, who to this day perceives people of Mexican heritage in a negative, derogatory manner.

Both my parents were told they could not speak their language in their one room school and when they traveled, they could not stay at the same hotel as their classmates. The level of discrimination they experienced is not always considered when talking about 'black and white' issues in America. Mexican-Americans tend to get overlooked or lumped into a greater argument, rather than their specific experiences being recorded. My mother was interviewed by PBS for the Children of Giant (the movie with James Dean in the 1950s that was filmed in her hometown) and she bravely pointed to these experiences, saying 'we can't erase history and we can't forget it either.'

Flash-forward to 2023 and America is predicted to be more 'brown' than 'white' within a few short years. Inevitable considering the higher birth rates, higher immigration rates of people of color who move to America. Despite being a 'melting-pot,' America remains at heart, a very divided country. We may have the United States, but our politics, and view-points vary radically. Americans as a whole, are not as aware of the rest of the world as they should be, their myopic perspectives mean our nightly news is focused narrowly and whilst the rest of the world has a greater understanding of world politics, we are encouraged to think only of America. The flaw in this is America is no longer the super power it once was, but most Americans don't know this.

For immigrants and people of color, flocking to America for part of the American Dream, they are just as likely to encounter racism and prejudice as they are opportunity. That's the harsh reality. And in my parent's case, they grew up in a small American town not far from the Border where segregation still existed and opportunities were scant for Mexican-Americans. My father was fortunate, but also incredibly hard-working, and the combination of this, enabled him with the help of some patrons, to climb the ladder from relative poverty and living in a 3-room home, to graduate from medical school and practice as a pediatrician. Understandably, his rise to the top influenced me greatly and inculcated in my psyche from an early age the value and love of education and learning.

In my own journey, I was less clear cut than my father about what I wanted to do with my life. All my siblings ended up with a degree, which is testament to my parents' constant vigilance and commitment to our education and success. We all played instruments from an early age, music being a wonderful counterpart to academia, both in creativity and discipline. Initially I considered a music degree but my straight-talking mother made it clear this was no easy road, with few opportunities. I switched to pre-med with an idea to follow in my father's footsteps. We were very close and I had begun working in his practice from my mid-teens, assisting him. The reality of pre-med was shockingly different and after a few years I saw realistically it wasn't for me, the personality required to deal with extreme sickness and loss was something I did not feel I could adopt. It helped me understand what my father had endured to become a doctor, and helped me avoid going into a profession that didn't fit with my personality.

After a serious bout of illness with thyroid disease, where I had to live back home with my parents and take an absence from university, I returned determined to find my place in the world. Taking a course in economics with no real idea of its value, I fell in love. For me, economics was music, it made sense, it opened my mind to understanding how the world worked in a profound way that other subjects did not. I determined this would be my course of study and never regretted it. For a Hispanic woman in the early 1980s, studying economics was not commonplace. It's still a male-dominated field, and has small numbers of minorities in high positions. These were realities I learned the hard way.

After completing my BA, I took a year to work in politics in Washington DC., with an idea of making political work my pursuit. That changed quite quickly when I witnessed the rabid corruption of the political system, and its sexist, elitist machine. The grind of expectation, what you were asked to do (especially as a woman) were things I hadn't envisioned and didn't want to be part of. I learned a great deal but ultimately quit to pursue my Masters. In fact, when I studied my Masters, I worked in administration for a trucking company and whilst that may not seem to be as valuable as experience, it taught me more about 'real' life and the ins-and-outs of profit/value/loss than anything else.

Armed with my Masters I was soon working in Bolivia, South America, for a development agency. This humbling work opened my eyes to the reality of 'economics' rather than the academic version of it. I began what is now a lifelong apprehension of statistics and traditional economics that hide behind these statistics, rather than get their hands dirty. Additionally, I came to see how easily manipulated statistics can be, and rather than being a 'fact' they are often a tool used to make an argument that is wholly subjective. For a social science, Economics is as subjective as a non-science, and we can take that further and argue that all science-based fields have a large element of subjectivity that many people are unaware of.

My time in Bolivia was edifying because I was out of America and learning what other cultures, other ways of doing things, actually involved and without going beyond your own borders, you really can't say you know things at a deep level, because you are only operating through the narrow lens of your (biased) culture. It was the most valuable thing I ever did and it encouraged me to become somewhat of a world traveler. Whilst some of my siblings expressed no interest in travel, I wanted nothing more than to learn how other people lived and to experience differences directly. I applied for the PhD program in Economic History at the London School of Economics and was accepted and paid my own way to London.

England was so different from how I grew up. I appreciated the cooler weather, but saw the inveterate racism when people asked me if I was Indian, Black, Israeli, Venezuelan. I wondered why it mattered 'where' I was from, as much as who I was? And why skin color was such a big determinant in other people's eyes. The irony being when I was among the native populations in Bolivia, these things were irrelevant, and there was a purer sense of self than in the complex social trappings of a developed nation. It showed me that when we think of developing versus developed nations, we don't really consider the moral and cultural development so much as the monetary and perhaps we should, since the worth is as much based upon the moral character and development of a population as it is their social standing.

I worked at the American Chamber of Commerce (London) and US Embassy, whilst studying and completing my PhD which was also a learning experience, with a combination of wealthy expat Americans and lowly paid English workers, clashing culturally. Each experience taught me more about perception and patterns, and in my work as an economist I keep returning to this, over statistics, which I notice, absent the personal experience in favor of a broad conclusion. When it was time to go for my Viva (oral exam for the PhD) I was in front of a board of two eminent economists. One of them asked me point-blank what the 'value' of my thesis was. My thesis was on cross-border trade between El Paso and Juarez Mexico. My examination of the micro-level of barter and selling, was a historical examination of outcomes that I felt added to the canon and exploration of US/Mexico historical trade. The English economists essentially told me the subject and purpose of my thesis was unimportant and rather than a PhD I received a MPhil.

To say I was devastated is an understatement. I am a reserved person and I just got on with it, but if I'm honest, it was a huge blow, as well as derailing my plans significantly. By this time, I had decided to return to the US without realizing I would leave two months after 9/11 occurred, which changed America forever, emotionally, and socially. I managed to get a foothold in academia for the first time, (since I had worked primarily in business until this point) with a community college in Texas, USA. I hoped once I received my PhD, I would be able to graduate to a 4-year University. Not being awarded a PhD thwarted that plan, as in America you can teach at community college level with a MA but need a PhD to teach at a 4-year University.

I made the best of it, working for a mostly Hispanic institution and helping disadvantaged Hispanics (often female) to get educated and gain independence and self-confidence. I was awarded several times for my initiatives and efforts in this field and it gave me a sense of accomplishment to know I was actively in the trenches, helping those most vulnerable and often overlooked. From the point of view of my career, it was stalled somewhat by not having a PhD. I worked as an adjunct for several prestigious Universities and was told repeatedly by the professors there that had I submitted my thesis to an American University, it would have been accepted without question. I believe this, and I know the risk I took learning in the UK, where there is a culture of failure without good reason in some fields and areas. I hadn't anticipated this because I believed in what I did and the veracity of my work but when you're in another culture, you are hostage to their rules and prejudices. To this day I know race and culture played a part in their decision.

What made it harder, also helped. I believe 'necessity is the mother of invention' and maybe if I had an easy ride gaining my PhD as I deserved to, first time around, I wouldn't have experienced some of the more in-the-trenches-work that solidified my commitment to help others. I also believe adversity brings things out of you that you didn't previously know you had. Disappointments can be turned around to learning-experiences. Granted, I wish I'd been treated fairly but when I compare where I am today to colleagues who sailed through because they were not diverse in their PhD, then I see how my challenges still got me to the table, it just took a different route and a lot of hard work. This helps me understand when a student comes to me explaining that they're having immigration problems or can't afford something, I get it because I have also struggled and it helps me help them by the compassion of shared-experience.

When I work with Hispanics, especially females, often from throughout Mexico, Central and South America, I empower them with a role-model who has broken through the glass ceiling and traditional roles expected of Hispanic women even today. There is no doubt Hispanics still have a long way to go to gain equality in education and the workplace. Likewise, women have a long way to go in economics, which remains a male dominated field, where alternative thinking is dissuaded. When I present papers that are original and disinterested in regurgitating the old economic canons, I am often met with bafflement or hostility, but this is part of why it's so necessary to keep pushing that envelope and challenging the status-quo.

A few years later I took a sabbatical and began a PhD at the University of Western Ontario, Canada, where I concentrated on Hispanic Studies. This may seem random but I was burned out on pure economics and believed this could expand my knowledge as well as prove useful and relevant in the fields I was interested in pursuing.

I graduated with honors in less than two years, having challenged myself in a field I was relatively unfamiliar with. My economic colleagues may have looked down on my choice but I was immensely glad of it, because it afforded me a greater understanding of how to work differently. Combining what I had learned from both seemingly diametric fields, I began work on networking models. Specifically utilizing network-representations to show patterns in creative ways, that can tell us as much as statistics can.

I have gone on to present my work and publish papers on this phenomenon with very positive feedback. Yes, I am always challenging the 'norm' and established rules, but I believe that's the legacy of my parents, who always said question everything, and don't assume anything. As a child of racism and prejudice I know the value of staying sharp and not just falling in line. I believe our world is healthier when we question and review the truth behind assumptions, rather than letting them stand. In my profession of economics, I see how we don't move ahead with new innovative ways of working, but remain wedded to our old methodologies. I want this to change and I want to be part of this change. As a Hispanic woman of Native American and Mexican heritage, and as a female, I am acutely aware I am a minority in my field and in general, and I push past stereotypes to add my unique perspective to this male-dominated field.

It now transpires El Paso / Juarez (Mexico) is the focal point of the global phenomenon of immigration. Currently people from 147 countries have crossed that border and it is the biggest confrontation between the third world and the 'advanced' world. While my first PhD professors may have refused to accept the importance of this, I am vindicated and continue to actively work as an economist and professor, now at a 4-year university that supports my work and promotes me as a valuable asset. It has taken a long time to get where I am, even after all that you still have to fight the biases of 'you didn't study in the US' or 'you didn't get your doctorate in this subject,' or serving under chairs that are threatened by my willingness to do the work, but this doesn't stop me. I see how I am a role model to younger Hispanic women, who see that someone like me, someone like them, can be and do whatever they want if they put their mind to it. I also believe 'failure' can either break us or make us. I turned what could have been a failure, into a learning experience and fought harder.

The irony being after all this occurred, I found it hard to break into the higher echelon of academia because shockingly, there is a very ageist aspect to academia worldwide, where newly minted PhD candidates are the ones who are mentored, whilst those who had valuable experience in the business world before getting their PhD, may be considered 'old' before their time. Again, this didn't stop me, but was a source of frustration nonetheless. I believe in true equity, and as such, we should not have closed doors based on age, race, gender, or things that have no relation to our ability to be useful.

I defy definition with almost every life choice (or lack of choice) I have made. I made my own category and it can be difficult or isolating but it's more satisfying than being pigeon-holed by everybody. More recently I now hold positions as President of SABES (San Antonio Business and Economic Society) give regular business interviews to the media in Spanish and English, am an economic forecaster for the Wall Street Journal, Coordinator for the Texas Latino Policy Symposium and I have my own economic impact and consulting research firm. I had a choice when my work was invalidated, to give up and agree with them, or keep going forward and find new innovative ways to challenge the dominant paradigm. I chose the latter. I had a sticker on my door for the longest time from a native American organization that said; *subvert the dominant paradigm* and truly, I think I am an activist in many ways through necessity and sheer outrage at inequity.

Selene Crosier

*Selene Crosier (not her
real surname because her
mother and she had to
change this for their safety)
lives in France with her
mother and their three cats. She speaks four
languages fluently and has a great job that
she absolutely adores as a translator. She
also graduated top of her class at university
where she majored in Islamic Studies and
Gender Studies. Selene's work was published
in SMITTEN This Is What Love Looks
Like, (Indie Blu(e) Publishing) and she has
also written for several organizations about
FGM (female genital mutilation) and she
is currently writing a memoir about her
experiences.*

My Mother My Hero

Crosier isn't my birth name. I was born in Africa, to
Muslim parents. Our heritage goes back to the Bedouin
and there is a proud tradition in our culture including the
bracelets we are gifted when we are born, that we carry

with us as a symbolic measure of our worth and value. I don't feel an attachment to the extreme element of my birth culture any longer and this essay explains the reason why.

In my culture girls are circumcised. This is said to be healthy for the girl and a sign of purity being maintained. The idea of a girl being sewn 'shut' for her husband is a matter of pride. My grandmother was circumcised. My mother was circumcised. When I was born, the only girl in our family of 3 boys, my devout father and his family were insistent that I be circumcised. My parents argued about this despite my mother taking a big chance by going against my father and his family. My mother lives with my father's family and they are in charge. She does not have any say. She still argued with my father because she was dead-set against the idea.

When I asked my mother years later why she took this risk of going against my father and his family this was her answer; She said she was already beaten down by the domination of his family and her lack of choice over who she could marry. All the girls in our family are arranged marriages by the age of 16. My mother was 14 when she was married to my father but she was betrothed to him from her birth. She did not ever have any rights or say in her life. Gradually she grew angered by this and when I was born, the last child she could have, and a girl, she knew she could not let what happened to her, happen to me.

My mother's arguments with my father were futile. He was not going to budge. His family, especially his mother, was very ugly to my mother, they shamed her, beat her and told her she was a whore for even suggesting this. They already were saying I was a whore of a whore. My mother knew what life this would be for me and she did something incredible. My mother ran away with me.

She had family in another part of the country, this was very lucky because without that she would have had nowhere to turn. That family was progressive. They were the black sheep of the larger family. My mother had corresponded by letter with them, and they told her to make her way to them. It was over 400 miles. My mother left one day with me taking nothing but one bag because any more she could not have carried and also it would have caused suspicion. Women are not meant to go anywhere without a man. The only exception is a woman's center where we would get charity handouts and the men were ashamed of these handouts from Christian organizations so they pretended they did not benefit from this by letting the women go together.

My mother and her sisters-in-law were there and she slipped away. To this day I don't know how she did this but she got a taxi with me and one bag and left. The money she had for the taxi was saved from her small amount she got for grocery shopping each week. The taxi driver looked at my mother and at me like we were whores for traveling alone without family but he was greedy and wanted the money so he did take us where my mother told him which was a coach station in the next town from ours. When we arrived my mother used the last part of the money she had and I think she also used some of her wealth from her bracelets to get two tickets on a coach. This was the only coach I had ever traveled on; we were careful to cover our faces and not attract any attention because the men on the coach could have raped us and we would be the ones to blame in the eyes of the law where I come from.

Although I was very young, I remember this journey,

I remember not being afraid but being very glad to be getting away. I did not have any love for my father. I did not like my father's family. They were always mean and cruel to my mother and to me. I held my mother's hand the entire way to give her my strength. Our bracelets were hidden beneath our long sleeves because we feared very much being mugged if not raped. A woman on her own is a target without any legal rights in my country and culture and she is to blame if something happens to her because the law believes she should know better than to do anything by herself. My mother's bravery on that day is something incredible to me even now.

When we arrived at our far away relatives, they were so welcoming. These relatives (I am not mentioning any areas or names to protect those involved) were Muslim like us but they were modern Muslims who did not believe in the more Bedouin ways especially in female circumcision which they thought was a barbaric practice. I did not know any of this and at the time I was only 11 I didn't even have my first menstruation. That is when I would have been circumcised. We stayed with these family members for a long time because everyone was putting money together to send us abroad for our safety. It was unsafe for us to stay in this country because we'd be found out and could be killed for leaving my father and his family and nobody would get jailed if we were killed because it would be seen as an honor killing. My mother was very jumpy and she insisted we both stay in doors so nobody did see us but I was young and spirited and would play outside with my cousins who I made good friends with.

In this part of my country girls could play, something I was never allowed to do back home and I could play with boys and girls and I could wear no full head covering. It was like the first freedom I ever felt. My mother was torn between two cultures. She was brought up very strictly and would disapprove of me not being properly behaved like a girl should be in her eyes but she also knew she was biased by her upbringing and that it was not healthy for girls to be treated that way so she tried to let me have some freedom. My cousins were so different to me, the two girls were like free girls without any fear of an arranged marriage or circumcision. I didn't even know what being circumcised was, I was told about this practice as it was a religious ceremony not something brutal. The details were spared me because it was considered indecent to talk about a woman's body parts that were unclean.

But my cousins told me everything in detail and I was disgusted at the idea that my father would let this happen. I did not know then about it taking away a woman's right to feel sexual pleasure, I just saw the brutality of cutting a girl for no good reason and for her future husband's pleasure and control. I talked to my cousins a lot about this because my mother would not talk about those things and they told me what happened to my mother and her mother and how they could not feel anything sexually and how bad the scarring was and the pain. I felt very badly for my mother. I had never of course seen her without clothes on and I did not know she was scarred or damaged but I did not understand how my father's family could have permitted this as part of the marriage arrangement.

One day I did ask my mother why didn't she leave my father sooner? She said she just was not able to because of having no options and nobody was going to help her. I asked her why did you leave now then? She said she could not bear to see me go through what she went through. She did not tell me the details but she did say she found it hard to urinate and it still hurt and it hurt to do her wifely duties with her husband. She said when it happened to her, she was taken to a woman in her village who did it with a sharpened piece of glass and a hot match and then much iodine and that she got a fever and was sick for a long time afterward and the pain was worse than childbirth.

My mother couldn't go home again because she would have been killed so she lost not only my father, which I think was not a bad loss for either of us, but her sons which did tear her to pieces. But she also knew her sons would hate her for what she did in saving me so she knew there was no way back. It did break her heart and she was not the same woman after that time. For me because I felt liberated from that future, I was glad and happy really despite being scared as well. I had things to look forward to, but my mother probably did not feel that way and it made her very sick inside her head and she was sad most of the time afterwards. I tried to bring her out of the sadness but I was a little girl and it was not easy to understand what was going on for my mother so eventually I got used to her being quiet and I tried to think of other things including going to school for the first time in my life.

After one year where I was going to the local school with my cousins and I learned some English there for the first time, my mother and myself were taken to the port and we said goodbye to our relatives and our homeland and we sailed on a big ship to France. The reason we went to France was because we spoke French and I only spoke a little English so we had to go somewhere we could speak the language to get work. My mother was very afraid.

We were accompanied by an uncle who was returning to France. He was our guardian on the ship which is lucky as you cannot be on a ship as two women without being in a lot of trouble no matter what. He helped us to get through the long sea trip where we were both sick from the savage waves and the bad food. I was excited as well because I had become a woman on that ship, I thought maybe that was a sign of a good future.

When we arrived in France we moved to a place where there were many Muslims but not the kind my mother's family comes from or my father's but the moderate Muslims who my uncle and other black sheep relatives come from. We lived in a small apartment that the French government gives to people fleeing their home countries for refugee reasons. My mother had to attest to the French government why we moved and it was very shameful for her to describe all the reasons but she had no choice. The translator, because my mother's French is not perfect like mine, was telling my mother please you must tell them everything or they will send you back so that encouraged my mother to do just that so they would let us stay. If she told the truth we could stay because we were in danger if we went home. That is the reason refugees like us are permitted to go to another country.

The apartment we had was luxury compared to anything I ever knew and it was very overwhelming to be in France after where we lived for our entire lives up until then. My mother did not like this place. She did not know anyone but some relatives she never met before and she did not want to learn French better so it was very difficult at first. We had a helper who was like a social worker for immigrants. They were the person who helped my mother most because this woman was Muslim and also had been circumcised and she really understood why my mother did what she did and was proud of her. Under her tutelage my mother went to French classes and also learned a trade of using her sewing skills to better income for us and she made friends with some of the women she worked with who also came from similar reasons for being refugees.

I went to school and I loved it. My school was about 50 percent Muslim so I felt at home there and I liked how the Muslims I met were not like my father's family back home. They were progressive and had fun and felt like it was ok not to cover up everything and women were not mistreated. One day in school we were taught about the prevalence of female circumcision and one girl who was older than us by two years, she did a presentation on this subject where she shared that she had been circumcised and all the things about it including frequent pain and infections. She told us that the reasons it was really one were not what we were taught about purity and they were more about a man having total control over a woman. This brutal operation was done without anesthesia on children and it caused some to die. She told us that the other reason was so a man who married a woman could 'break' the woman's sewn parts so they claim that woman and the last reason was the worst reason, because the woman's clitoris was removed, she could not orgasm and feel sexual pleasure so she would not run off with another man, so her husband thought.

I was in shock when I found this out and I really hated being a Muslim then util I talked to my friends and they said not every Muslim is sexist or abusive like this! And then I hated my father and his family for permitting this and wanting this for me too! But that is their culture and they are not going to change because it suits them to have women subservient in every possible way. My mother is the one who defies her tradition and her culture by going against this and escaping with me. My mother is my hero for this reason, she is the strongest woman I have ever met. I am so proud to be her daughter and to say she is my mother.

The end of this story is that my mother did finally find a home in France. She never married again because she was really sick of men and she did not want to be touched ever again by a man. She was happy because we were free and she could watch her daughter grow up in a country where for the most part there was no abuse like that. I did hear about some parts of France going back to the 'old' ways and I joined a group that protests about female circumcision, it was set up by an Egyptian activist who campaigns against this cruel practice throughout the world. Besides my mother she is my hero. She has done more for women than anyone I know and it is our service as the next generation to support her and help her spread the word.

Now as an adult I also am involved in the Orchid Project which helps to spread awareness about this practice. I feel it is my duty to help other girls and women to avoid what was nearly done to me and what was done to every female in my family until my mother had the courage to put a stop to this by running away. But it doesn't stop it happening so people like me who have the advantage of living in a safe country must do what we can. I defy my culture in this way because I am proud to be a Muslim but I refuse to go back to the old ways of my ancestors. Female circumcision used to be around 70 percent in some parts of Africa, now some statistics have it as low as 8 percent. I believe it is higher than this but I do think it is trending downwards and I believe it's thanks to women like my mother who say NO even when they have no means, no safety, no money, no voice. Still, they are successful.

According to the World Health Organization over 200 million girls have been mutilated through this practice throughout Africa and the Middle East. I suspect it is far higher than that. It is typically carried out between the ages of 0 and 15 by unlicensed cutters who do not use pain killers or sterilization. It is also a cruel practice that robs girls and women of the rights over their bodies, many of them have life-long problems and cannot experience any sexual pleasure. There are no religious reasons that justify doing this to a girl and no parent should let their faith make this bad choice. My mother was never educated. She didn't know better but something inside of her told her this was wrong and her courage saved my life. I will take care of my mother for the rest of my life to honor her sacrifice of losing 3 sons and her husband. I can never thank her enough for what she did for me. I am now a citizen of France and I speak 4 languages and earn a good living and have a degree. I am in a relationship and am free to love who I choose. My mother gave me all of this from the kindness of her heart and sacrifice. Often, I wonder what would have happened to us if we were not able to escape. I wonder what happened to all my cousins who are still there, and how long this is going to be permitted. I am proud to be Muslim but ashamed of this practice. I defy this practice as part of the Muslim faith and ask other Muslims to join me in saying this must end.

Adrija
Chatterjee

*Adrija Chatterjee
(Preferred name
Adrija C.) writes
from India. She
holds ass Master
of Philosophy degree in Foreign Policy and
Peace Studies. Her creative fiction, poetry
and nonfiction pieces have appeared in The
Active Muse, The Alipore Post, Life and
Legends and elsewhere. She has been a
contributor in an anthology titled Narratives
on Women's Issues in India: Vol 1 Domestic
Violence published by the IHRAF, New York
and a global feminist anthology, Looking
Glass Anthology Vol. 2. She is the author
of the chapbook titled Beyond The Night
Jasmine, September 2021. Her piece was
recently selected in the Ukiyoto Publishing
anthology, Words That Remained Unsaid
and Wide Awake Vol 2.*

Childfree by Choice

Dear munchkin,

I know you shall be reading this on some yet to bloom cherry blossom, nesting upon a tree probably melting away the snow. Drop after drop white after white, as pristine as mom holding you in her womb. By the way do you know what mom means? I assume you do not, yet. Mom is just like an M & M: one that feels softness underneath it's crackling shell. Your grandmother, my mom seems to fit in as an epitome of whatever I said right now. My thought to hold you close and upright grew with me well into my adulthood. An inexplicable desire to raise your grandmama's bar, filling in the gaps she unintentionally created, the hope to improvise upon her unique style of smothering me. Anything I ever wanted was to fill your life with a kindness that you could never find a parallel with. All this till the day when I first encountered the rebuke my father, your could have been grandfather heaped my mom and me with.

On a humid late evening of autumn 2008, your grandmama and I cowered in a corner of the large mansion of a quarter assigned in the name of my mother's husband (you know I am so tired and agitated to tag him a father). Both of us exasperated in fear of when that man could strike again. After all the pegs of cheap whiskey he filled his intestines with.

"Mamma, am hungry..." unable to bear the hunger anymore, I was this scared piece of defenceless chick, with nothing but the hope that my mom would go to the kitchen and bring me some food. You know what munchkin, she did. Knowing well she shall be crossing that man's path in the middle. By the time we had dinner, she had endured countless slaps and cuss words to fill our already dizzying heads with. It was almost three years later when your grandmama could finally gather the bones to confess I was the child my father never wanted her to have. I was a reluctant piece of life to the man who valued wealth building at a time my mother wished to create life inside her.

That was the time I understood had my mother considered this future once, the consequence of her magnanimous decision to prize life over wealth, I would not be around. An overwhelm stupefied me when I realized how much better it would have probably been. I could be saved from the destiny to endure a violent parent, be a witness to mundane obscenity and above all probably, just probably a life free of diseases that crept on me through chromosomes on stress.

Here hon, look at me, your mom, in some other world, I know you are crying, I know you are probably defying every definition I have for not bringing you. I know you are resisting me. But I don't feel ashamed for any bit of it.

The day I was diagnosed with severe asthma, unexplained spondylosis and a host of other hormonal disorders, all my doctors were concerned about was how a young female like me could endure all this and still be able to conceive biologically. I felt like a piece of luggage that day. Was I just my fleshed womb and vaginal pathway? Was my identity only and only for doctors to bring out another flesh and blood regardless of whether the cellular permutations and combinations made my child, as defenceless, as sick as me? Was I just an agent for procreation at a time I was chasing my ambition to evolve beyond such trivialities? Was my love for you so large that I had no right to love people who could need me, those who were already around!

Hon, look into my soul, your mother's soul, do you see how much love it still holds for you, but hey my sweetheart, we haven't met each other. Aren't some loves just like this? The mortal world would have probably made you hate me at some point, me hating you at the other… but this way we can never let hatred creep between us.

It's weird how humid autumn days became the backdrop of my most intimate and life changing confrontations. In one of these in the year 2013, my mom finally made me awake to the biggest identity paradox of my life, that I was *her own very own* choice. Probably the biggest reason my father never learned to love me or my identity as his own kin. On the second, in a similar humid autumn afternoon of Houston, me and my husband, married only for seven months then, agreed over our regular evening coffee to stay without a child, our biological one. It never hit us hard, except for the fact that long before our marriage when we had been seeing each other he once told me, "We will see life together, we will create life together".

That last part, I was far from convinced in that calm look behind the spectacles when I said,

"I don't think we can *afford* a child".

Not long after that day I asked him back,

"You once said we shall create life together! Are you okay with this?"

To which his reply resonated my innermost idea:

"Creating life does not always mean a human child of flesh and blood. We can love our unborn child in ways most people won't."

In choices, that is where we need our partners.

Partners to legitimise a child, not socio legally but mentally, emotionally and of course financially.

Little one, you now probably see from the world you never came from that your mom cannot forget for a single day the horrors she had to endure for everything denied to her. An emotionally unavailable father, a mother going through a series of misfortune, financial difficulties so much so that your mother had to endure every bullying the family put her through.

The first time I made *our* decision to go childfree in public was to my gynecologist. I visited her for my polycystic ovarian syndrome. It was almost three years since I last visited a gynae's clinic in my city, Kolkata, India. After studying my medical records and suggesting me all the meds, she finally said,

"So, when are you planning the baby?"

Nothing had changed and it was clear. The expectations from me, my body and my cognitive abilities.

"I do not want a baby, it's a decision between me and my husband."

My voice cold, sharp and my words far from minced, the lady doctor it seemed, faced her sharpest scalpel so far. That was in 2016, I came out of her clinic, promised myself to never visit her again because she said I cannot be a woman if I did not want a child. I came back home, told my mother everything, she said it would be my next struggle. The next red flag people would chase me for, but I should not be bothered.

"I know that art maa! To develop this thick skin, because nobody paid for me so far and nobody's going to pay for my child as well."

You know honey, what is the only thing that latches me to my spouse, you could have been father? Our mutual consent to respect you by protecting your dignity that's questioned even if you aren't around. Your dignity to be raised as per your dreams, which we knew could be legitimate enough and at the same time probably unachievable by our mortal financial means.

My mother-in-law once said to me,

"Never deny your man in bed".

The same woman who made sure her fury and rage be known to the world because her son, my husband, decided to get married to me. She cursed me for as long as I remember, froze all relationship but when it came down to my intimate equation with my husband, she was oh so concerned. The same mother, who never batted an eyelid before hurling every curse to traumatise my husband for life, to silently agonise me with her mental and emotional abuse, thought it was a mother's well-defined role. The right to abuse, the right to inflict enough harm to destroy a conjugal life just because she procreated her son. In her I saw the liberty, privilege and drama procreation could bring.

Stone after stone hurled at me, sometimes they did not even spare the man, the husband. Unfortunately, the darkest encounters and ugly interrogations happened inside a doctor's chamber.

"You do not want a baby?"

"You know not having a baby raises your risk of getting breast cancer?"

"You are being silly, if everyone thought like this there would be none left to fuel humanity."

"There are so many medications now, to ensure even

if your child inherits the disease causing genes they will be leading a good life."

Good to whom? Good for whom? It's my child, I myself cannot guarantee their good will be equivalent to my standards!

Repulsive is the word that hit me every time I opened a social media group, all groups slowly converted into groups of well-meaning parents. I finally realised how it felt to be the *ugly duckling*, when people asked me how could I miss out on my biggest accomplishment as a woman. I don't know, probably I saw my mother's life close enough, dissected my mother in law's maternal domination too instinctively. With all that and my above average cognitive skills (which as a matter of fact am a little protective about) than the mediocre, I could deduce being a mother and having your own child could actually be *two separate* phenomena. My expectations from myself and expectations from me by the people around never converged and beyond a point I was happy being the arrogant headstrong Armageddon people never expected me to be.

Know what sweetheart, every day I miss you, a little bit and am allowed to do that. Every woman deep down probably craves for a daughter, one who takes upon her, so she can relive a metamorphosed life stage after stage. But then what if when I have you around?

I probably could save one soul, from this chaos called the socio capitalist life. The system needed to change before more thoughtful pregnancies happened and were executed to create a formidable society. Unfortunately, as a mother of a child of my own I knew I did not have the power to ensure it.

School running business in the name of education.

Higher education thriving upon a vested corporate agenda.

Realpolitik and Neo liberal institutions sucking intelligence into a black hole.

In the other part the syllabus is getting reformatted to suit a given jingoistic agenda.

Old age getting harsher and mortality rate nowhere down.

Families becoming a semblance of the macro problems just foraying into my thoughts.

I was raised by my grandparents, probably one of those last pieces of human in my life who understood nothing but love for me. What about my child? What family could I give them? A maternal grandfather obsessed with his own patriarchal existence or a paternal set of grandparents obsessed with the ulterior motive of property, power dynamics and probably on the lookout for a chance to poison the child's mind against me. Friends? Logically I would have preferred home schooling, but honestly could I afford it? I mean there would come a time my depth of education no matter how formidable, would clash with the societal definition of examination and grade centric life.

Then could I pull them out of the system, the answer unfortunately is a *NO*. As one wise person once said no matter how far you get in the rat race the truth is you are still a rat! Temperamentally I would not allow that, practically I would be left with no other option! Yes, my son or daughter could be the agent of change but from my own experience I know that's anything but a cakewalk. And being a *mother* deep inside I would choose a human's convenience over their unnecessary struggle. Be it any human, any living being.

On days I read about rape incidents in the country and across the world, I read about women used as the bait to win and

*lose wars, a nausea fills my mind. Is this what I shall be giving
a child, this overpopulated world, human pitted against human
for the scarcest of resource. It's a primitivity I am ashamed of as
a human. I read of Elon Musk trying to build a colony up there
on Mars, I closely studied the shareable income of global wealth,
the top one percent populations own over half the world's wealth.
They alone make the system. And you know what munchkin, your
mother could have been a rebel to the system with each birthday.*

Yet am forbidden to discuss all this and so much more,
for the sheer minority I have turned into. From the doctor's
chamber to office talks to casual meet ups with old friends.
My only hope is a few people who probably can resonate
to my rather universal human concern of overpopulation
and inherited disease. How I wish doctors could come out
of their self-styled cocoon of orthodoxies regarding life.
There is too much life around us and more unhappy than
the happy ones. Who cares about a bloodline, kinship when
lives perish in war even today. What comes through buying
new clothes for my own bloodline when a morsel of food is
all a section craves for in a day!

Immortality through preservation of my generational
chromosome is passe in a world where the environment is
crying to get unburdened. The mother nature that sustains
me and all of us never gave us the umbilical cord. Instead,
it nourished and nurtured, so that we could wake as
humankind. In my own small way I just wish to be beside a
mother, in my own capacity I just wish to be more inclusive
of love that isn't measured by just my womb. There is too
much paucity of love around. As a mother with this defied
definition of staying childfree am just trying to be more
kind beyond selfish ties of my blood alone.

Rondalyn Whitney,
PhD, OTR/L, FAOTA

*Rondalyn Varney Whitney,
PhD, OTR/L, FAOTA,
is a poet, writer, occupational therapist,
and researcher. Her writing narrates the
lived experience of defiant healing. She
writes across various genres, from scholarly
journals to professional texts and creative
works. Her poem Amazing Grace appears in
the anthology The Healer's Burden, essay Is
this The Wife in Intima and Time is a Fluid
in The Examined Life Journal. She holds
advanced certificates in Narrative Medicine
from Columbia University, Cognitive
Behavioral Therapy for Insomnia (Colorado
State) and Sexuality and Intimacy. She
recently retired after over 20 years in
academia. She lives in Hamden, CT where
she enjoys the sound of tree frogs and insects
and watching the occasional black bear from
her porch. Facebook: @RondalynWhitney /
Twitter: @DrRDub_writes /
www.rondalynwhitney.com*

Lies in the Afterlife

Lesson 1

Maybe I'm the one who died.... No one tells you how to judge what is real and what is an illusion in life, in death, if you're alive or dreaming or dead and in a purgatory or suspended waystation. That's a lie – Margery Williams knows what is really real and she told the truth back in 1922 in her story *The Velveteen Rabbit*, and while she claimed it was a story about how toys become real through being deeply loved, the truth is this is a story about how anyone becomes real, that we are loved into a reality.

It's also true that *The Little Prince* by Antoine de Saint-Exupéry tells you the truth about the afterlife and *Good Omens* by Neil Gaiman and Terry Pratchett which was written about being thrust into the afterlife when one of the two authors was in fact thrust into the afterlife so you can trust it as solid reporting. But what happens once we die? Who knows? It depends. It is different for everyone. The lack of certainty and predictability makes it hard to understand. Margery Williams did not talk about what happened to the stuffed rabbit or that ratty Skin Horse shell of a toy (I mean, we're to believe he's left behind unloved in a heap of toys while a splendid stallion is out galloping in the field, right?). Now, THAT would be a good story... Steven King would have to write it, I suppose.

I died last year, all my cells got shattered when a car hit and shattered all the bones that should have been a femur and tibia and fibula but then became a lot of splintered osteoblasts, osteocytes, osteoclasts, and bone lining cells. I died when all the coagulant cells were insufficient to coagulate the blood that ruptured from vessels in the legs and then drained all the blood that was supposed to nurture the chordae tendineae and keep oxygen going to the brain. The chordae tendineae in case you don't know, are the tiny but strong inelastic fibrous cords in the heart, stretched between the edges of cusps of the atrioventricular valves to the papillary muscles within the right and left ventricles. They open the heart to receive and to let go. Most of us call them the heart strings, we do have heart strings that flutter and strum when we are anxious or in love or overwhelmed by a feeling. I died that day, or a part of me did at least who I knew myself to be.

They say you have to live a year and a day after a traumatic death of a loved one. That's just another lie the 'they' in life tell to keep us from tearing our skin off and gouging out our eyes and to keep those heart strings from pulling clean out of their anchor points. The day after the longest year of my life was a day of exhaustion: I'd run a marathon that ended with a tilted non-stopping treadmill right at the finish line. *Other lies in life?* To get up in the morning, you just need to open your eyes. Waking up with dry eyes means the lid of your eye fuses with what is supposed to be a lubricated layer over the cornea and when you open your peepers, you rip off a layer of cells. If you cry at night, in your sleep, the salty tears dry into crystals that layer over pores and you get frequent styes until you figure it out and learn to wipe your eyes religiously with expensive, rough eye wipes every single morning of the rest of your days. Here's another one: It's best to have a baby naturally. What no one tells you about having a baby *naturally* is that the alien will tear a hole in order to pass or that midwives measure the tears, compare them, and use the centimeters as a way to gauge their own skill set. Perineal tears work like golf: Smallest numbers are winners.

Life is full of these lies, outright ones and those that are lies of withheld information, unspoken but known horrors and out and out myths spun around us so we will continue to breathe, our hearts will continue to pump rhythmically and send oxygen to the brain and even strum a little tune once in a while to make you feel like is worth it. No one tells you why you faint – you faint because the body, your body, is a traitor – yep, it has one mission when the oxygen levels dip: Save the brain. In order to do this, the brain (an egocentric tyrant) will surrender everything else (the femur, your eye, it doesn't care) in order to save itself and to save itself, it gets the head onto the ground where the blood, from the heart, can more easily get to the brain and deliver the oxygen needed for neuron survival. So, you faint, and hit your hip and back and head and eye all along the path of resistance as you fall to the floor of a cold bathroom.

Another thing no one tells you is that teaching your teenager how to drive, helping him transition from a learners permit to a license can be fatal. I lost my husband of 30 years when my son took a left turn into 3 lanes of traffic which dad said was clear and was not clear. Here's what else isn't clear: Did he die or did I? We had grown together for so long, ripping off the symbiotic part of the him of me- him killed me, or part of me, or was it all of me and I'm dreaming he was the one lying on the blacktop while caring passerby folks stopped to perform CPR? Nothing is clear when the threshold between this life and not life rips open, it's not clear what side you're left on. No one tells you that, I'm sorry no one tells you that, I think someone should tell you that.

It's not clear what to do when an officer at the scene of a fatal accident asks you if you want to sit in the back seat of his cruiser. No? I mean, who wants to sit in the back seat of a cruiser with lights blasting overhead? Behind a cage? Will he shut the door and forget you? Are you in trouble? It's best to say no, a lot. It's not clear how to answer when so many people say *not to you, but around you,* Is this the wife? It's not a direct question for you, what is the social rule here? Do you answer, let them answer, do they know the answer? Are you a feminist and try to avoid the possessive wife nomenclature? It's correct to say *no* if you don't believe in living a life as a possessive but it's best to say yes on this one, it gives you power and authority you'll need along the path of so many decisions, so many decisions....

It's not clear how to answer when the undertaker asks you if you want an urn, if you want to be there to watch the burn, if you want to see how the facility will turn the body. Just say *I don't want anything* and take a friend who can make decisions in your behalf – I'm sorry no one tells you all this, it's information that will come in handy someday and all the decisions are harder if the questions are about someone you loved like life had given you something precious and special and you don't get a handbook on this. As it turns out, there's not much that's clear. In the end, you just have to make a choice a hundred times a day and move forward without regret. My younger son moved forward into the intersection, he and dad made a choice, and we grieve now but have no regret. Mostly.

Lesson 2

Regret is a strange thing. As a verb, regret means feeling sad and disappointed over a loss or missed opportunity. As a noun, regret is the emotion, the wistfulness that one should have made a different decision in the past, that now you have the consequence you don't like. We loved dad, every day, and we told him so. My sons ruffled his hair when they passed, said he was a true Chad (which apparently is a compliment). I loved my husband every day, made sure he knew he was loved in words and actions and tiny gestures. He died knowing he was loved, beloved. We regret nothing except wish we had more time.

Time is another lie we should talk about. The physicists know a lot they do not share, mostly I think because we cannot understand their language. Physicists get overly excited by lines of math running across pages, they can distill a universe into a series of numbers and symbols and it makes perfect sense to them. My husband was a physicist and he would read page after page of mathematical equations and laugh! Laugh, imagine that, over pages of numbers, equations, graphs. Physicists named the smallest particles discovered *Truth* and *Beauty*, *Strange* and *Charm*, after all. Physicists are quirky poets who love and understand the language of the universe, of math and the essential parts of life. That *Truth* quark? Truth quarks are literally 40 times as big as everyone else in the quark family and still they are the hardest ones to find: You know the physicists named it Truth as an inside joke. Maybe it's a hidden clue that they hope we discover, that truth is hard to find but also most essential even in a quark. Essential things are hardest to see – The Little Prince told us that in 1943. Two decades later, physics playfully dubbed the most essential particles quarks, the largest one Truth, the one most essential the most invisible to the eye.

Entropy is the natural law, that the universe wants to push a person out of their cohesive *I know and love this man* state, or make a bowl teeter and fall off the edge of a table given the energy of a house rumbling or a car slamming into a body. Without energy, particles will not return to a cohesive, orderly state: No, it turns out that's a lie. A group of physicists (they humbly call themselves time-crystal tinkerers) have learned how to arrange atoms in a crystal in the fourth dimension, *Time*, where they blast a crystal with a finely tuned laser to make atoms dance, flip back and forth from one state to another without absorbing any energy from the laser. This laser blasting allows the particles to be in different states simultaneously and interact at impossible distances, breaking apart what we used to think of as entropy, disorder. I am sure they dance with awkward scientist moves when they do this.

Hell, as a place outside of the day-to-day life on earth, is a lie. At least, I don't believe in hell, I gave up that belief when I sat with Quakers at Baltimore. I don't believe in heaven either. I think all of that is a form of magical thinking. People outside the afterlife say *I'll pray for you* when you find you have arrived in the afterlife – I don't know how that would help me. A bottle of good Berkshire Bourbon, some nice cheese with good crackers, a soft scarf or hat to hide behind maybe? But a wish tossed into the void? Not so much use for that in the afterlife.

Children grow out of magical thinking in second grade, that's also when they stop believing in Santa, Elves, and Spooks under the bed are forms of magical thinking. I wouldn't want to work for or receive health care from someone who believes in Green Elves or a flat earth. Similarly, I am leery of those who believe in a white male puppet master in the sky with a long beard who grants the prayers of one person to move traffic out of their way but lets the prayers of starving children go into the spam folder. I grew up in the Bible Belt, raised in the church back when Christianity meant truly caring for and loving others without ego. But the first bitter bite of truth came when my Sunday School teacher, Mr. Weeblin, said everyone who isn't baptized will burn in hell for all of eternity. I raised my hand and asked about the Pygmies (I must have read about them in the set of World Books my mom bought for our home) and he said yes, even those little people in a world far away. I didn't want to be part of a story that would damn innocent people I had never met; that was the first time I began scratching my way out of a big ball of tangled lies. I've come to understand becoming an adult is nothing but finding your way out of all the lies and realizing, if you're going to live in a world full of lies, you might as well choose helpful lies, narrate your own story.

Lesson 3

My husband of 32 years died; the quintessential 'dad' armed with a battery of infinite bad dad jokes. He could juggle. He made great lattes. He used his knowledge of physics to suspend ropes from trees and create swings that hurled boys through the air like air-stream surf boards. He filled notebooks with small, precise penmanship of equations. When we were cold, he would run over and rub us briskly, and narratate his signature *friction treatment* to warm us. He left the earth, and we were left here in the chilled afterlife, the after time of his life.

Salut! Cheers – we raise our glasses and toast to long life at the end of a year, retirement, the end of being single and moving into a state of marriage. Also, a lie, Salut is a toast to good health, not long life and while they can go together, you really, we all really need to understand tomorrow is a lie. You can have good health and die in a car wreck – you've heard this, right? As an excuse for having a juicy burger with cheese and fries? Well, *Salut!* Have the burger or don't at some point you'll either die or be thrust into the afterlife and it's a lie to think you have much control over any of it.

Fate: We made up a narrative about that too, that a supernatural being has scripted our life's plot and we just walk through the various scenes waiting until viewership wanes and we get cancelled. Fate or destiny, if you go back and look it up, was a myth spun by the Greek's, a story of three goddesses who presided over the birth and life of humans. Your destiny was a thread spun, measured, and cut by the three Fates; Clotho, Lachesis, and Atropos. So destiny, all that is a lie unless you DO want to believe ancient goddesses spin a thread, cut it and hand it into the world that you are born into. See, there are just so many lies and we don't take the time to follow the threads of the stories until we find the truth.

After telling you about lies, I'm guessing you want to know what is the truth, as in THE TRUTH. You might feel entitled to know the truth of life or at least the afterlife, like I owe you something. Okay, let me pay the debt. Here it is: Truth is the name of a quark, the largest of the smallest known particles and the most elusive. That's all we've got. And the physicists, they made that up to poke fun at the rest of us mere mortals who do not know how to sit with and contemplate the wonders of the universe, to see all of everything in an obit of electrical charges or to understand that all the light we love and call stars are from something that likely died lightyears ago.

The poets and artists have tried to help us understand

truth, giving us metaphors, but that got hijacked by too many, watered down and overused tropes without judicious wielding of a pen honed to be mightier than a sword. Metaphors are used to teach us, but they obscure, muddle, obfuscate, and blur the lines of what is true and real and count-on-able and what isn't. Even the definition of metaphor is opaque: *a metaphor is a figure of speech in which a word or phrase is applied to an object or action to which it is not literally applicable.* Like that makes one bit of sense, isn't that a circular definition? An exemplar of circumlocution? one that uses the term(s) being defined as a part of the definition or assumes a prior understanding of the term being defined? When someone dies, death is real – you are either dead or you are not. The question is, who dies, someone should tell us about that.

Lesson 4

True story. In January 2020, I got up early and went downstairs for my morning coffee. As is my habit, I brought it back upstairs to sit at my desk and write. This day, at the top of the stairs I felt the presence of my father, dead for 4 and half decades. Now you might have dropped your coffee or at least felt afraid, but I had nothing of that reaction, instead just asked, "is it time?" It's all that came to to say, *is it time?* He told me no, it's not my time, I had more to do but to be ready, death was near. And just like that, the moment was gone. I remembered that moment when I took a plane to Columbia, New York at the end of February. A week before the first person was diagnosed with Coronavirus. I thought that was what he was talking about but it was a lie to think that, a misunderstood why do spirits speak in metaphor moments.

I don't believe in God, but I do believe in the Angel

of Death. And I imagine he might at times need a holiday. One of my favorite movies is *Death Takes a Holiday*. In the movie, one of the characters, Baron (the Angel of Death) says *I think you're all wrong to be afraid. I talked with him about dying and he said, 'Has it ever occurred to you that Death may be simpler than Life and infinitely more kind?'and when he spoke, I had a curious feeling that somehow, he knew."*

This 1934 black and white film, was an invitation to my teen self to understand shadows in a new way, that they may be kind spirits to turn toward, that I should long to know them, know their character, to lean in or learn from them when it is time to turn away and seek out the light that created them, remove what might be in the way of them and the light. This film was about the membrane, the threshold, that between-world clearing. Through watching this film, I came to know, somehow, the threshold itself and the displacement that lives there in the in-between. I learned early to *be wary of the angels and what they promise* that Death might wait if we ask, that angels ruthlessly kill innocent children behind non-blood splashed doors to appease a vengeful god and there is a threshold that will reveal itself to us if we seek it.

When my father died, I was 15. I was getting ready for an end of the school year party at the pool. I was ironing the curls from my hair, not with the flat iron that we have today but with an iron, on an ironing board, and in the humid heat of the south. What hope I had for control back then! That call, the last time I heard his voice, his call was to say he was returning home after a long stay in the warmth of Florida. Casey Kasem was announcing the top song of the year, *Joy to the World* by Three Dog Night. I can hear that song, smell the summer air, smell hair being burned and hear my father say he loved me. For the last time. I knew he was dying that day, I felt it in his tone, something... it was like final words, "take care of your mother" and "don't be afraid to love people". I didn't recognize it as death speak like I understand now. I wish someone had told me then how to know when I heard death speak – in the afterlife, anyone in the afterlife knows what death speak sounds like. I think we should tell others about that but I'm not sure they can believe us. Stories can linger on us, sometimes for a lifetime, an earworm, or a scent: I'm not sure what invisible mark is so enduring and visible to the initiated.

Death came early in my life. Angel of death, one to long for or struggle against or to fall in love with, I had been given a gift to know all these paths were a choice I could take. Death whispers to me even now, I can see it when I look into the eyes of those who gesture with age-knotted fingers to what seems, to the uninitiated, at uninhabited spaces. Some stand still until water overtakes them and they drown, others beat against the undertow. I hope I welcome the waves. Death comes *for* us, he doesn't chase us down, he stands on the threshold offering, maybe, a friction treatment or warm blanket. *Death Takes a Holiday* is a story about being at home in the in-between, the simultaneity of the in and the out, and love the innocence on each side, forgive each of us as we cling to what we know, celebrating when any of us let go and drop into the nothingness of destined paths. I think what I loved about this movie was the confirmation, that when we near death or times of cataclysmic transition, if we soften, if we open, we can sense another is with us, someone or something removes the veil, if only for an instant and, in the threshold, an instant is eternity is there, and if we look closely, a greeter at the top of stairs and a soft message to prepare, to *pack*.

When someone you love dies, you are in the afterlife, the life after life of the one you loved who died. That is not a metaphor, that's the soul-punching truth of life, that love is dangerous, losing a love hurts more than any other wound and the afterlife is where you turn into a gas and you know this to be a truth because you feel it as you float around, aimless in the afterlife; you feel yourself expanding or contracting and there is no pressure because there isn't a flesh container for you anymore, you are in nothingness and you know all this is true because gas particles are farther apart and more weakly attracted to each other than when you were attracted to and able to touch a beloved solid who is, now, dead. The only truth is that all of this is a lie and, in the afterlife, you learn, I hope, to choose the empowering lie, push the day's boulders up the day's hill and find a way to love the absurdity of it all. It really is absurd, that we choose to love and wait to lose. I hope I never see you here, in the afterlife, but if I do, I hope you bring me a lie you've discovered, and we can laugh about being gassy and edgeless on this side of the invisible threshold.

Afterthoughts

I lied about this being the end. You probably figured that out on you own, knowing, by now, that time is an illusion and so too would *beginning, middle* and *end* be an illusion. There is no ending in the afterlife as far as I can tell, it just slogs on and on and on, like Sisyphus rolling that boulder up a hill on and on and on. Camus told us, try to find a way to be happy even in that fate your spun thread has brought you into. Try to be happy in the absurdity of your afterlife – that is the only thing you have control over.

Nina Chari

Nina Chari hails from New York City, but was raised for the most part in Iowa...and hence where her snarky sensibilities were cultivated. For the past (*cough, cough*) decades, Nina has had a very successful career in the technology space but her true love has always been writing. As she embarks on this next chapter of her life, Nina looks forward to being able to focus on that particular area of expression, exhibiting her deeply felt compassion for others along with the ability to laugh at the absurdity of life itself.

No Regrets: The Barren Spinster Chronicles

"Nice to meet you! So, tell me about yourself! Are you married? Do you have any kids?"

"Nope."

"Well, you're young. You still have time."

"Not really. My uterus was captured by a gang of rogue tortoises when I was 17 to be used as an alternate source of roofing material. They featured it on the show Ancient Aliens. You should check it out! I'm the one with the hair."

One would hope that there would come a time in every woman's life where people around her would cease scrutinizing her life choices. At that point, she would be considered "too old", hence no real potential harm could occur. An alternative would be the realization that this woman knew what she was talking about and was able to own her own path.

What age would that occur, if ever? Your mileage may vary.

Making the decision to be child-free may arguably be near the top of the list of decisions that apparently require societal board approval and airport tower clearance. Bracing oneself against the slew of commentary, judgement, and unwelcome pity should be considered a skill worthy of prominent placement on a resume or at least Marvel comics character superpower. Cue The Amazing Teflon Woman with her impenetrable snark armor.

In the spirit of complete transparency, I always thought I would have kids. It was never awaited with tingly anticipation, however, like it did for every other woman I knew. It was more a casual presumption, much like how I would envision my first colonoscopy prep.

I was *supposed* to get married, garner a prestigious career, and have kids to whom I would pass along my family's traditions. I really did not have an objection to any of it occurring and figured it would just happen when it was supposed to.

And therein was the issue. Looking back, I realize I did not want to become a mother enough to make it happen. I was waiting for a magical sign from the universe indicating that this was time. For me, that sign never arrived and that was an overwhelming relief.

When it came to my career path, I pushed. When it came to cultivating my friendships, I put in the necessary effort. When it came to eating that remaining slice of cheesecake, I rose to heroic heights. I was capable of relentlessly attaining anything to which I set my mind. Regarding having children, however, I was decidedly and thoroughly apathetic.

"I can't imagine my life without my kids. I don't think I could ever be that self-absorbed".

"I totally agree. But...the others...they hate children, and I try to run our coven ...sorry...book club... as a benevolent fascist dictatorship. By the way, I have a spell that can remove that nasty wart of yours..."

I have been surrounded by friends' kids for years and enjoyed playing with them and helping them with their homework. But not once did I have this evolutionary-driven desire to have one or at least not one that was not instantly squelched with a subsequent tantrum.

Meanwhile, I was also bombarded by many pressure vectors, societal as well as cultural. And oh yes, my own insignificant preferences were buried amongst all of that somewhere.

Those societal pressures assumed many forms and

tapped into many emotions, ranging from legitimate concern, snide judgment, passive aggressive guilt, to outright accusations of selfishness, immaturity, and emotional deficiency. Everyone felt they had license to weigh in, including random relatives, neighbors, a random drunk woman at a Sonoma winery who apparently felt we were "ride or die", and even my employers. I was informed that I was disappointing my family and my heritage. Astoundingly, if my child-free status was deemed palatable, I was instead asked "why aren't you further along in your career then?"

I was eviscerated from all directions.

Do not think for a moment that these tactics were not effective. A lifetime of being a dutiful friend, family member, or romantic partner had trained me very well to put others' needs above my own. I was the undisputed champion in justifying my decisions as altruistic instead of seeing them for what they truly were: self-destructive. I was miserable but I had initially felt it was out of guilt for not being the mother everyone wanted me to be. Only much later did I realize that my sadness stemmed from my feeling stifled in a world that was supposedly "modern", but still maintained deeply held mores of what appropriate female roles should resemble. Decades of this ongoing assault manifested itself as persistent panic attacks and depression. I was trapped and could not find my way out of a room in my mind, even though there was a well-lit door right in front of me.

At first, my people-pleaser sensibilities led me to believe if I simply explained my reasoning, I would find acceptance from those who questioned me. Through this I discovered a painful truth- nobody cares about my justification. I have been deemed guilty by the village elders and thus no acknowledgement or clemency would be granted.

I had collected quite the catalog of reasons for being hesitant in not wanting children. I felt if I had kids, it would have been for purely selfish reasons, e.g., needing someone to take care of me in my old age, obtaining some narcissistic satisfaction of producing a miniature version of myself, living up to the expectations placed on me by my culture and family, etc.

"That's so sad you did not have kids. You would have been such a good mom!"

"Yeah ...I know. I had hoped to have multiples so I can conduct psychological experiments on them. You know...for science."

In addition to my questioning of any underlying motivation, I had some legitimate concerns about bringing children into the world, e.g., missing out on my life's ambitions to focus on child-rearing, the endless expense, and sharing a life with someone just for that reason. I also had concerns I would develop additional health issues because of being pregnant. The cons outweigh the pros by a mile. This was not a shallow whim of a decision, despite public opinion. All I craved was some measure of empathy and advocacy. Unfortunately, none was forthcoming.

So sadly, I did what people who did not feel they had a voice in the world did, I played the waiting game with my fertility. My biological clock could not sound the alarm fast enough. So finally, when I was officially "old" by societal child birthing standards, I was finally released to the peace I should have fought for harder decades ago.

So alas I stand here now, "victorious". However, I do not consider it a true victory. I won by forfeit. I lost precious time and effort in my losing battle to win hearts and minds instead of finding my voice sooner and living my truth, regardless of what others thought. My hope is with the current political climate de facto forcing pregnancies, more is done to give these women a louder megaphone to speak their mind and not cower under untenable pressure instead.

Elizabeth Jaeger

*Elizabeth Jaeger's essays,
short stories, book
reviews and poetry have
been published in various print and online
journals, including Margate Bookie, Caustic
Frolic, The Blue Nib, Capsule Stories,
Watchung Review, Ovunque Siamo, Peacock
Journal, Boston Accent Lit, and Italian
Americana. Her memoir Stolen: Love and
Loss in the Time of COVID is forthcoming
from Unsolicited Press. You can find her at:
https://jaegerwrites13.wordpress.com and on
Instagram @jaegerwrites.*

Fired

When I started teaching English at Plainfield High School in 2006, I was excited. I had begun my teaching career in first grade, but after several years, I realized I was far more suited to teaching older kids. Sure I enjoyed reading Dr. Seuss, who doesn't? But the idea of delving into works by Steinbeck, Golding, and Marquez was far more appealing. My enthusiasm, however, lasted about a month, long enough for me to learn that most of my students hated books. Words defeated them, and the concept of actually sitting down and painstaking dissecting an author's words was too overwhelming. While I was ecstatic to have moved on from children's books, my students were not as advanced as I had initially assumed. Though they were in twelfth grade, the majority of them were reading on a middle school level.

It was this, a desire to remain employed, that motivated me to say nothing about my personal life. Neither my students nor the administrators needed to know that I was queer. They knew I was married, but by using the term "spouse" instead of "wife" and avoiding pronouns, it was easy to evade the truth. My students would sometimes ask me questions or ask to see pictures of my "husband," but I avoided details that might hint at the truth. This was before the era of smartphones, so it's not like I was carrying photo albums in my pocket. The students were disappointed, but by redirecting them to their studies, I was able to deflect follow-up questions.

Some of my colleagues, including Barbara, knew the truth. Keeping secrets from my students was one thing, keeping them from the people I ate lunch with and occasionally hung out with after school was impossible. Barbara had been teaching at the high school for many years, and since I was a first-year teacher in the district, she became my unofficial mentor, walking me through standard procedures and advising me on how to best overcome student apathy. She was also fiercely critical of my desire to remain closeted. "What good are you to the students if you're afraid to be yourself?" And when I tried to defend my stance she wouldn't hear it, stating instead, "There are students in this school who need to see you for who you are. They need to know that you accept yourself." But discrimination was alive and well, and there was no way I was going to crack open the door and invite it in, at least not until Dante tore the door off its hinges.

Along with reading novels with my students, the curriculum tasked me with reading certain chapters in a World Literature textbook. One of those chapters included an excerpt from Dante's *Inferno*. Getting my students to read prose was hard enough, getting them to read and comprehend Dante was virtually impossible. They weren't able to read on their own, so I ended up reading it to them. After each stanza I paused, and we discussed what I read. Mostly, that meant clarifying Dante's words, simplifying the text, and making it more digestible for my students so that they could analyze it. On day two, one of my students, Darnell, refused to open his book. He sat at his desk, arms crossed in defiance and eyes set in a stoney piercing glare.

I knew better than to confront him in the classroom. Surrounded by his peers, he would have been apt to put on show or ignore me completely. So, I asked him to come speak to me in the hall.

"What's going on?" I asked, standing with one foot in the classroom and the other in the hallway.

"I'm not reading this, and you can't make me." He kept his arms crossed, only now his eyes were on his shoes, unwilling to look at me.

"Okay, but why not?"

He shuffled uncomfortably, crossed and recrossed his arms, "Because I don't want to read about hell. I can't. My grandmother told me it's where I'm going and I don't want to know how bad it will be."

"What do you mean, your grandmother told you that you're going to hell? Why would she do that?"

"Because I'm...I'm..." he leaned against the wall, slowly lowering his body until he was sitting on the floor, legs pulled up into his chest, elbows digging into his knees, and his head in his hands. "I'm gay," he spoke in a broken whisper, his voice barely audible. "And my grandmother hates me. She said I'm going to hell."

I sat down next to Darnell, momentarily forgetting the rest of the class, my responsibility to them, but more importantly, forgetting my promise to myself. "I don't believe that. I'm pretty sure your grandmother is wrong."

He turned his head toward me and I could see that he was crying, "How can you say that? You have no idea. She goes to church every Sunday."

"And I bet she's a really good person, and she probably means well, but that doesn't mean she knows everything."

"She knows the *Bible*."

"I'm sure she does, but that doesn't mean she has the right to make you feel badly about yourself. I'm confident you're not going to hell, because I know that God, if there is a God, wouldn't send me there."

"But you're not gay."

"I am, and if I let religion make me feel badly about myself, I'd be pretty miserable."

"You mean you're like me, and you're okay?" He ran the back of his hand across his eyes, wiping away his tears.

I smiled and nodded, wanting to believe he'd keep my secret as I would keep his, but I knew that wasn't likely.

"Why don't you go take a walk to the bathroom, get some water, and when you're up for it come back to class."

Later during lunch, I joined Barbara in her classroom. The second I sat down she laughed, "Well, that didn't kill you, did it?"

"What are you talking about?" I asked with a sinking sensation in my stomach.

"You did the right thing. He needed to hear that. He needed to know that his sexuality doesn't matter."

"And I'm guessing the entire school now knows."

She waved her hand and chuckled, "Nah, it's only lunchtime. It won't be common knowledge at least until dismissal."

I groaned. The prospect of being out was completely unappealing to me, but Barbara told me not to worry. "You did the right thing," she assured me. But, all I could hear in the back of my head was father, *No good deed ever goes unpunished*.

Two years later, my tenure year, I had become the unofficial guidance counselor for the queer kids. By then, everyone—staff and students—knew I was a lesbian, and since I had thus far not suffered any dire consequences for being out, I was a little more open about myself in class. Students who were struggling with their own sexuality came to talk to me. I was conscious of the fact that I have no training as a counselor, and so I was careful not to offer advice. I simply gave the students what they needed most—an adult to listen and care about what they were experiencing, how they were feeling. If I felt a student wasn't in a good place and I felt concerned for his or her safety, I spoke to the official guidance counselor, one with whom I felt comfortable, knowing she would provide the student with a safe space and give them what they needed.

One afternoon, the assistant principal, Mrs. C. called me into her office. Teachers like getting called into the principal's office about as much as students do. We experience the same dread, the same cold sensation, the same sense of foreboding. Sometimes the anxiety is misplaced. This time it was not. I walked in and Mrs. C. wasted no time in getting to the point, "Your job is to teach English literature. If students want to talk to you about anything else, you send them to guidance."

"Excuse me?" On more than one occasion the administration had told us that for many students we were their lifeline. We were expected to make ourselves available to them, demonstrate on a daily basis that we cared about them. And that's exactly what I was doing.

"Your lifestyle is your business, but you don't need to bring it into the classroom. The students hear you talking about being married to a woman and think it's okay."

"It is okay." I objected

"Not for everyone. Not for our students." She sat up a little straighter, folded her hands primly on her desk, and smiled a fake smile, showing off her yellowed crooked teeth.

"What?"

"When you tell them something that conflicts with what their parents say it causes a conflict. We want to avoid that. We want parents to know that their children are safe in our school. That their morals will not be challenged."

"I've never—"

"But you have. If you so much as mention your significant other again—"

"You do realize that many teachers here have pictures of their spouses on their desks. They have no qualms about sharing stories with the students. So, if you want me to keep my personal life quiet, then you need to tell every teacher in the building to remove pictures of their loved ones."

"I have no problem with pictures."

"So I can put one on my desk."

"That's different."

I wasn't going to win, and I didn't want to get fired, so I left before my temper got the better of me.

A few weeks later, students in one of my freshman classes started to make hurtful derogatory comments in class. One kid had the audacity to stand up and claim that his mother told him that all gay people should be killed. I was too angry to confront him myself, so I called security to remove him from my room. He was gone for less than five minutes and when he returned, Mrs. C escorted him. She gestured me into the hallway and told me that no one should ever miss instruction time because I felt offended. "It's your own fault," she told me bluntly. "You were the one who told them about your private life."

Fury, unlike anything I'd ever experienced, made teaching impossible. I gave my class a writing assignment to keep them busy and stood by the window, looking outside, and willing myself to calm down. During lunch I consulted Barbara, asking her advice about what I should do. She recommended that I speak with the head principal. That meeting proved to be only marginally better than my initial discussion with Mrs. C. The principal told me that students were entitled to their own opinions, but he promised an intervention. As for what that intervention would be, he needed time to think about it.

The following week, the students were all called into the auditorium for an unscheduled assembly. The principal, after consulting the guidance team, decided the best course of action regarding my complaint was to show a video about bullying. On the surface, it was a fabulous idea. Then the video started and I couldn't help laughing at the irony. It was produced by the non-profit organization where my ex-girlfriend had once worked as an intern. The video followed three people who had been bullied: one for being overweight, one for a reason I don't remember, and one because she was a lesbian. The lesbian was my ex, and most of the stories she shared in her interview were either about me, or had taken place when I had been part of her life. Mrs. C. had told me not to bring my personal life into the classroom, but now—under the direction of the principal—it was being broadcast to the entire school.

When it ended and we returned to our classrooms, my students had questions. The questions that pertained to my ex I answered as well as I could. The discussion lasted the entire block, and by the time it ended, my students knew more about me than any class ever had. To cover my back, I wrote an email to both the principal and Mrs. C. expressing my dismay at being told that I should keep my life private, only to have it spoken about in front of the entire school. Neither of them responded via email. I suppose neither of them wanted to put anything in writing. Mrs. C., however, called me back into her office.

"I gave you explicit directions not to talk about your life outside of school," she said the moment I sat down. "Why is it so hard for you to follow directions?"

"What did you expect when you introduced my ex to the student body? I didn't choose the video. I didn't press play. I didn't plan for the students to see it. I sat in the auditorium completely blindsided." My mistake, I realized too late, was not asking a union representative to sit with me while I spoke to Mrs. C. But at the time, I didn't realize it would escalate. I also foolishly thought anti-discrimination laws would protect me.

"Let this meeting serve as an official warning. You are here to teach. Nothing more."

I nodded, and returned to my classroom, but that was not the end of it.

In May, the administration fired me. The official reason they gave was budget cuts. But I knew that wasn't the reason. They let me go because I was an out lesbian. Upon receiving my pink slip, I went directly to the union representative. The woman I spoke with shook her head when I finished explaining my perspective and said there was nothing she could do. I was not tenured, which meant the administration could let me go without giving a reason. As for my complaint that it was being discriminated against, the union representative asked me to present proof. I had none. The administration had been smart enough not to leave a paper trail.

Barbara was enraged—irate—but she remained staunch in her belief that I had done the right thing. "You made a difference in the lives of several students. You might even have saved one or two," she said, dismissing my regret. I wish I could have taken some comfort in her words, but I couldn't. Doing the right thing wasn't going to convert into a mortgage payment or put food on my table.

The worst part of getting fired was that I was pregnant. Finding a new job proved to be impossible. I spent the summer searching…and nothing. My quest to find full-time employment lasted more than a decade. Part of my difficulty was the fact that I was overqualified. Three masters degrees plus experience meant that I would be more expensive to hire than someone right out of college. Another problem was my appearance. As a non-binary lesbian, I wear men's clothes. Men are expected to show up for job interviews wearing a tie, biological females are not. Again, I have no proof that I was discriminated against in the hiring process, but I am confident that if I were a cisgendered, straight woman, I'd have landed a job much sooner.

If I had the opportunity to do things over again, would I do them differently? I wish I could give an altruistic answer and say that I wouldn't, that I have no regrets. I'm sure there are students that benefited from me being out and honest, students who gained courage and a sense of self acceptance. But the penalty was steep. Years of not working full-time has put the prospect of retirement in question and they wore thin my own sense of self worth. The hit I took to make sure one student felt better about himself cost me dearly.

Even if I would do things differently, I must also acknowledge that unemployment had its benefits. I raised my son and had the pleasure of homeschooling him during the COVID pandemic. I earned two graduate degrees—one in history and one in creative writing. Perhaps most importantly, I found my voice as a writer, publishing my work in online and print journals. (My first book will be out in 2025.) And last fall, I finally landed a full-time teaching job. The road to get where I am may not have been smooth, but there were lessons to be learned, and the detours I took were not without some reward. I probably would not be the writer I am today if my life had gone differently. Adversity breeds creativity. And today I write for some of the same reasons Barbara wanted me to be out and open nearly two decades ago, so that others might find solace in my truth and my experiences. So that others may know they are not alone.

Goutam Saha

Dr. Goutam Saha
is an Associate
Professor with
the department
of Fashion
Management Studies and the Campus
Academic Coordinator for NIFT
Bhubaneswar. He is a PhD in management
with marketing specialisation. He
joined NIFT in the year 2012 at NIFT
Bhubaneswar. Before that, he worked in
different multinational corporations as a
marketing professional and various business
schools as a faculty member. At present,
he has more than 20 years of experience
in industry and academics. In NIFT, he
specialized in teaching entrepreneurship,
sustainable business practices and models,
philosophies for sustainability, luxury
business, neuromarketing, etc.

His research interest lies in handloom and
handicraft clusters, local and informal
economy, sustainable entrepreneurship,
sustainability issues in the fashion industry,
etc. Apart from getting international
awards for his research work, he has several

publications, which got published in Scopus, EBSCO, Proquest indexed journals with considerably good impact factors. He also contributed many chapters in different edited volumes published by Emerald, Bloomsbury, Springer, Elsevier, Macmillan, etc. He writes popular articles in English and Bengali for Business Today, Fibre to Fashion, Odisha Review, Ananda Bazar Patrika etc.

The Diary of a Doubtful Agnostic

After fifty years of life, generally, people look back on their journey with some introspection. I am not an exception. Great people do great things, they achieve success in the name of wealth, fame and they create the pages of our collective history. When I look back at my life, though very insignificant, probably one thing I have done committedly is; I have not compromised on my thoughts, my truth, my doubts under the pressure of bigger narratives. I put my doubts out there and raised questions. These thoughts may be very insignificant, but they may help in posterity, for others to think on their own, and avoid getting bogged down by the big institutions and organizations of our politics, society, and history. These references of my agnostic journey come from the torn, yellow pages of my old diaries, preserved with utmost care and love by my wife. In the era of loud post-truth and biased polarization, they may murmur honesty. On a lazy Sunday morning in my reading room, I started going through those pages and scribbling a few points.

My Living Room and my Parents

My journey of doubt started around 40 years ago when I was ten years old with an experience in my parent's living room when my Bengali parents were not on talking terms for a couple of days after a verbal tussle. My communist trade union leader father told my Sanatan Dharma gurubadi mother about a few quotes from arguably the most famous Indian monk from Kolkata where the idol monk was clearly supporting patriarchy, Sati and British Raj.

My mother was equally assertive by accusing the legendary communist leader of Bengal of sending his granddaughters to an English medium convent school after taking a pathbreaking decision to prune English from the syllabi of all the government primary schools of West Bengal. After two days, my parents went back to normal as they were very committed to raising me and following other Indian middle-class family values and most importantly, they have huge respect for each other for their contributions towards family and larger society. But I developed a habit then, of not believing everything that great men or great philosophies preach.

Being a teenager, believing in anything completely, is easy and having any doubt can be disturbing. In the next forty years, my habit of having doubt did not leave me, but gradually I have learnt to live with it. I am happy with my doubts; like a believer who believes absolutely in a person or political or religious philosophies. My various experiences in life helped my life journey to remain happy alongside those doubts as I started accepting and loving the inevitability of imperfection.

My first visit with my mother in Puri gave me some valuable exposure of the commune living in a Bhakta

Sammilani of my mother's Gurudev, one of the famous East Indian spiritual stalwarts. I had very simple vegetarian food in common dining areas with thousands of people in those days. I slept in a tent with many women and their children, just like my mother. All were from different castes, classes, creeds, and different states of India, speaking different languages. My father was very protective of me, but my mother with her farm religious beliefs did not have any doubt about giving me the great mini-Bharat experience that enriched my personality. Consequently, I became interested in my mother's late Gurudeb's works and his Bhakt community. However, gradually I saw very senior saints enjoying a very cozy comfortable life which normal Bhakts and saints cannot imagine for themselves and witnessed their power-mongering politics. After seeing these, I could not have unconditional faith like my mother used to have in Gurudev's community. But I still like some of his great advice.

Another experience relating to my mother was her very puritan approach toward the opposite gender. She used to tell me and my dadas and didis (elder brothers and sisters) to always have a one-foot distance when you are speaking to people of the opposite gender. It helped me and my siblings to avoid a lot of issues. But in my adolescent period, my mother used to motivate me to read a good number of books by different saints of India on celibacy. It created huge unnecessary tension in me. The tension was reduced when my father took me alone to a local park on a summer evening and educated me regarding sex education with a very scientific approach along with some book references. From that, I understood the limitations of my mother's approach and the books given by my mother, but I still love to follow my mother's one-meter rule for all females apart from my very close ones, especially with my first love who gave me non-identical twins (a wonderful boy and girl).

I started learning physical sciences in college with honours in Chemistry and joined a leftist student union (a student wing of the then ruling party of West Bengal). From my student union connection and my father's support, I came to know many communist leaders, trade unionists, student leaders, etc. Many of them I found were very knowledgeable, dedicated, and honest. But I thought it was strange that I was nominated and elected as class representative of Chemistry Honors. The student union did not ask me whether I was interested in that position or not. They nominated me without my permission. They always tried their best so that no opposition members could try to participate in the students' elections.

In my locality, I saw how our own respected Bengali language and Rabindra-sangeet teacher were brutally harassed verbally and physically by local ruling communist party leaders at his home as he had some rift with her sister-in-law. Her sister-in-law's father was an influential ruling party leader. My teacher could not tolerate this assault and died within a year. I heard the same voice of hatred in many highly educated leaders of the ruling leftist party later for their opposition. Later, I read Nobel laureate Rabindranath Tagore's interview after visiting Russia, where he criticized the Russian then-ruling Communist Party for bringing class hatred into the social system. I have respect for many facets of Communism, which have a proven track record and potential to address a lot of social issues like healthcare, and education well. But my objection regarding his jingoist class hatred may not be invalid. So, on that basis, I could not become like my father with total commitment towards communism.

Institutions

One of my sweetest memories of childhood was with a very well-known religious Mission that focuses on education and services to humanity, where my elder cousin's brother was a student. My mother used to go occasionally and chant Sanskrit prayers and Bengali devotional songs in front of the white deity of a very popular spiritual leader of Bengal. When my mother passed away, I used to go there to listen to those very beautiful songs and to experience the serenity of the place beside the Ganges. I saw very disciplined students, and their dedicated sanyasi teachers and how a culture of excellence is nurtured in that very renowned mission.

But like any other Ashram, the spiritual leader, his wife, and his most celebrated follower monk became the Gods there. In spite of their immense contribution to Indian philosophy and society, they should not be beyond the critical thinking exercises of the students as they are part of our society and history. After reading many published works of those spiritual leaders, along with some criticism of them by many rationalist social activists, I developed a habit of personally reading great people as human beings from the perspective of the then socio-economic reality, learning from their strength and accepting their follies, rather than idolizing them. The Mission does not give that platform to the students to analyze these great personalities. I think this habit of critical thinking may empower the students' thought processes for being the agent of change and not becoming another co-holder of unchanged status.

I still remember my sister-in-law, who was an

ashramite in the Ashram of a very popular freedom fighter turned saint in South India. How she used to fill a huge number of glasses with drinking water with love, affection, and utmost dedication in the big dining hall of the Ashram where more than a hundred people take breakfast, lunch, and dinner together. When I asked her about the reason for such dedication, my sister-in-law told me one of the quotes from the internationally reputed saint and founder of the Ashram. She reiterated that in Ashram, all the work is worship and Ashramites do not have to perform any extra worship to get divinity.

I was spellbound. However, the saint's attempt to bring super consciousness seemed very poetic to me, much like beautiful literature. But the city, which his spiritual partner founded, is an amazing city of research where many people have been experimenting very passionately with how the future of the earth can be built more sustainably. Our governments never took a great initiative to study that city and its social enterprises as knowledge repositories. They thought it was a religious place only. I spent and will spend, many days in that city to learn from those social enterprises. However, I feel, there is some sort of cultural hegemony present in those organizations too. Mostly local people's involvement in those organizations remains at shop floor level. However local people have not been empowered to take leadership positions in those social organizations.

Personalities

My wife and I have a thing in common from our fathers. Both of us heard a lot of Gandhi bashing in our childhood by our fathers. My trade unionist father was very critical of Gandhiji. He was positioned in my house as selfish, backdated and impractical. My religious Hindu father-in-law always taught my wife that Gandhiji had aimed to destroy Hindus through a conspiracy. I have not researched their claims enough. But being a researcher of sustainability, I have understood that Gandhiji along with Tagore, perceived the challenge of the climate crisis very well in comparison to all their political colleagues. Since independence, Indian governments used Gandhi as an icon of peace, and cleanliness, but cared little about his environment and economic vision and Tagore was perceived very narrowly as only a poet, the author of our national anthem, and the Nobel Prize winner for the country. However, I failed to agree with Gandhi's thoughts on art appreciation and Tagore's assessment of the Italian Fascist dictator Mussolini. I think their understanding of these two areas was narrow.

I got my first exposure to Netaji's thoughts from a gift from my father on my 14th birthday. The gift was a book in Bengali, titled Taruner Swapno (The Dream of Youth) by Netaji Subhas Chandra Bose. Probably he is the bravest freedom fighter of India, who led our freedom struggle. My grandfather was in Forward Bloc under the leadership of Subhas Chandra Bose, and I still remember, in my younger days, I heard a discussion between my grandfather and father. My father used to assert to my grandfather that if Hitler were the winner against the Allied powers in the Second World War, then Subhash's partnership with Hitler might become more costly for India. In that case, India had a high chance to become a colony of Nazi Germany. I found my father had some logic in this presupposition.

Though my parents were living in two polar-opposite ideological positions, they have a common thread in between, which is Geetobitan, the collection of songs of Rabindranath Tagore. Both of them used to read them and share their feelings about the songs with one another. Thus, they sorted out their conflicts. I am always obliged to Tagore for reducing conflict among my fighting parents. I did not read Tagore too much, apart from listening to his songs. But I read his short stories and essays. They shaped my thought process. I tried to read some of his dramas, which I felt were boring. But criticizing Tagore as a Bengali is a blasphemy.

My only support came from the great dramatist, the late Girish Karnad, who asserted that Tagore's dramas were mediocre. In Varsha Mangal (rain welcoming festival), Tagore used to plant thousands of trees and organize cultural events. My Bolpur-based friend tells me that nowadays the Tagore established institution Visva-Bharati, organizes Varsha Mangal with a great cultural programme but plants only a few trees. Visva-Bharati clearly missed Tagore's concern about deep ecology.

Trying to find the perfect ideology or ideal person is an inherent trait of us humans. My father's perfect state was the undivided United States of Soviet Russia (USSR) whilst my father-in-law's utopia is ancient India. Still, I remember the glossy magazines titled Soviet Union that used to come to our house. Those periodicals were used to publish all the impressive events and good news of the USSR. The publications empowered my father's belief system. My father-in-law was equally empowered by the videos from WhatsApp University, which claim every knowledge of the modern world comes from Ancient India. Once Prafulla Chandra Roy, a very famous scientist, entrepreneur, freedom fighter, and author, lamented that whatever he was doing as a scientist, some people of India used to say that everything was in the Vedas. However, he read the four Vedas but could not find the answers. My mother also had the same type of question for my father, "if in the USSR everything was so perfect, why did it collapse?"

Dialectical Conclusion

Being a researcher, I came to know about an organizational development strategy called Appreciative Inquiry, while interviewing Ms. Sumita Ghose, the founder of Rangsutra, a 10-crore craft brand in India. The philosophy, proposed by David Cooperrider and Suresh Srivastva in 1987, appreciates the strength of every stakeholder to chase the goal of the organization without focusing on the weaknesses. Ms Ghose's husband was abducted by terrorists at a very young age. As a mother of two very young kids, she started her social venture Ranngsutra. She managed many stakeholders ranging from capitalist corporations to socialist NGOs through Appreciative Inquiry, to empower a few thousand artisans by providing them with livelihood opportunities.

I also studied the world's largest informal organization SEWA and its huge success in generating livelihoods for millions of women in South Asia. In SEWA, the philosophy of organization development is quite similar to Rangsutra. Around five hundred years before, long back before Appreciative Inquiry was proposed, there was an illiterate but great king of India who tried to get knowledge from different religions, even from the atheists and agnostics to strengthen his empire.

I understand no one is perfect, no political or religious philosophies are perfect. Our world is also a big organization, we have to love ourselves as a bundle of imperfections and focus on our strengths to reach our goals to save humanity from its big and pressing crises, ranging from climate change, unemployment, and inequality.

Oh! My study time and scribbling time is over. Suddenly I heard a chilling voice saying from our bedroom *"Today also you kept your towel on our bed. And you have been doing it for the last twenty-two years since our marriage."* But we have a very successful married life with two kids and plenty of good times. Appreciative Inquiry works on my domestic front also. Otherwise, there were enough reasons for my wife to divorce me as an imperfect husband. I appreciate her love for imperfections.

Vanessa Rowan Whitfield

Vanessa Rowan Whitfield is a Celtic mutt who resides just outside of Manhattan. She is an internationally published poet and author who dabbles in photography, and through her art she uses nature to try to heal. Her work is centered around flares of her Celtic background, pagan beliefs and ecofeminism.

Some of her recent publications include Shashi Kadapa's Women Power anthology through NYC's International Human Rights Arts Festival and Sweta Kumari's Efflorescence: A Florilegium of Humanity, Nature and Peace.Updates on her personal poetry books, publications and photography art can be viewed on her Instagram handle @ nessanthemum

Moon Music

"What is that song you're playing?," my honey skinned friend asked as he lowered himself onto the repose that was my yoga mat. He sat gently beside me, and the mallet I held in my hand echoed across the circular hang drum in a rhythm that I had not premeditated. I felt the pollen and the wisps roar across my cheek, and I was reminded of the lion that is March that was on its way to the lamb. "It sounds so familiar."

"I don't know what it's called," I responded. "I made it up just now." My hand kept up the beat as if it was the only reason that the hollow sounding seconds had continued to pass, and I looked up into the empyrean fishbone clouds within the blushing womb that hung over me. The fileted carcasses of past lovers waiting to disseminate into lavender night. One defiant would find his way to the flower of the season's Pink Moon who had waited patiently to become full and glow ever so brightly. That harbinger of rebirth, I watched her become a white crow with the purest of intent. The Earth below her was wormy and she could see the ribbon-like entozoons. I stared up in awe at the ancient messenger, so swollen, so filled with songs of life, and a mischievous verdant laughter rolled joyfully from my own lips. "Moon Music."

During this meditation, I became suspended in the web of recollection and I waited patiently for my wings to form on the subject so that I might fly freely though the film. A series of women appeared before me. Women that I had encountered on my path that were waiting like the moon to give birth. I remember conversing with them about their pregnancies, and I felt their excitement as they expressed to me their anticipation and nervous anxieties about becoming parents.

On one of several such occasions in particular, a duo of the expecting had asked me about my own relationship to child bearing. After I had expressed to them that that archetype of womanhood presents differently in me than it does in some others, that I sought to have a child free life, the two women looked at each other knowingly and then greeted my gaze once again with smug smiles like maggot shells which started on one of their faces and then spread over to the other. A grin that sustains itself on the rotting of others. They began to ask me a series of questions and then devalued my responses with their only excuse for their changedness toward me being, "It's a Mother Love language. You wouldn't understand." This was not the first time that I would be infantilized or denigrated in the future by others of any gender for my choice.

I once had a dream that the world around me was set in a bluish gray hue and that I was walking up a long path where there was an orchard on either side. The trees were filled with voluptuous fruits, and a little girl with long orange hair danced barefoot in a rainbow colored dress around the firefly lit branches. I recognized this phantom child, and as I loomed further up the path, I recognized my destination as a white house that I remember from my youth. I walked along the stone path to enter the door, and I passed by a greenhouse in the distance and a large garden filled with porous loam soil. It was dry and crumbled to the touch and very little would grow there.

I stepped through the doorway, and there was an open room with robin's egg scolored walls. I did not recognize this room from waking life, and in the center of it stood a trifecta of women holding hands back to back in a circle, their red hair standing upward on top of their heads and all bound together by one thick braid that stretched nearly to the ceiling, suspended by something indiscernible. The whites of their eyes were all that showed as their irises were rolled back into their heads, like dried flower petals placed onto their sockets. The long dark dresses they wore served as a contrast to their pale skin. I recognized these figures as some of my relatives. I stared at the still figures before me, this symbol of three generations permeated in my memory like a prophecy, and when in my waking walk recalled the painful social fallacies that I have heard uttered from the mouths of each one considering women of my position. Women who cannot or will not have children.

From the mouths of the toxic mesh of messages from generation to generation, the image of the pitied spinster arises. The question of how any woman would know anything about life or being a woman without having had children is a common one. Women without children are lazy, unintelligent, inept, irresponsible. We are not good enough for partners to keep us long term. We don't have more to offer someone than our wombs. When taking up a passion such as creative writing, we are greeted with questions asked in patronizing tones like, "What else would you do with your time?," letting us know that someone else should be directing us on how to spend our time, and that the way we fill our time is wrong and our lives are being wasted.

Someone else should be controlling our bodies. There is the idea that there must be something wrong with women who value their pleasure over their fertility, and who enjoy sexuality without procreation. We become demonized in the eyes of others, and the truth of our wisdom and work to plan our lives without children being included is overlooked. Our bravery is ignored and confused with something other than what it is. Strength comes in many forms and the ignorance of this knowledge leads to mistranslation.

I reach deep inside of me and I hold myself in child form. Some girls were playing with dolls and nursing them with little bottles. I am the one wearing fantastical costumes and writing stories or plays. I pretended to be an explorer and I was curious about plants. I was all knees and elbows. Taller than all of the boys, I always wanted to be everyone's husband. I knew one day I'd be some kind of writer, and I carried around a notebook like Prairie Dawn from Sesame Street and was always accompanied by stacks of books. It was never my dream to be a parent.

I conjure this ambitious little girl. I hold her and I tell her that I love her and to please always keep herself, because she is invaluable and amazing just as she is. I encourage her choices and I tell her that she is worthwhile before she sets off on her great adventure to define what it means to be a woman in her own words and on her own terms. I travel beside her as she grows into who I am today.

I gaze into the mirror now, and see my face, my dwindling thirties. I examine my Mom-Bod, no children included, and affirm to myself all that I am. I am a lover and not a mother. I am a dreamer, a nurturer and am maternal to many and to myself. I have the right medicine for many but not for everyone. I am meant to love many and not just one. When I mother myself, I change the world. I remind myself that it is okay to lose yourself as long as you try to find your way back. That my ancestors watch me and that they smile when they see me taking back my body from the depths of rivers. They are proud when I choose what is best for me and reach the peaks of the tops of those mountains. That you can be a birth parent and still identify as child free, and that you are not a wicked witch of fables because you have chosen a different way.

Each igneous circle of monthly melodrama and blood tells me of my choice and my voice. The hibiscus dew reminds me that I am childless for another cycle. That I have come around another time and that I have reached my fullest moon. This egg that I shed. The divine mother goddess that resides in each of us becomes prominent, and I welcome the new souls coming through to time with the hollow sound of my birth drum. My palm opened like hello as it pounds like an open heart on canvas. I am a big, beautiful Mother. Like the ocean or the sky. I am a fertile soil and the Earth needs to heal as well as I need to heal.

Pallavi Deka

*Pallavi Deka
is primarily
an academic,
engaging young
minds with critical
thinking. A researcher on ecological politics
and society of North East of India, Deka has
an Mphil and PhD from Jawaharlal Nehru
University in the same. She presently teaches
Political Science in Handique Girls' College,
Guwahati. Her latest book from Routledge
publication is "Environment, Climate
Change and Migration in South Asia."*

Dawning a Special Life

Nights were sleepless, as is said, after she arrived.
Though it was an unexpected realm for me...a never
thought out before zone in my life.

JNU, I describe as a Hogwart of Harry Potter and
like all others, I too had the fullest part of my life there.
Exploring the world, exploring my possibilities; it gave me
everything- the name, fame, degree, job, good friends and
my life partner. Coming from an extreme eastern corner

of India to becoming a known entity amongst people in JNU (academics or activism) or overcoming the caste and cultural barriers to enter into an offbeat nuptial relation, all these were no small feats for me. As if life was so nicely penned.

I lived this life of extreme fulfillment from 2005-2013...where I was everywhere; in libraries- in fields (finishing off my PhD); in conference halls, in my job, on the streets- sloganeering, asking questions, clearing doubts. Then in 2014...everything stopped. I cocooned myself for a new life in the lap of hills again in the easternmost corner of India.

When she arrived, I could hardly understand anything. The pain of the C-section was still persisting and the cry seemed unstoppable. The poor little thing was so clueless about the new ways...not knowing how to get her food (she did not know to suck). She cried and cried and it continued for three of the longest months of my life. Thereafter things became relatively normal. My daughter coped with everything so well...she was cheerful and intense, splashing pure happiness with her every act.

Gradually she attuned herself so well that it was possible for me to go back to join my job by leaving her for longer durations and she was exposed to television too early; maybe that triggered what has occurred since to some extent.

The Early Signs:

She was detected with Autism Spectrum Disorder, as early as three years of age. I suspect something different in her actions when she was barely 18-19 months. I found that she was too carefree and active, not knowing to rest. She was oblivious of anyone's presence and when she found something really interesting she would sit down quietly for hours again oblivious of anyone's presence. A slightest response from her will need a hundred time repetition of the query. Because the condition is in mild form and her too young age made her actions natural to some extent. So, for some time, us, as parents, were expecting that things would fall in place gradually when she grew up; That her not speaking sentences till three years of age is something she has inherited from her father due to the family habit of loving to be a lonely pig (not needing to associate or talk with others).

No one really knows the reason for the condition she acquired. To everyone, I went to thereafter for help and suggestions, they ended up asking me thousands of questions about what the pregnancy period was like; did I eat well, was I in a stable mental condition, were there any physical complications? And I did not remember anything beyond the normal. I was engaged too much into academics- completing my PhD thesis, lecturing in college and there was average urban life tensions, nothing more- this was my answer. The possibility of a genetic carry over of the condition could be there from some distant connections as we have not seen such people around us in the immediate family. The hypothetical explanation these professionals could point to, is her severe neonatal jaundice or a possible chromosome mutation.

But it hardly matters now...why she has this condition. As soon as someone has the smallest of doubts that her child is a bit different, a bit slow, a bit too silent, a bit too naughty...means one needs to engage more time with the child. One needs to talk, play in groups and pull her away from being idle by herself. In our case Reeha in most times was all by herself till two years of her age when we suspected that she was a bit too hyperactive to listen to anyone. Then the time we took to sync into the reality that she has a condition, again took almost a year more. Only after that did the practical years of her getting proper attention start and my journey of a special motherhood begin.

Days passed when I started introducing myself to the materials available on the internet about the condition Reeha is living with. There are so many of them...but nothing conclusive. One thing that was made clear was that it is a lifelong condition and she has to learn everything with great effort. Days were grim and many nights went by when myself and my mother changed shifts in sleeping time as Reeha would wake up in early morning to not to sleep again. However, because she has the condition called autism in a mild form (as suggested by medical professionals) our hope is still alive that she will overcome some of it someday.

The Social Encounters:

People (pediatrician, psychologists- my first encounters) suggested that she should be mixed up more with her peer groups and to let her play more in a social environment. So dragging her to parks, malls, and city buses was my daily routine, to make her be among people. She enjoyed these outings very much and she enjoyed the fun and games involved. But, all by herself without involving others was her preference. The best part was that she was a happy go lucky child. In pre-school she rarely sat in a closed classroom. Her charming nature made her a lovable kid among the teachers and *ayas*...who let her play in the first year. However, she was rarely playing with other kids. Gradually complaints started coming that she did not sit to write a single word in the classroom and did not want to learn about classroom etiquettes.

Reeha was only 4 years old at that time. The school and the teachers did not have the slightest training to handle a kid who was a bit different from others. They did not have any technique to make her work playfully and most of the time she was left alone to do whatever she wanted. In the least deviation from her being under control would bring me rushing from 15 km away from my workplace by a single phone call. Things became worse when in a parents teachers meeting, her nursery class teacher suggested that I should be thinking of a second baby to look after Reeha when she grows up. Then and there I made it clear in my mind that whatever may come, it would be foolish for us to keep our daughter with such naïve people. There is the end to her pre-school episode. Me as a mother understood that this was not going to be easy for either me nor her.

Gradually I understood that there was a need to stringent my timetable along with my daughter. There will be strict division between my time in college (where I work) and rest for Reeha. Overtiming, soft skill management for professional growth, interpersonal workplace bonding started having less priority in my life. My academics and urge for activism lost their space. I started getting quiet so that I rarely became engaged in an active professional life as I had previously been. After my stipulated lecture hours, I rarely had a second to spend in college; since it would be time for Reeha to be dropped in or picked up from her special school or therapy centres. The psychological and therapeutic centres were crowded with people. Parents carrying their little ones with hopes that the child will lead a normal life eventually with all the efforts they are putting in. The grown-up teenagers and even a few adults also come for interventions, counseling, and training to these centres with their guardians, waiting for some miracle to happen in their lives.

As I visited these places with my daughter I felt as if she was not meant to be there, she just needed a little more push in learning how to socialize and be comfortable with others who weren't severely autistic. This is the mother in me that believed and told everyone that she is better than others on the autism spectrum. However at the same time the conscious human part of me always reminded me that each time we talk of inclusivity, why shouldn't my daughter be mingled with the child with severe traits of neuro-a-typicality/neurodivergence. Such realization pushed me to openly accept that Reeha is neuro diverse and she is a special child. My family members sometimes tried to project her as being too naughty for her age, so that they will escape people's questions on her condition. And we all have every reason to do that as long as we can.

At first I was not ready to accept the ways by which my parents wanted to project their grand-daughter as being normal when they talked to others. But when I encountered people in society who had the least knowledge and empathy for people with such differences; when many of them tried to convince us that it is a disease that leads to mental retardation and when many of them avoided Reeha just to make sure that their children did not come in contact with her (who knows it can be contagious they wrongly thought); it made me realize how heart wrenching it must be for the grandparents to cope with such a society they did not see before. For me it is even harder; on the one hand I have to face the ignorance of society everyday and on the other hand I cannot even show to my parents that I have ever felt the pain of raising a special child. Otherwise seeing their daughter in such a condition would be an added misery for them. So even if I am broken someday with all the thoughts of Reeha's future…all these emotions can't be reflected on my face. I need to gulp those tears and fears away all by myself.

The Best Seeker in Me:

Things are turning out to be so much more serious that my life became the total opposite of what it used to be and who I used to be. I was…a non-serious life leader. I took life as it came to me; but it never was so unpredictable. From choosing what to watch on TV, to coming to JNU, to instant decisions on life partners, getting married, having a child…I accepted what life had to give me. But it has been kind enough for me.

Now I count each step and decision I take. As if I want to make the best decision because I know there may be no second chance. Reeha is now 9 years old and the school we chose for her is an inclusive school. We all had high expectations initially…slowly we are losing that. Any school, including hers, takes these children for granted. As if they are ignorant of everything and they can be pushed to the corner doing nothing and schools become no more than crèches. They just keep our child for some hours, guarding them against any untoward incident; the children lose the chance to learn anything substantive in their formative years. Therefore, most parents prefer classrooms with 'normal' children, though it might lead to lower self-esteem for the child in later years.

My idea was initially to provide her with special assistance along with giving her an opportunity to be with typical kids for some time. So the choice was for an inclusive school, which we have realized, is in reality, barely inclusive. Now, not only as a special mother but also as a vanguard to this community, I am trying to build up some reformatory ideas and put them before concerned persons to bring some necessary changes to the service providing agencies for special people.

Everyday is a new learning opportunity with Reeha; like seasonal changes…she has new mood in every season. As she is growing we are able to predict her temper. I can now prepare myself to soothe her, to handle her in a better way. I have travelled with her alone to almost all states in India, just because she loves travelling. Many a times in awkward circumstances, when she would behave age inappropriately and people would stare at us. But all these have hardly mattered to me anymore. I have learnt to be with her company as she is. I have learnt to behave normally in such situations and not feel ashamed. I feel this is my greatest experiment with myself, being so poised in accepting Reeha's condition. The silly things she does, I laugh them off and the more serious, hostile things she is up to, I sometimes brush it off or put on an annoyed look. I am with her as if she is four or five years old and why not? Her mental age is that and she loves that warmth for a little girl.

Am I a Good Mother?:

Perhaps this is the question that haunts every mother as they raise themselves up with a special needs child, or for that matter, any child; mothers are under constant self-scrutiny as well as by society. It is a tightrope to walk because the first blame will always be on the mother's shoulders which is unfair. First of all it was not planned motherhood; my partner and I never really wanted to be parents. And now since she has happened and so specially, our only intention has been to let her grow as safely and fully as she likes. Many times, due to the lack of my involvement with her, it makes people ask me why I have not decided to quit my job. I suppose that would have been too suffocating for me and Reeha as well. Teaching is something that I love and those few hours in college makes me rejuvenated to be more meaningfully a mother when I am not at work. For me the question is not whether I am a good mother anymore, but to attempt to be a sound human being that gives me the strength and patience to be with a special kid.

Taking her to all social outings is not a privilege but a priority; so that she does not miss out on anything even if Reeha rarely tells her yearnings to us. Sometimes she avoids those gatherings and we have had to return from some events from the very start, as she could not handle the crowds. Many of my associates say I should have my 'me' time too. But things are pretty set...college is my time for myself and other than that it is with Reeha whom I do things for and with. She enjoys these outings afterall. However, we miss out on movie nights or drama festivals as dark ambiance is what she refrains from. So then it's a solo movie night for me, though it does not come often.

I disassociate myself to the whole idea of branding or rating motherhood, however the natural self-scrutiny remains. This new dimension of myself began very early in me when Reeha was more attached to her grandmother than myself when she was 2 months old! It might also be the postpartum symptoms I experienced, as I felt constantly neglected by my child. Now I have started enjoying my time when she is with another person in comfort. However, the self-inquiry remains as to being able fulfill my role in bringing out the best in her.

Postscript:

Being with Reeha has been the greatest learning experience for me; it has given me a whole new dimension of realizing my unexplored side and learning to be compassionate and patient are the greatest ones. I had a life fine throughout, till Reeha happened and whilst it has changed it still has much value. Days in JNU remind me to be grateful, how can anyone's life be really hard if someone does not have to beg for their daily bread and butter? Mental trauma, anxiety, stress etc seemed to me like middle class privileges at times. Back then I could multitask on things without getting perplexed or stressed. My mental zeal was perfectly agile so I have sometimes wondered at the psychological struggles of some of my friends and associates.

I am as headstrong as I ever was, but these days with even more positivity thrown in. Now it is clear to me that mental troubles are not someone's privilege but they can come to anyone and at any time. I have come to understand that there are lots of backstage dramas in people's lives and personal stories of growing up are so varied that we can all have diverse mental responses. Neurological a-typicality is real and my daughter's condition is an eye opener for me. Now if she is not being able to act or think in a balanced way, it is not always due to her lack of alertness or clumsiness, but due to the different kinds of tuning in the nervous system. That is all we need to acknowledge to make a room for everyone, to every neuro diverse person.

In this whole new process of becoming more humane, I honestly admit not to being able to be a superhuman. The short temperament that I still struggle with, the non-strict, non-disciplinary lifestyle of an average human being have persisted in me, and the spirit of flowing with time and situation has remained. These also accompany the grief and guilt of not doing enough for my kid. I am still trying and there are still miles to go for this special mother…

Jennifer L. Gibaldi

Jennifer Gibaldi is a poet and author. She has published two poetry collections, Perfectly Imperfect, and 24 Hours of Transformation, (EMS PUBLISHING, 2023) both available on Amazon.com.

Jennifer is currently working on her third poetry collection, as well as a debut novel. She draws on her real-life experiences for inspiration, writing with pure heart and raw emotion. She looks forward to sharing her story with the world in hopes that she can comfort and inspire those who are in similar situations.

Jennifer can be found performing at various open mics throughout Long Island New York. You can follow her on Instagram @ iamworthit82 and her Facebook author page I AM Worth It.

Beating the Odds

I may be white, but I am far from privileged. I grew up with the eyes of the world watching, judging, waiting for me to fail. Like it was expected, given my circumstances. The youngest of four, I was raised by a single mom on Welfare, living in a two-bedroom apartment. Our street was lined with businesses and bars. We didn't have neighborhood kids to play with or fancy toys. We had each other and our imaginations.

I was teased daily for where and how I lived, how I looked and dressed, and the dynamics of my family make-up. My one sister had Autism, my other sister was African American, my brother was rebellious, and I had extremely bucked-teeth and spoke with an odd accent. We all had different fathers. None of this was considered normal for the town we lived in - a town primarily made of middle-class white families. All the kids in school lived in nice houses, had their own bedrooms and two parents. They had cars and money, took vacations, and ate out.

Although I loved learning, I hated school and often came home crying. By the time I got into High School, the separation of our two worlds became more apparent, the teasing more personal and hurtful. I started having health issues that no one could figure out. Days turned into months, with the doctors telling my mom I was faking it. The school would not give me home tutoring and rumors started swirling the hallways that I had died. By the time I finally had a real diagnosis (bowel obstruction and impaction), I had started going septic. Once my course of treatment was complete, I had already missed more than half of the school year. I had no choice but to repeat the 10th grade. Over that summer we moved to a new town, and I started my 2nd attempt as a sophmore in a brand new school with no friends and new teachers to disappoint.

It was a long road, and no one thought I would make it. I was destined to follow in the footsteps of my family members who came before me. My grandmother, mother, sister, and brother all dropped out of High School at the age of 16. My mother and sister both had their first child by the time they were 17. I spent most of my childhood promising myself that that would not be my fate. I was determined to make a life for myself, determined to prove everyone wrong. I took that determination, stubbornness, and strength, and used it to push forward. I fought long and hard, never letting my various illnesses take over, and I walked across that stage. With my head held high, wearing my cap and gown, I proudly accepted my diploma as my family watched alongside the many teachers who never thought the day would come.

I used my graduation money as well as money I had saved up from babysitting jobs and bought myself a car. I enrolled in Community College on a public grant. I found myself a full-time job. I had kept my promise and could not have been prouder.

I went on to study writing, psychology, and developmental disabilities, eventually working in the latter. While I did complete various programs, and earned Certifications in these fields, I never did obtain an actual college degree. Life, as it often does, got in the way. I started my college path majoring in English and education as I wanted to become a creative writing professor. While in school I got a job working as a Direct Care Staff in a group home for Developmentally Disabled adults and simply fell in love with it. I no longer wanted to teach writing. My path was now changing, and I needed to decide where I wanted it to go.

Amid all this, I got married and gave birth to a beautiful daughter who had Down syndrome. Due to her diagnosis and the unknowing, I left both school and work to focus on taking care of her full time. I spent the next year navigating doctor appointments and therapy schedules. By the time I had settled into my new life and routine, I could not afford to go back to school. Instead, I went back to work, again as a Direct Care Staff in a group home. Within a year, I had proven myself worthy and was promoted to House Manager. Over the span of my career in that field, I was promoted two more times – once to Residential Coordinator, overseeing multiple houses, then to Assistant Director, overseeing the entire Residential Department. My knowledge, experience, and work ethics stood out and were recognized and acknowledged over the fact that I did not have a college degree.

When a new director was hired, they did away with the Assistant Director position and put me back as a Residential Coordinator. Unfortunately, life happened again. A back injury that I had sustained in High School had flared up and caused me to become immobile. After 3 months of being bedridden, I was admitted to the hospital for emergency back surgery as I had lost all feeling from the waist down in my right leg and was on the verge of becoming paralyzed. While the surgery was successful, the recovery took a lot longer than expected. It was still another two months before I was able to start Physical Therapy, and yet another two months after that before I was cleared to return to work.

By this time, another new Director had been hired, and they had filled my position as Residential Coordinator. The only position left open was either House Manager or Direct Care Staff. I took the Management position, with the hopes of eventually being able to work my way up the ladder again. This, I would later learn, was not to be the case. When an opening for Residential Coordinator came about again, I applied for the position. I was granted an interview as a "required courtesy", but was told flat out that I would not be getting the job. I was informed that for the Residential Coordinator position a college degree is required, no exceptions. A House Manager position, a college degree is preferred but not mandatory.

Therefore, House Manager was the best I would do with this agency and I would not be getting promoted again - ever. It did not matter that I had previously held the position and had the experience and knowledge. It hurt knowing this, I was with that agency for 16 years and had given my heart and soul into every position I held. I found myself starting to withdraw and not wanting to get out of bed in the mornings to go to work. I was making myself physically ill, and it felt like High School all over again. I had yet again become the unpopular girl who was only there because I had to be.

Eventually, I had to make the very difficult decision to leave this field. I could no longer handle the physical requirements of the job and did not want to stay where I knew there was no room for growth (I won't lie, there might have been a bit of spitefulness and hurt pride that helped to push me into this decision). I needed to move on, but to what?

It was not an easy transition and took me three years

before finally finding my place again. I started looking for office work, but now not only did I not have a college degree, but I also had no knowledge or experience. Going back to school was not an option as I still did not have the funds and did not qualify for any grants or loans. I started looking for free courses online and at the local library for anything office related. I enrolled in as many as I could and applied for every entry level receptionist position that I could find. No job was too small or "beneath" me. I needed a job, and I needed the experience. I landed a few gigs here and there that didn't last very long for various reasons, but each job gave me a little more experience and understanding of the role. I asked a lot of questions, eager to learn. I used that to help me in my future interviews. I am far from a salesman, but I figured if I could sell my good points such as being a team player and a fast learner, I could talk my way through the door, and let my work itself show them that they made the right choice once hired. Although I wasn't having much luck with this plan, I never gave up – even though I wanted to, and often felt like a failure.

Eventually, my perseverance paid off. I interviewed for an Administrative Assistant position and, although not everyone was initially on board with hiring me, I talked my way through the door and was offered the job. What started out as being hired to do billing and assist with some clerical work, turned into me helping to create new departments, workflows, and schedules. My bosses have asked for my input on how to restructure and grow their company. They listened to what I had to say, and valued my suggestions. I have now been with the company for two years and it was recently expressed to me at my annual review how I have by far exceeded their expectations. I am currently in the process of building my own billing department with them, and continue to assist in developing new policies. I have also been asked to assist in the interviewing, hiring and training of new office staff.

I have learned throughout the years that, just as there were many people who were waiting, expecting for me to fail - there were also a few people who were waiting for me to succeed. No matter how many times the odds seemed to be stacked against me, and I wanted to bury myself under a blanket and give up - I kept my head held high and never let those nay-sayers have the final word. I never gave up and fought my way to the top in everything I did. I still do. To those that had faith and took a chance on me, I am forever grateful.

B.A. Brittingham

*Born and raised in the
grittiness of New York
City, Brittingham
spent a large segment of her adult years in
the blue skies and humidity of South Florida.
Today she resides along the magnificent
(and sometimes tumultuous) shores of Lake
Michigan.*

*Her poetry has appeared in Kitchen Sink
Magazine, the ocean waves, Words for
the Earth, the Crone's Words, Green
Shoe Sanctuary, Halcyon Days, and The
Emblazoned Soul Literary Review.*

Oeuvre

Late in the evening of my life I often think
of those I chose not to allow to enter
into being. Understand: this is not regret
or remorse, guilt or even disappointment
in my selection. It was, quite simply, a preferred

option predicated upon where the world was
in that time of potential post nuclear lunacy.
(That, and the memory of prolonged
maternal callousness.) No, I am proud I
chose to never let you live; for though the
general population scorns my attitude,
still do I maintain that not everyone is cut
from that unique, unruffled parental cloth.

To be sure, I recognize that you are all
deceased now, that whatever aptitude with
which you were endowed was spurned by me;
that as sizeable as you were — human eggs
are the largest living cells, though barely
the width of a strand of hair — I think I was
justified in not allowing you to be more.
For what if the *more* involved a vile twist?
What if it circulated around your becoming
something evil, a malevolent being, someone
who enjoyed the imposition of torment,
or who merely didn't consider the immorality
of acts of agony, be they mental or physical?

Do you suppose Mrs. Manson or Madame Dahmer
or Senora Mussolini or Frau Hitler knew what
they had expelled from their bodies? Had
let loose on an unsuspecting society? And if they did,
were they appalled or sufficiently humiliated

to want to plunge a carving knife into their child's
tiny heart? Perhaps they simply didn't care.

So, by developing into part of me, you were doomed
to shrivel on the vine. Huddling deep within, did
you wonder where the other half of you was lingering?
Perhaps those twenty-three additional chromosomes
would balance with affirmative traits, my negative ones.
Can you hear me laughing? My aptitude in choosing a
man to father you was nearly as abysmal as my desire
to take a chance on the emotional brutality that so often
accompanies those 'forever' options. If I was amiss
in my decision, then so be it; regard yourselves as
fortunate in that you sidestepped that anguish.

You will never have to face the decisions
that straddle the fickle line between
desire and ethics; nor that between virtue and
vice; nor even the Shakespearean one between
life and death (when life becomes too terrible);
that has been made for you. *Nakazora*, little ones,
be thankful, I seized the selection from you.

[Dictionary Definition of Nakazora (Jap.): *The space
between sky and earth, the place where birds, etc., fly. Empty
air. The inability to decide between two things. Midway.*]

Dr Paromita Mukherjee

Dr Paromita Mukherjee, Associate Professor, Visakhapatnam, India.

A voracious reader, passionate painter/ crafter, philanthropist. A participating author/poet of more than forty national / International short story and poetry anthologies. Winner of multiple literary contests. Participated and presented more than 25 research papers on Literature/ HR/ Cultural Studies. Book of poetry titled 'Sylvan Fragrance' available on all major online platforms.

Wordpress-paromitamukherjeeojha. wordpress.com

Twitter Handle- @paromita2906 / Facebook Page-www.facebook.com/paromita2906

Saga of Colour

These days we all are discussing the problems of marginalized groups of people all over the world-their social, ethnic, economic and cultural problems. Marginality in all its aspects is indeed a major problem despite progress achieved in all other spheres worldwide.

Most countries and cultures have empowered groups at one pole and impoverished groups at the other. The form and nature of marginality depends upon the degree of impoverishment-economic, social, or cultural. Marginality based upon gender, caste, creed, colour, religion, or race is a kind of disability or affliction. Colour bias or "colorism" is believed to have been coined by novelist Alice Walker in 1982. It is an apt term that refers to the preference for lighter skin between different racial and ethnic communities, and also *within* those communities. Colorism is an enduring remnant of colonialism and white dominance around the globe and consequently has harmed self-belief of dark-skinned women.

I grew up in Barrackpore, West Bengal in the 90s. My extended family of relatives still proudly carried within them vestiges of the white man's burden of racial prejudices and superiority complexes. Growing up in close proximity to such relatives I would be bewildered at their various epithets for me ranging from 'coal mine', to 'Ba-Ba black sheep' etc. My grandparents tried to elevate my status in the colour hierarchy by insisting that my skin tone was 'wheatish', I feel maybe it was their way of comforting themselves about my otherwise doomed prospect in the future marriage market.

To quote from Kathy Russell Cole's book, The Color Complex: The Politics of Skin Color in a New Millennium: *Many people from lower castes have darker skin because for generations, they have been subjected to hard physical labor in the sun. Since caste and class often intersect, fair skin is also perceived as being evidence of "better financial and social status of a person.*

So by virtue of being born in a class conscious society it was my duty to be born with a fair skin. My mother was regularly fed with age old "wisdom" from well-meaning relatives to attain that elusive fairness for her daughter. *Apply gram flour, milk, and turmeric on her face daily, a Brahmin girl cannot be dark-skinned like this.* My childish mind failed to connect the dots between what someone's caste has got to do with complexion? The rejections and castigations were endless. I cursed myself and my skin tone. On birthdays I was gifted with banal fairness creams. My mind was bogged down with the guilt of having been born dark –skinned.

In India, "fair" is proclaimed to be virtuous, while anything dark has negative connotations. In India TV programmes, billboards, advertisements, all reinforce the ideology that "fair is beautiful". India's skin whitening market is dominated by 'Fair & Lovely', a fairness cream that was launched in 1975. Fair & Lovely has strategically marketed itself as the saviour for dark –toned unmarried women in their quest to find grooms — and for married women to keep their husbands interested in them. Ironically, Hindustan Unilever, the multinational conglomerate that produces it, has blatantly used 'colorism' to sell its products. This kind of colour bias has created a mental health epidemic. Dusky -toned women desperately try to look fair by using makeup that is not meant for their skin tone or bleaching their skin chemically. Most women here do not embrace their natural skin tone.

It is an established fact that western stereotypes about ideal skin tone have been coercing young Indians to struggle for their identity, loss of self-esteem, and hopelessly retreat into a shell. Colour discrimination is also propagated by the humongous Hindi film industry coined as 'Bollywood'.

Hindi movies often feature songs that glorify fair skin and deride darker skin tones.

The pressure thus was immense and I searched ways to rationalize my 'skin colour' to people around me. I had unfortunately internalized the 'black sheep' tag. I was convinced of my inadequacy and thought that 'I was never going to be good enough to be noticed by anyone'. My descent into self-pity and self-loathing was inevitable. My studies suffered, my self-esteem took a beating. I tried to distract people from noticing me or judging me by their parameters of beauty.

As I grew up I started believing that I should never marry anyone dark-skinned as my progeny would also then have to undergo this kind of mental abuse. I readily forgot the true meaning of beauty and subscribed readily to the problematic and disdainful notion that 'fair is beautiful'.

So, what turned the tide for me? It was a quote from Zora Neale Hurston that I read and imbibed:

I am not tragically coloured. There is no great sorrow dammed up in my soul, nor lurking behind my eyes......Even in the helter-skelter skirmish that is my life, I have seen that the world is to the strong regardless of a little pigmentation more or less. No, I don't weep at the world – I am too busy sharpening my oyster knife.

My perspective towards life changed, it did not hurt when someone complimented me by saying 'you are a black diamond' whatever that was supposed to mean.

I concentrated more on my academics. All those years my studies had suffered due to my low self-esteem, failure to concentrate and then miraculously the tide turned when I literally burnt the midnight oil for my XII(ISC) examination,

I stood third in my stream and my Alma Mater lauded my achievement on stage. Suddenly people were crowding around me hailing my parents, my efforts, no one that day noticed my skin colour. It was a life changing moment and I treasure that experience till date. That day gave me the necessary impetus to overhaul my outlook and the road was paved for further academic achievements leading to my Doctorate.

Fortunately, wheels of time are in motion and idealization of white standards of beauty is changing too. After sustained campaigns against fairness cream and related products, the Advertising Standards Council of India has issued guidelines stating that "ads should not reinforce negative social stereotyping on the basis of skin colour". There have also been campaigns worldwide like "Unfair and Lovely," which encouraged women to post their pictures on social media celebrating dusky and dark skin tones.

In 1994, an 18-year-old dusky girl changed the misconception regarding beauty by overshadowing a fair, beautiful, crowd favourite girl. She till date serves for me as a source of inspiration. She was our first Miss Universe title winner Miss. Sushmita Sen. She strengthened my belief that more than complexion or outward beauty what matters more is your wit, composure and holding your head high against all odds

We are slowly creeping out of our obsession of associating beauty with fair skin. Young people now are less haunted by the unrealistic standards of superficial beauty and coming out of their closet of insecurities and uncertainties. Dark-skinned people are now judged based more on their intelligence, educational qualification rather than on inane beauty standards.

I have pledged not to ill-advise my two gorgeous dusky babies to apply turmeric, milk cream to become hypothetically fairer. Why should they need to change themselves by applying fairness creams and potions? I vowed not to let them feel less valuable because of the colour of their skin. I constantly reiterate to them that a person's worth is not determined by their looks or skin colour.

I escaped from my insecurities after lots of internal struggle and trust me it was a tough fight. I am determined to celebrate my daughters' inner beauties and not let them tumble into vortex of insecurities. I want them to grow up in a progressive society that accepts them the way they are – recognises their strength of character, individuality and values.

I know that there is no magical potion to heal my inner traumas so I consciously decided to be free from the shackles of colourism. I still fail sometimes to oversee someone's comments about my skin tone but I persist in accepting me the way I am. I have crowned myself as my own favourite after confronting my insecurities point-blank. I am teaching my daughters to be free from shackles of colorism and that I believe is my contribution towards giving hope of an inclusive society to our future generations.

Nancy Dunlop

Nancy Dunlop is poet and essayist whose chapbook, Hospital Poems (Indie Blu(e), 2022) explores the realities one faces as a patient in a mental hospital. A finalist in the AWP Intro Journal Awards, Dunlop has been published in a number of print and digital journals, including Swank, Truck, Green Kill Broadsheet, The Little Magazine, Writing on the Edge, 13th Moon, Writers Resist: The Anthology, and Through the Looking Glass: Reflections on Madness and Chaos Within. Her work has also been heard on NPR. She received her Ph.D. in English from UAlbany SUNY, where she taught for 25 years. She resides in Upstate New York with her husband and two cats.

Dear Child I Never Had

Apologies for the lateness of this letter. I am 46 years old, and this is my first communication with you. I recently got married, for the second time. My new husband is 56 years old, and this is his first marriage. He has no children, either. Some might call us childfree. Many would call us tragically childless. Lately, I don't know what to call us.

When we started dating a few years ago, a window of opportunity cracked open for the first time in my life. A window I could slip through to enter the world of parenthood.

I remember the moment vividly. It was over breakfast at the Blue Ribbon Diner on Rte. 55. We discussed children. He was then 51, physically healthy, and wanted a child. I told him I had never wanted children. We sat quietly, considering the other's wishes. I then said to him what I had never said to a man: "I would like to have your child." And he, almost in unison, said, "You're more important to me than having a child."

I looked down at my pancakes, astonished. The window opened, and then closed. I allowed it to.

I know it's outside the norm to be a 46 year old woman, married, without children. Many of my peers have children now in college. How could this possibly have happened? I share this with you with some bitterness, because I suspect how I am sometimes perceived: An anomaly, a freak of nature, a statistical outlier, far afield from the rest of the data tribe. "What exactly is she doing out there?" the rest of the tribe asks. "What could be taking up her time? Her thoughts? Her *life*?" Assumed to be relatively free of a sufficient inner and outer life, my purpose seems to be to attend to those with a "full" life. My job is to listen. Listen to parents or parents-to-be. Perhaps they use me as a hollow valley that shoots their own happy words back to them, like a reassuring echo.

A few years ago, my husband and I attended a political fundraiser. We sat at a giant round table, like we were at a wedding reception, staring down at the obligatory prime rib, pink and flabby and spilling over the edge of the plate. The woman next to me was an attorney, running for a second term on the City Council. She was a good bit younger than me. Smart and eager and engaging. I found her pleasant, and we chatted about this and that: Our lives, our professions. She said that she and her husband, who was also running for public office, were planning on starting a family soon. And then The Question: "So, do you have children?" I answered, "No." Just like that. No emotion one way or the other. I didn't tell her I made a decision years earlier not to have children. I didn't go into the reasons. And judging by her sympathetic yet encouraging expression, I didn't bother to tell her that I actually kind of liked my life. And then she said those words I've since grown to dread: "Well, don't worry. You still have time." I stabbed the slab of meat on my plate, holding my tongue.

Considering a woman without children permits feelings of pity and elicits words of gentle encouragement. "Well, don't worry; you still have time." To know that someone considers herself, not "childless," but possibly "childfree" is far more intimidating, as it challenges not just the status quo, but someone's life goals. If someone who wants children hears that someone does not want them, that person might be forced to consider why exactly she does want them. It forces that person to consider what she might choose to do with her life if she *didn't* have kids. What might she be giving up? As a little girl, did she always want to travel the world? Raise animals on a farm? Become an aviator? A writer? A dancer? Did she want to run off and join the circus? In short, did she ever dream of having a freedom most people don't dare assume they have a right to? Solitude requires a certain fortitude.

That might be why the young councilwoman might have said what she said. It was emotionally easier to feel pity. It allowed her to be the bigger person and offer encouragement someone like me must be in need of. "Well, it's okay; you still have time." She didn't know that this "encouragement" was actually calling my decision into question. She didn't know that my silence in response was, in part, merciful. Imagine if I had said, "Well, don't worry. You're not pregnant yet. You still have time." No, dear child, I stayed quiet. I allowed myself to be the one who was somehow flawed and incomplete. I allowed myself to be outside the norm, to absent myself, to become invisible to her frame of reference. While the young councilwoman remained polite, we had nothing left to discuss.

My role as listener occurs in the oddest and most inappropriate of times and places, instituted by people I am close to, and who are otherwise lovely and intelligent. Take holidays (often challenging for people without children). Christmas seems particularly given to children and grandchildren. Those of us who are single or who are in couples but without children are either forgotten in the festivities or stand out like sore thumbs. At least I feel this way. I'm also surrounded by reminders that I don't have you to share the celebration.

This past Christmas was particularly difficult, as my mother-in-law passed away over the holiday. She would have been your grandmother, and you would have loved her, as she would have loved you. The wake was held right after Christmas. A close friend came to the wake and probably felt uncomfortable talking to me about the reason she was there, grief and death being something people aren't trained to discuss. Instead, she chirped happily about her little boy and how fun it had been to open presents on Christmas morning. She gave me a list of the toys she had given to him and how he responded to each one. Then she said, "Children are what make life so worthwhile and happy." I looked down at the floor, and I could feel her eyes follow mine. She realized what she had inadvertently done.

I forgive her for this brief interlude—for her display of personal joy in place of condolences. I know she was aware of our pain and in other ways showed kindness and a sense of proper occasion. I would like to assume that she thought this story—the only words she spoke to me at the wake—would "cheer me up," rather than simply cheer herself up in my presence. But while listening to her that evening, I felt robbed twice. Doubly bereft. For now, my mother-in-law lay silently in her coffin. And there was no childish excitement—no you—to go home to, on this or any other Christmas.

But you do have surrogates. My husband—his gentleness, the press of his warm body, his artistry and talents, and his quickness to humor and fun—keeps my heart filled. I also have three cats, so I suppose that could make me an odd cat lady. I collect what remains of my own infancy and early childhood: the cradle my father built me from knotty pine; the tightly woven tartan throw from my aunt; tiny dresses my older sister made for me. All now stored in a corner in the basement. The cradle that would have held you stores old stuffed animals and cat toys and CDs. At one point it held potted plants.

Beyond these few things, I don't keep many mementos

from my family of origin. My two siblings both have grown children. And now, grandchildren. On a recent visit from my sister, I was deluged with photos brimming out of a stuffed album, all of them of my new grand-niece. I listened to story after story. Viewed photo after photo. Each one seemed the same as the one before. It was an exhausting visit. After my sister left, I found a stray photo of her new granddaughter, which had fallen to the floor. I took one more glance at this stray photo that fluttered down from the baby album. Then I threw it in the trash.

I confide this small sin to you, feeling rather ashamed. I threw out a picture of a baby. Does this symbolize I am capable of tossing out a baby? Couldn't this mean I also tossed you? Bear with me for a moment: Did I do it out of frustration at the idea that parenthood, and now grandparenthood, dominated everything? Did I do it out of despair for a lost connection with my sister? All of these explanations work in a way. But not totally. I should be more mature, I know. Less petty. But I admit: I get angry. Angry at the external prejudice I face because of my decision, while I also must deal with inner ambivalence and sometimes grief connected to that decision. It's not that I threw out a baby when I tossed that photo; it's that I was throwing out the conflicts I felt. I was tossing out the insistence about my invisibility. And yours.

The external prejudice doesn't come just from women who have chosen the traditional role of wife and mother, as my sister has done. I feel it from those women who have chosen both children and career—those who "have it all." I feel it in expectations made of me (the one who doesn't "have it all," and therefore apparently doesn't "have enough"). When their children are in grade school,

I hear from colleagues that they are unable to carry out their professional responsibilities because they need to leave early to meet a "child at the bus," implying, whether they know it or not, that those who don't have such a need should somehow make up the slack. Colleagues who beg out of work because they have made plans with their children explicitly state these plans to their supervisor and colleagues. By contrast, I feel the pressure to remain vague if my plans involve "just" my husband, as if I'm hiding something. A husband is not really as "family" as children. And not as legitimate a reason for needing personal time. A child on the other hand….a child is always legitimate; always proof of the full definition of "family."

I know I am getting political, but I also notice social expectations beyond my family, friends, and colleagues when it comes to not having a child. In many middle- and upper-middle-class white communities, there is the general feeling that "it takes a village" to raise a child. But sometimes I can't help but think that the child everyone is thinking about is their own. Their village doesn't necessarily consist of children of color. Or children facing poverty, homelessness, hunger. No, that part of the "village" is invisible (and threatening).

Forgive me my bitterness. What right have I to judge? Who am I to talk about such things? And beyond that, who am I to talk about such things with *you*? Who knows how protective I would have been of your helpless baby life? Who knows how solipsistic I would have become? How much your care would have totally circumscribed my universe? Maybe I'm telling you this here, so you see how political this issue can become—how there are ever expanding layers beyond just the private ambivalence and grief.

This letter is not meant to elicit special understanding from you. I suppose I am using it to reach a state if not of peace then of some understanding. If I've never had the opportunity to tuck you in each night, then maybe I can, through this writing, put my grief and ambivalence to bed.

But what does this letter really hold for you? It is to offer, hopefully, an explanation, even an apology. As you know, I never lost you to a miscarriage. And I never aborted you. I don't know if it's kind or cruel to tell you this. True, you didn't enter me only to be wrenched out again. But at least that would have been a one-time rejection. Instead, you're faced with knowing that I practiced neurotically protected sex, barricading myself for over 25 years. I chose to reject you over and over again.

I hope you are willing and able to listen to what I am telling you, without feeling pain. I hope this letter lets you know that, yes, I have thought about you, often, but had reasons not to bring you into this world. Frankly, for many years, I thought it would be selfish to have you, given my upbringing: a physically violent father and an emotionally absent mother. I honestly didn't think I could raise you without becoming them. I couldn't stand repeating their pattern for another generation. So I chose to let it stop with me. It was my burden to carry, not yours.

And as you can tell from what I've revealed already, I have always noticed friends and family who had children and watched them turn away from the external world to form a tight circle around their newborn babies. They can't be blamed for this. But I have lost friends to parenthood; I have only seen their backs. This will be painful for you to hear, but I didn't want to turn my back on the world to nurture a single child. I wanted to nurture many. So I began to teach. Over a hundred children a year—freshmen in college, to be exact.

My work with them sustains me, and (I hope) nourishes them. And you know what? I simply like being with 18 year olds, perhaps because that is the age you would have been today, if I had had you. I grow attached to these students. But I know them for a semester or two, then send them back to their parents. Many, I never hear from again. Sometimes, out of the blue, I get a note from a former student who still thinks about me, grateful for what I provided years ago. This is rare. What I provide is ephemeral. Sometimes it doesn't seem real.

You, on the other hand—you would have been real.

When I was in my twenties, I visited a psychic. She said she saw you hovering around me. You were the soul who wanted to be my child. You wanted in. This frightened me. At the time, I was in my first marriage. My husband, then, was a cold man who lacked affection. If he was unable to hold me, how could I expect him to hold you? No, he wouldn't have been a good father. I really thought I was sparing you…from both of us.

That conversation with the psychic was 20 years ago. I divorced the cold man, and led a life filled with opportunities to do many things, except for you.

Now in a happy second marriage, I sometimes think back to that dinner morning several years ago, when my current husband and I discussed children—when the window had cracked open to the point where I could see you—the window I allowed to slam shut. Gazing through the closed glass, I see not you, but my own reflection. I see a grief counterbalanced by a sense of relief, like the right course had indeed been taken.

But what about you? Did you mourn my decision not to have you? Did you stay in the ether, seen only by psychics? Or did you find another mother—another open window—to slip through into the world?

Perhaps I will meet you. Perhaps I already have. In fact, I know I have seen you, year after year, in the small pleasures and love I now have in my life: in my husband's eyes, in art and writing and creativity, in my work, my students. In fact, on a good day, when I am feeling most open to life, I see you in everyone who crosses my path.

So I will end this letter with a word of thanks. I want to thank you for the gift of sight—for those times when I am able to release my resentments, my grief, and my anger, and I am permitted to see everyone, not just a single child, as worthy of patience and encouragement and nurturance. To see everyone, even if only in brief moments of grace, as family.

Signed,

"I Love You, Dear Child"

Kimberly Burnham

A brain health expert (PhD in Integrative Medicine), Kimberly Burnham grew up in tropical Colombia; Belgium during the Vietnam War; Japan teaching businessmen English; and diverse international Toronto. Now, in Spokane, Washington, Kimberly speaks extensively on peace and brain health. She is the author of Awakenings: Peace Dictionary, Language and the Mind, a Daily Brain Health Program and The Red Sunflower Diaries, Why Everyone Should Garden and Share Seeds, a fictional story where people trade seeds making the world a more beautiful and just place. Her next book is Mistaken For a Man: A Story for Anyone Struggling to Feel Comfortable in Their Own Skin, Clothes, and Community. Follow her at https://amzn.to/3RLeMvY Contact her at nervewhisperer@gmail.com

Mistaken for a Man

The waitress in the nice sit-down restaurant in Spokane, Washington, looks right at me and says, "What would you like, sir?" My wife, who loves the way I look, gently corrects her assumption about my gender. The restaurant was busy and loud with clattering dishes in the kitchen, piped in music, and conversations over a late morning brunch. When our food came, the same waitress looked directly at me and said, "Is there anything else I can get for you, sir?" Realizing her second mistake, she laughs, and apologizes.

I didn't feel malice or embarrassed. I realized that she was just too busy to pay attention. I self-identify as a butch lesbian. I didn't freak out, get mad, or decrease her tip because of her mistake. It is something that I am used to by now. I have been living in this body for more than 65 years. But I always wonder, should I correct the person, clarify my identity, and contribute to greater awareness and understanding. Should I help challenge assumptions and break down gender stereotypes? Should I let it go, be the man she thinks I am, avoid the discomfort of pointing out someone's mistake and simply enjoy an omelet with a side of hash browns with my wife?

With more life experience, I find I am prioritizing my own feelings and safety. I also realize what it has taken for me to be more comfortable with who I am and how I am seen in the world— It is Love. I feel tremendously loved at home for who I am, inside and out and so those people in the world who don't love me, or even hate the idea of me, aren't powerful in my circles.

In my 20s, friends would ask me what is your type? *"What is your type? What type of person are you attracted to?"*

The answer often starts with gender, although I suspect that is evolving. When you fill out the questionnaire on a dating site, there are questions about your gender and the gender you are attracted to and for a lot of people those questions are easy to answer. They are for me but not for everyone.

When I came out as a lesbian to my cousin, one of her first questions was, "Are you attracted to me?" I gave a nervous laugh. I had more or less grown up with her. It didn't even occur to me to be attracted to her. No, she was not my "type," even if societal taboos about a relative too close to kiss, had not been weighing on me.

Gender is only one factor, and for some people not even an important one, in who we are attracted to and who we attract. Authenticity, kindness, curiosity, and a good sense of humor are also attractive. How we define those characteristics is vitally important and distinctive. I think I am very funny and have a good sense of humor. I remember jokes. My timing on punchlines is good. I select the joke from my memory at the appropriate time, but even so, I am sure not everyone would agree with me about my sense of humor. Some people might even find my jokes annoying. We are each unique in how we present ourselves to the world and who we attract.

I met my wife in my fifties. We have a magical love story, but what stays with me always is that I feel unconditionally loved. I feel attractive. At home, I don't have to be realistic about how attractive a 65-year-old woman, who is on the heavier side, with white hair, who is sometimes mistaken for a man—how attractive, really could she be?

I don't know how I got so lucky, but I have never felt so loved unconditionally. And that is in part what enables me to explore who I truly want to be in the world. If being a butch lesbian means I get mistaken for a man, so be it. I am at peace with who I am in the world. It wasn't always that way, though. I have never wanted to be a man. Would I like to have the privileges that are extended to men and denied women. Of course, but I am happy with my body. I am also happy to be able to dress and move through the world in the way I want.

My parents love me unconditionally, but parents and siblings are different from society in general. We expect them to love us no matter who we are, how we look and what we do. Some of us test the strength of that love more than others. I feel particularly fortunate with the family I was born into. I come from tough, smart, resourceful stock, Mormon pioneers, five generations back. I am a daughter of the Utah pioneers, an honor bestowed on women whose ancestors came to Utah before the railroad. It means they walked or rode in wagons or on horseback from the East coast to Utah.

I am sure it was a much more dangerous and difficult journey than the one I took in 2013 when I rode my bicycle in the opposite direction from West to East. My trip was well supported with food and accommodations planned out from Seattle to Washington, DC. I had a question for everyone I met as I bicycled over 3,000 miles in support of the environment and food security. "What do you love about where you live?" The answers were as varied as the people I met. "The mountains. Wheat fields at sunset. The strong community feel. Pizza. Bread. The lake and surrounding environment. That everyone knows each other."

We each see the world we live in differently. We focus on different things.

I wonder if my great grandmothers and great great grandmothers would admire my toughness. I wonder what they would think of me today. Would they be proud of me, of who I have become, of the good I have done in the world. Would they be disappointed that I converted to Judaism, that I married a woman? Would they think I should be more lady-like? The first time that I know of, that someone mistook me for a man is nearly 50 years ago. I was at an airport with a group of Brigham Young University students. One of the chaperones came over and introduced herself as I stood waiting in the gate area for our flight to be called. I was excited. I was on my way to BYU's sister campus in Hawaii for the Fall semester. I was in comfortable white painter pants and an untucked loose-fitting collared shirt. My brown hair was short but curled down a couple of inches over the top of my light blue collar in the back.

Referencing BYU's dress code for men, the chaperone said, "Are you going to get a haircut as soon as we arrive? Your hairline needs to be above the collar." I immediately realized that she had mistaken me for a man and mumbled something like, "Sure." The last thing I wanted was to draw attention to myself, my introverted self. She was insistent and incensed that I would have shown up at a BYU sponsored trip without a proper haircut. She made sure everyone at the crowded airport gate knew it. I felt certain that people two or three gates away could hear her scolding me. I wanted to crawl under one of the unbreakable plastic chairs or lock myself in the bathroom, but our flight was boarding soon. I just stood there and let her humiliate me.

Finally, she walked away with these parting words. "When we get to Hawaii, I will pay for the haircut, if you send me a picture." I nodded my mortified ascent then watched her slowly walk away. I was still watching as one of the other students approached her and corrected her misconception about my gender. "Nooooo!" I thought terrified as she turned and looked at me, really looked at me and started marching back towards me. I shook my head. "Please don't let her come back!" I prayed. My prayers unanswered hung in the air crisscrossed by planes. I wanted to be on one of those planes. Anywhere but here. She apologized loudly. In my mind just making more of a scene and drawing further attention to my androgynous look. After the plane ride, I thankfully never saw or contacted her again. One of the students who had witnessed the exchange did commiserate with me later when it turned out we were roommates in an eight-woman campus apartment at BYU Hawaii. My roommate asked me if I was a lesbian. She was. I said, "No," because I wasn't yet.

There is something about the sensory overload, the stress, the rush of airports that turns off people's ability to pay attention and correctly guess my gender. I can't even count the number of times that I have been told, "This is the ladies" or "The men's bathroom is over there," by people at airports. I would completely avoid airports if I didn't love to travel and see new places, so much. Once while traveling in Malaysia with my girlfriend, I got so sick, I might have died if she hadn't been there to take care of me. I was constantly running out of our tiny cabin on the beach to the outhouse. I felt slightly better a few days later when we stayed at an endangered turtle rescue center. We paid them to wake us up in the middle of the night on the off-chance leatherback turtles showed up. We hoped that someone would bang on our door to say, "there are turtles on the beach laying eggs. Come quickly."

The knocking came.

We got up and walked quietly across the moonlit beach crowding together a few feet from where a huge mama leatherback turtle used its legs to dig out a depression in the sand above the high tide mark and laid her eggs. After she covered them and scuttled down the beach disappearing into the dark water, the turtle rescue team gently dug up the eggs and moved them to incubators where they would hatch and be returned to the deep waters of the ocean when they were a few weeks old. They told us that the most dangerous time in a baby turtle's life is when it hatches and has to run down the beach to the water.

Going into or out of a public bathroom leaves me feeling like a baby turtle. Will I make it into the bathroom without someone stopping to stare or saying something like, "this is the women's restroom," or leaning back to look at the markings on the doorway to make sure that she is going into the right bathroom because she thinks a man is coming out. Since 9/11 airport security has been on higher alert and people are more fearful of strangers. Airports of course are full of strangers. Strangers getting on and off of planes, running to find their luggage, grabbing a quick meal or snack. There are people everywhere but very few people are paying attention.

I am 5′ 9″, the height of the average American man, with the broad shoulders of a girl who grew up swimming competitively. No one would mistake me for a man in a bathing suit but when I cover up with clothes, there is something about my height and stance that makes people think— a Man. One time, I got pulled aside for extra screening. My first clue that they thought I was a man was that the screener assigned to me was a man. He had already started the process before I registered their mistake, so I went with it. But seriously, he made me take my coat off, stand with my feet apart on the shoe print marked mat. He wanded me and patted me down. Without really looking at me, he handed my coat back and said, "have a nice flight, sir." I was not impressed with the security at that airport.

A few months ago, I was at a water park in Southern Idaho with my extended family. I was in my street clothes, jeans and a button-down shirt and headed into the women's change room. Just as I was at the entrance, I heard a voice behind me. "Excuse me, the men's changing room is across the hall." I turned to see a woman in her 40s wearing a knee length skirt and red blouse. She smiled at me. She was intent on being helpful, helping a man not to embarrass himself. Something mischievous welled up inside of me and I reached for the bottom of my shirt as if to lift it up and said, "Did you want to see my breasts?" "No." She sputtered, turning as red as her blouse. She spun around and scurried down the long hallway away from me as fast as she could. I proceeded into the changing room and put on my swimsuit knowing that for the rest of my time there, no one would think I was a man.

It is not just stress that turns off a person's ability to pay attention. We sometimes don't pay attention to things that we think we know. In many religious communities we make assumptions based on strictly binary dress codes and responsibilities. Men wear suits and women wear dresses, unless they don't. But when the community standard is men wear suits then anyone in a shirt and pants becomes a man in the eyes of community members. I usually wear khaki style pants or tailored slacks and collared shirts with the long sleeves rolled part way up my forearm. When we can't imagine anything different from the standard binary, that is all we see.

One of the younger people at the Orthodox Jewish services, I sat towards the back of the large synagogue. with my friend, her sister, and mother, who resided at the assisted living facility associated with the synagogue. An orthodox man walked into the row behind us and put his hand on my shoulder, handed me a kippah or yarmulke (traditionally male head covering) and said, "I will take care of the ladies." He proceeded to pin a doily-like head covering on the women in the family.

I hadn't grown up Jewish or yet converted, but it wasn't the first time I had worn a kippah, because in the renewal or reform Judaism congregations where I regularly attended, it was considered a unisex head covering. Both men and women wore kippot. So, I sat there in this orthodox service wearing a head covering indicating male gender. I didn't want him to be embarrassed by his mistake, but it quickly became a slippery slope. When we came to the part of the service where someone, usually a man in orthodoxy, lifts the torah scroll, I was invited up onto the bimah (raised stage at the front of the synagogue) to lift the torah. It is considered an honor, to face the torah laying on the table, lift the slightly unrolled torah scroll, hoist it above your shoulders and turn your back to the congregation so that all may see the letters on the scroll. It was an honor I had never been offered.

I imagined what they saw, a tall, strong-looking, youngish man sitting with his wife and elderly mother-in-law. Why not invite him to be part of the service and give him the honor of lifting the torah, which was too heavy for most of the elderly men, who lived at the assisted living facility? Quickly shaking my head, I declined because another image came to mind. I could see into a future where I was standing on the bimah with the Torah raised above my head, when somebody realized that I was a woman, and then they felt compelled to snatch the heavy scroll out of my hands. Of course, I also knew that I was not yet officially Jewish, and they would never have invited me up to touch the Torah if they knew that. Instead, I sat with my friends knowing that the rabbi thought I was a Jewish man unwilling to be helpful when in fact none of those things were true. I was a non-Jewish woman, happy not to cause a scene. I wanted to do the right thing and respect these people's traditions and their right to live their lives the way they feel comfortable.

I want that for everyone: a trans child and their parents in Texas, a gay teenager in rural Kansas, a lesbian or non-binary person in Alaska, an African American in Chicago, a Native American in Oklahoma, a neurodiverse child in New York City. We are not hurting anyone by showing up in the world in a way that is uniquely comfortable for us. We are so much more than how we look to strangers. Our friends know we are poets, doctors, lawyers, artists, police officers, teachers, elite athletes, comedians, and dancers. We, who do not fit into binary boxes are everywhere, trying to live our lives and love in nurturing ways.

Don't make us lift up our shirts and show you the wounds.

Iris Ng

Iris Ng is a British Chinese writer and ESL teacher, who currently resides in the Czech Republic with her Czech husband and two children. She has dabbled in ghostwriting, work-for-hire inspirational writing and bespoke poetry with @Tinkelei on Instagram, though her passion remains with writing her own novels. Aside from that, she enjoys drawing, singing, and origami. Nothing makes her heart happier than snuggling her two babies, though finding her favourite Chinese and Japanese snacks in the middle of Europe certainly comes as a close second. She can be found under @writerkayan on Twitter.

Through a Coloured Lens: Overcoming Racism and Building a New Life for the Sake of Our Children

I learnt of the term 'third culture kid' when I was already an adult. No one ever told me the displacement I felt all my life was a natural phenomenon considering my history. A third culture kid is someone who grew up in a culture that is not their parents'. Thus, immersed in both the culture of their parents at home and the local culture in which they live, a third culture emerges: neither of the parents nor of the local community. One entirely their own.

I'm an immigrant twice over, with a childhood in Hong Kong, an adolescence in England, and finally, my adulthood and subsequent motherhood in the Czech Republic. I did not always speak English, though I call it my mother tongue now. People like me are not supposed to be writers, nor to enjoy writing at all, because I am a third culture kid. Chinese, or Cantonese, had suddenly become obsolete, and no one had heard of the things I knew and loved. My Chinese education had ended overnight, and my English education had to be picked up from a British native child's level when I hadn't even learnt to blend letter sounds. Before the time of YouTube and the internet, I had no access to what I knew as 'home'. Home was England, a land I knew nothing about, with a language I did not speak.

I waited with barely contained excitement each month for the VHS tapes my dad would send from Hong Kong, with Hong Kong dramas and dubbed Japanese anime shows I hadn't been able to finish, even as my own writing increasingly became punctured with English words. It invaded, like a second plant taking root in my mouth, until it replaced all my Cantonese words—at the encouragement of my parents. We needed English to survive, and survive we will. My parents knew what racism was. We couldn't change the colour of our skin, and my parents were middle-aged without hope of losing their Chinese accents, but we, the children—me and my sister—we had a chance. We were only children. We had a chance to be *normal:* By acquiring an English accent and speaking as the natives do.

Where are you from? It's a culturally loaded question. At its heart, it is asking for your identity. Who are you? How may I understand you and your story? Which boxes do you fill? The average European might give you the city of their birth. The average American their state. Standing in the middle of the Czech Republic, with my Chinese skin, my straight black hair and dark eyes, I am asked, "Where are you from?" England is not the right answer, not to them. "No, where are you *really* from? What's your *real* first language?"

But ignorance isn't unique to any one nation. Back in England where I grew up, I distinctly remember a time when I was fifteen, my English friends clutching their stomachs in hysterics because I'd claimed 'mortician' was a word. Newsflash: it's American English, which I'd picked up from a novel at the time. My fellow English native friends just thought I was stupid. But nothing could make you appear dumber than the sound of your own language in the ears of those who don't speak it. I dare you not to splutter at the sound of this Cantonese word: *Gay ho.* It simply means, "I'm quite well / It is quite good." More well-known is the viral story of Professor Greg Patton, who scandalously spoke a Mandarin word that resembled the N word in sound and had hell to pay. Languages do not often overlap well.

One of my favourite movie moments is from Rush Hour 3, when Chris Tucker demands to know the name of the Chinese master he is speaking to, and the master's reply is, "I am Yu." Because, more than a comedic moment, it is closer to illuminating our ignorance of each other and where we have all come from, individually, than most movies have dared to. Beneath the laughter is the discomfort of the alien and an acknowledgement that there is no such thing as normal. What is normal for you is not normal for me. Common sense is not really common sense. My parents cannot tell German apart from Czech, but why should they? Can the average Brit or American tell Chinese apart from Japanese or Korean on sight? Don't be shocked when someone does not know what you consider as 'common sense', because they might be just as shocked when you show the same ignorance of what they consider 'common sense'.

I have come to accept this, and many others things, nor am I above my own splutters. In accepting that, sometimes, the laughter is not malicious, it has allowed me to live in peace in the cultures I dwell within. When the time came for us to name our first child, my parents suggested a perfectly mundane Chinese name: Ah-Man. To my ear, I heard nothing wrong, and there is nothing wrong. To my Czech husband's ear, it may not have been the best choice of name for our daughter when we live in the middle of Europe. We laughed about this a lot. When time came for us to name our second child, we considered the Chinese name Kwok-Ting. *Kwok*, unfortunately, resembles *Kvak* in

Czech, which is the sound of a frog: *ribbit ribbit.* Imagine the child's name would therefore sound like *Quacking*, or perhaps more accurately as *Ribbiting*. We went with a different option.

Never did I imagine I'd emigrate again after England. The thought of leaving never occurred to me until I met my Czech husband, who wanted to go home for a variety of reasons. We were graduates and England was in the middle of recession. Just like before, I thought nothing of what I'd be giving up—no one had explained to me when I was a child that I'd be leaving a whole language and culture and way of life, and I lived with the same obliviousness as a young adult embarking on my first adventure. Upping and leaving a whole way of life is something I've already done once and survived, so how hard could it be to do it again? Truth be told, I might not have done it if I'd known—I'd simply thought nothing of it.

My experience in the UK was to my advantage in the Czech Republic, because when I became frustrated, when I became disoriented and confused, I told myself: *this is all normal.* I'd lived the same thing when I first moved to England. Things take time to accept, so take a breath. *Breathe.* The biggest mistake a foreigner can make in a foreign land is to insist on the way things used to be, and yet where does that lead eventually except a forgetting of oneself altogether? There is give and take here. If there's one thing I have learnt, it is that nothing is quite so absolute. To allow yourself to change, to be moulded, while holding dear a part of yourself that shall never change, and never should. To do this requires a breaking and remaking of oneself, finding all the essential parts that make you who you are, and dissecting the facets of your identity to the point where you can pin the words 'cultural upbringing' to the parts where they apply. That's the magic trick, and no one can really teach you how.

When I see expats complaining about the Czech school system, I can't help but think: *You don't get it yet.* You still wish things could be different, when this is just how things work here. Acceptance does not mean liking it, nor does it mean no change is necessary, but you must find your way to work within the system.

And every now and then, push a little out of it.

My daughter goes to Czech school, and she's insanely bored in her English lessons as a child from a British-Czech home still stuck learning how to say, "My name is..." I tell her, *Listen to your teacher.* But in the same breath, *I'll email your teacher and send a book with you to read.* Her teachers tell her she must speak only Czech at home or her Czech won't improve, but I tell her no. However, Czech is indeed important. Even as adults, we crave dualities, the mutually exclusive, and I'm trying to teach her the world is more nuanced than this, and our minds more capable. I know, because when I was a child, British teachers said the same thing to my parents: *Iris must read English books at home.*

But losing a language means losing a culture with it, and being Chinese is part of me. If Chinese was obsolete, then so was part of my identity, and that isn't right either. Having said this, it is a question whether my English would have got to this level if my parents hadn't abandoned our Chinese education. I was not a regular bilingual child, since I was already eight when I emigrated. Would I have withstood the pressure of learning Chinese at home on top of regular British school? Would I have had the time to explore my creative writing to this level in English if I'd been saddled with keeping up my Chinese literacy? Would I have assimilated as quickly as I did into British culture and picked up the language as fast as I did, if I had been allowed the crutch of my true first language? Did anything worthwhile come without a measure of loss?

I cling to the good that's happened to me by growing up in the UK—not least of those that of meeting my husband and having our subsequent children—though sometimes I wonder if I haven't exaggerated these positives in my head in an attempt to justify what I'd lost.

We defied expectations: Chinese parents who worked regular English office jobs rather than Chinese takeaways; my father, a foreigner who climbed the ranks shoulder to shoulder with English natives despite his heavily-accented English; my mother, who obtained her first university degree at 63 years old in her third language in a completely new educational system than the one she knows; their children—me and my sister—who acquired English to native level; me, who should never have been a writer according to the theories of the third culture kid with their disrupted linguistic education and gaps in the cultural understanding in language. My family's achievements are many, most of them things people usually take for granted, but then most people did not move their families halfway across the world.

It was a gamble my parents took, to give up one life in exchange for a better one on the other side of the globe. It was reckless, ambitious. *Courageous.* To think all that I'd lost, but I was only a child when I moved—what of what my parents had given up? To live as foreigners forever for our sakes. My dad sometimes says, "Natives don't want a foreigner telling them what to do." He does not elaborate, but I wonder what passive discrimination, what small jibes, what side glances, what barbs in the unspoken played a part in forming the foundation of that statement. Meanwhile, my mother had no university degree as a foreigner when we first arrived, and one income wasn't enough in England with two children. All by herself, she learnt to drive, got to grips with how the school system worked and how to get a mortgage, all in her third language before my dad could move to England to be in England with us. In effect, operating as a single parent in a foreign land where she barely knew a soul. She went back to school studying entirely in English to obtain her GCSEs, all in order to get a job.

I've experienced racial prejudices; I've experienced what it's like to be plunged into the deep end and told to start swimming in a completely new system, but this is only the dregs of what my parents took the brunt of. They are the ones who paved the way before me. They are the ones who bore the burden. They are the ones who truly faced adversity and thrived. Not only succeeded, but *thrived*. They are the heroes of this story.

Aishwariya Laxmi

Aishwariya Laxmi's flash fiction, drabbles, essays, and poetry have appeared in more than 25 international anthologies. Aishwariya's bio is included in the Who's Who of Emerging Writers 2021 by Sweetycat Press, USA. She was one of the top three winners of High 5 - The Great Poetry Hunt Contest organized by WriteFluence in 2021. Her poem was featured among the 'Best of the Best' in an anthology by Sweetycat Press, USA in 2022. She was chosen as a finalist for the Orange Flower Awards 2020 in the category: Health Writing/Fitness Writing.

*Twitter - https://twitter.com/aishwariya /
Instagram - https://www.instagram.com/
ashtalksbooks/*

*Facebook- https://www.facebook.com/
Aishwariya1*

Childfree in Chennai: Childfree by Choice – A Single BIPOC (Black, Indigenous, and people of color) woman's account

My earliest memory is of me in a pinstriped blue frock in a pre-school. Then fast-forward to me in class four in another school, when the class monitor wanted to write my name in the detention log for some minor thing like maybe talking in class. And I actually gave him or her (I forget the details) my notebook to copy my name from. Notebook labels were handy that way since my name was Just. So. Long. Until class four, I hardly spoke with my classmates.

Throughout my childhood, I've never played with babies. Cat babies, yes, but never human babies. I just did not feel the need to coo over a child and I was honest about it and refrained from doing so. Now, please note, it's not that I hate children and wish them horrible things and I'm an evil monster because I keep children at bay. I love children but from a distance. I like sending them books or talking about books with them or preventing them from going the wrong way (for instance if a child is writing about drugs, etc., I try to alert the mom), you know…things like that.

But I have a string of health problems: rheumatoid arthritis, anxiety and other issues, obesity, etc. Taking care of myself is tremendously challenging and the only reason I'm able to manage is due to hugely supportive parents and sensitive and responsible domestic help, not to forget kind neighbors and some other good people. I really don't want to take on the responsibility of even a plant, leave alone a human child. I'm just not up to it. I have some dreams and goals for my future. I'd like to write every chance I get. I'd like to write books whenever I am able to. And I want to remain immersed in this world of books. Books and music have saved my life, apart from the actual human beings who have helped.

Another thing to note is I'm not fit to bring up a plant or a cat or a child. I can be very loving and sweet and kind and shower the plant or cat or child with love. But if I start undergoing stress for any reason (and the recent pandemic is a prime example), I can go off the rails. I went through some kind of mental torture during the pandemic. At one point, I was convinced we were all going to die and I was terrified that I would lose my parents. When my dad had to be operated on, I was not feeling "all there", but I didn't have a choice but to somehow reach the hospital and see that he got medical attention. When we stayed at the hospital, sheer terror bubbled up in me. I locked myself inside my room when my dad went into the operating theatre and kept imagining horrible scenarios straight out of a Robin Cook novel. I found it nearly impossible to find my way from the room to the canteen and back. I know, right? Sounds ridiculous. But it was a huge challenge. My friend told me to use technology to do it. But there's another thing I suck at.

Computers and phones hate me. They absolutely decide to conk out only when I touch them. The maximum contact I had with a human being outside of parents and strangers on the internet was the tech support guy at the place where I work as a consultant editor. Every day I would ask dumb questions about technology to him, and I struggled to communicate in Hindi since especially during stressful times, I forget all the languages I know and I can only communicate in English. The messages of doom and gloom pushed out in various WhatsApp groups fed into my terror until I told my former house help that the world was indeed going to end. Somehow, I have made it alive to the "other side" of the pandemic. I'm definitely not up to facing any more pandemics since I don't have the emotional wherewithal to handle it.

A child needs emotional support and security, not a mother who loves the child one day and yells at the child when things go wrong. So, I'm very clear that I will never biologically have a child or even adopt one. They deserve a better home.

Regarding stigma, prejudice and criticism in relation to my decision; I'm just doing my own thing and living my life. Nobody anymore tells me to my face that I should get married or have a child. If they are talking about me behind my back, I really don't care.

My college friends were extremely inclusive and supportive of me at a time when I was struggling with emotional issues. From age 40 onward, I have been living with my parents in suburbia and reading and writing have helped me cope with life. Since I moved to the suburbs, another close friend from college has also been instrumental in helping me maintain my sanity and happiness. Those who read my writing make me happy. And finally, the writing community has been amazing!

Thinking and reflecting on this subject has made me consider the following; whether a person is fit to raise a child and I've already answered that. Another is does one really want children around when they haven't been raised around children and have no idea how to look after them or care for them? Children are not to be just popped out and left to survive in the world on their own. They need a lot of emotional support and the first 1000 days of a child's life are crucial in determining the rest of the child's life.

In respect of our society; one is expected to get married at the latest at twenty-five and have a child before thirty. I have done neither.

Khwrwmdao Basumatry

Khwrwmdao Basumatry is currently working on his PhD in Electrical Engineering from Indian Institute of Technology, Jammu. He has obtained his Master of Science from Chalmers University of Technology, Sweden in 2021 and B.Tech in EEE from KIIT Deemed to be University, Bhubaneswar in 2017. He has been awarded National Overseas Scholarship for studying abroad by the Ministry of Tribal Affairs, Govt. of India in 2018 for his pursuing Master of science from Sweden. He has been awarded Garla Bata Talent award by Garla Bata Trust among the first from Bodo community. He also earned Certificate of Excellence in Republic Day for his outstanding performance in national level 16th National Children Science Congress-2008.

Cultivating Dreams: Paving the Path to Pursuing Abroad

It was Sunday; father went to a teacher association meeting, which happens once a month. I remember my father came drunk late at night. Mother worried about Father being late to come home, so she used to feed us dinner early, as the situation was not pleasant in those days, and at any moment, the situation may go even more wrong. The police used to come to our village for counter-insurgency and sometimes used to ask about whether insurgents visited our village for their food. We were scared to talk to them, so we ran away. One day, things went very wrong; we were going to school, and in between, the police came over and warned of punishment if we didn't tell them about the name of an armed activist who had come last night to have dinner. We had no idea why we (children) were targeted by someone else.

It was already late at night; Father came home drunk. At that time, myself and my younger brother had already been put to bed. I saw mother wake up and ask father why he had come home late. Father had quarreled with mother every time he got drunk as he had a desire to educate their children. He complained about the parents of the village not educating their children and allowing child marriage. Mother always tried to console father to talk slowly-but father had to talk rapidly and passionately when he got drunk. Repeatedly, he asks our mother to promise she will take care of the children and educate them. I was in 1st standard; my brother had just started walking! Father wanted us to study well so that he could send us to Nippon

(Japan) for higher studies. I listened to my father telling my mother, so I woke up and came to my father, asking him to have some dinner and go to sleep soon. Father used to cry whenever he got drunk -so I requested him to not be so loud. It used to happen whenever father went to his association meetings. Even though my father got drunk-hearing that our father wanted us to study well, I kept that in my heart! Maybe because of that, I never scolded father for being drunk-rather I promised never to get drunk myself.

I remember my mother's story, telling me that she used to prepare 'Jou-gishi (rice-beer)' and 'Jou-gwran' to maintain our livelihoods before my father got an appointment at the village primary school as a teacher. With this, there is the story of how we survived communal violence in the late 2000's-now it is a real family story for us. Mother had her passion for preparing 'amao' as the main residue for preparing 'Jou-gishi'. 'Amao' is not edible-not normal for direct consumption by children, which is prepared by grinding soaked rice and mixing it with plants. Father was not at home, as usual, and went to his association meeting; he did not come home, and the village was targeted by other community living in the neighbourhood. We had just had our dinner around 7 pm; mother said I cried and did not take dinner; it was dark moon-no electricity, and that's when the communal violence broke out; mother knew about the incident and she packed a meal for us and kept herself in the kitchen before deciding to leave.

Mother carried my little brother on her back with a 'gamsa'-a bodo tribal traditional attire, and held me on her right and held a meal for us. We merely escaped the enemy- running through a locally made 'canal' and joining with others who were also escaping. I did not understand the situation, so I cried in between even though I was able to run fast. Mother asked me to stop crying. I felt hungry, so I asked mother if I could have some food, Mother knew she had carried food for me, but she realised she picked the wrong 'amao'. Mother had no option other than to ask if someone had extra rice among the escaping groups. I was given rice by my mother finally. Things may seem normal now that I understand all the situations I have faced. Even my father telling me to go to Japan to study to be a scientist makes sense and I have been determined since then and keep focusing on studying- but was all that happened imaginary?

The situation eventually became normal; we returned home after a week. As usual, days passed playing with friends, and I loved going to school. Father was an assistant teacher in a primary school where I attended, a pure 'Bodo' medium. It was the time for my 1st standard exams to happen; I got an assignment to make a lotus and papaya with a piece of earth; my mother accompanied me every time I prepared such assignments. Mother had her good art while painting the walls with mud in our home. I remember there was no electricity in our village, so mother got ready a kerosene lamp for us to study. Sometimes, when kerosene finishes, my mother would light up a diya for me to study. I appreciate now how much my mother did for us, when she tirelessly fought for us to complete all our studies.

Finally, my first exam in life came; I went to the exam holding a new slate and pencil, bought by my mother in the Thursday bazaar. During the exam, we were told to write the answers to each question and submit them one by one before attempting the next questions. I was a good student, so I followed my teachers. I attempted to write the answer being asked in the first question, which was Devanagari 13 vowels! I was the first to submit my first answer to the table for checking; after that, only then could I attempt another question. I waited till all the students submitted the first answers. Teachers checked answers from top to bottom- I was first while submitting, but last to get my slate back to write the next answers.

Until I got my slate returned, my fellow classmates submitted another answer; I got nervous thinking of being defeated. So I cried in the examination hall loudly till the exam was attempted except for one. Father took me home-I was crying still. Mother asked my father about me and why I was crying. Father told mother that I was late submitting the next answer because the teachers were late checking my slate even though I was the first to submit the first answer. Mother scolds my father for not taking care of me in such a situation as important as merit. I used to be afraid of my mother, as she was strict, but my mother was always by my side when I was right, not doing anything naughty. My mother advised me not to worry about failing in the early stages, as this encouraged me to achieve more and go more carefully next time. I knew every answer; I could attempt everything.

I failed in the first standard, my first failure in life. I was unaware of the future, but this incident served as a lesson for my entire life. As I grew up, I passed my examinations-finally in 4th standard, securing first position in all standards throughout. It was the last level in primary school before attending middle education (M.E.) schools. At the same time, I saw my little brother start going to an English medium school; it was 5-6 kilometres from home, so he was sent to a hostel later. My parents were also discussing where to send me for my 5th standard and for further education, as I would be passing my 4th standard.

When that happened, I was far from home now, studying in a rural school after passing my 4th standard. A completely new environment in rural-where I could not hear the birds singing in the village, only the sounds of noise. Mother wanted me to study in a place where there was no disturbance, communal clashes, and insurgency. Me and my little brother's school was just a kilometre far-still we could not meet each other to play like we played before with mud. I missed everything in rural schools. Now Sunday was our happiest moment; mother came walking 5-6 kilometres from home to our schools, carrying delicious meals for us. Mother got us edible stuff along with study materials and left us back home. I never realised how far Mother can walk for us with food to feed. Mother had my father's words to us in her head- study well!

I adapted myself to the new environment and loved going to classes. I performed well in examinations and developed a hobby in extracurricular activities, poem recitation, writing poems and debate competitions. It was the sixth standard, and we were taken to a literacy event for poem recitation and debate competition. I was excited and determined to perform well. I secured first prizes in both events. People started talking about my talents in the quiz competition, and I answered many, including earning bonuses and answering others' questions. My school felt very proud of our performance. Likewise, I reached 8th standard- we were the senior most students. So, there was an election for a student secretary who was responsible for student development activities. I got support from the majority, so I won the student election.

In between, people had their imagination and minds this wrong-headed-idea that; 'studying in Bodo medium, students cannot excel in education and subsequent jobs'. I was participating and leading my fellow students in different literacy events organised by Bodo Sahitya Sabha (BSS) and All Bodo Students Union (ABSU). There was a time when debate competitions were concentrated on the 'future of Bodo medium students. I had strong words to say regarding the topics in those days; I still remember that a learners' duty was to learn and language alone does not decide our success. A person may speak a language we do not, but it does not mean that he knows everything and exploits our (bodo medium) opportunity. Strong determination and willpower only decide where we could reach!

I got the 'Best Student award' for my performance in study and extra-curricular activities at school. I was very motivated and inquisitive to do more! For the 2nd time, I won a student secretary'ship. I promised to take the name of the school higher than before. I did not forget my studies and even devoted more to my studies than extra-curricular activities. Since childhood, I heard my father saying-'I will send my son to Japan for higher education to be a scientist.' I remember we had an amazing General-Knowledge (GK) and Social Science (S.Sc.) teacher for the first time who told us about Missile Man of India. APJ Abdul Kalam. After listening to this legendary scientist, I was motivated by his determination and struggles. My brother, who works for ABSU, got me the 'Wings of Fire' book- I read the book and completed it within a week. I so admired him and wanted to meet him in my lifetime. I promised to find ways to reach the position to meet the person whom I admired the most.

I just started my 9th standard classes, my GK and S.Sc. The teacher called me to the chamber regarding the opportunity to participate in the National Children's Science Congress (NCSC) 2008. I agreed to prepare a project according to the theme 'Planet Earth: Explore, Share and Conserve,' given under NCSC-2008. I was very thankful to my guide, who tirelessly helped me start and successfully complete the projects. I was determined and morally so high that that chance would never be missed if I could help it! Along with my guide, we then took our poster to district-level NCSC-2008; luckily, the venue was near our school. I guess we prepared the poster very well; I was guided on how to start, engage the evaluator and end the presentation. I was confident and looking forward to the present. Finally, my turn came; I explained our project, its scope and how society can benefit from it. It was nice interacting with the evaluators; I was praised for the presentation! It was the time for the declaration of results, and find out who would represent the district at the state level. My name came out in first place. My school, along with my guide, was so happy about the news! For me, it was path-opening to meet someone!

I was about to finish my 9th standard and was preparing for the level NCSC 2008 to be held far from my school. Except for my mother tongue, I could not speak any of the other languages. So, I was a bit nervous, but my morally high spirit helped me beat this problem. Along with other participants from the district, I, too, started the journey to the venue of state-level NCSC-2008. Two considerations and goals always reminded me to keep trying- Father wanted to send me to Japan for higher studies to be a scientist, and I, too, had to meet someone whom I admired the most! This motivation encouraged me to focus on my aim and present my poster just like I did earlier. There too, the evaluator praised me for my confidence and way of presentation and simplification. Before announcing the results, we had an interaction with the scientists working in different organisations. That moment was something special for me. Honestly, I could read English but speaking for a while was challenging; I had in mind this idea of inquisitiveness about framing the question regarding the objective of the Large Hadron Collider (LHC), the largest and most powerful man-made particle accelerator, which opened in 2008. I am thankful to the GK teacher, who updates us with trending and important scientific developments. I got the answer right, amazingly. It inspired me a lot and whilst I interacted with the scientist in broken English; they pushed me to ask more...and I requested them to give me their autograph! Finally, results were announced- there, too, I made it on the list, only two to three teams from our district were selected to represent the state at the national level.

In the same year, I, along with fellow child scientists, reached the venue for the 16th National Children's Science Congress 2008, which was in Nagaland. After getting there, we were welcomed by the organisers of the state and offered programmed sheets. I first checked at the guest section- who would ignite our minds? I saw the name of a scientist whom I admired the most. Unimaginable- within a year, how my wish was going to come true! I was excited and felt morally high. It was confirmed I would be getting a chance to interact with Dr. Kalam. I focused on the poster presentation and did it as well as I did previously. I explained in my Bodo language about my project to evaluators, so I had a translator to narrate my words to them. I regretted not being able to explain in English...at the same time, in the same room where I had my presentation, I saw kids crying while explaining their own projects even though they knew good English too.

This situation enlightened me, and I realised that determination and self-confidence beat any problems, no matter who you are! The information I heard about how Bodo medium students can not compete with English medium students- it was wrong. I have proved it. Still, I must be strong enough to prove that studying in any medium can also excel in their education. Finally, the event was about to end with open session meetings where we will have our respected Missile Man of India as a chief guest to ignite the young minds. I was so attentive during his delivery speech with soft and easy English that I was able to understand most of the words. This Chief guest ignited the minds of the attending youth to face the problems, urging them to have big dreams and focus on perseverance! I noted down his two quotes in my diary, which I am quoting here: "If you have an aim in life, continuously acquire the knowledge, work hard with confidence to win and have the confidence to defeat problems and succeed with a righteous heart, you will definitely succeed in all your missions. It doesn't matter who you are" and "When you wish upon a star, it makes no difference who you are, anything your heart desires, will come to you."

I was so happy that day at being able to fulfil my desires to meet and interact with someone whom I admired so much. This instilled in me to have more and more targets with specific objectives in life to achieve. This time, I got good grades for my presentation but could not make it on the list for further presentation... I was satiated with what I had done so far...achieving my targets. The word perseverance, which I heard from Dr Kalam, motivated me;

I accepted the problems with positivity to work out a better way to come up stronger. After the session meeting, we were given a chance to shake hands with Dr. Kalam. I was fortunate to take this opportunity and have his autograph in my diary!

I came back to school with medals; I was welcomed at the school. I am very thankful to my co-worker (classmate) on that project for giving me a chance to present our presentation. I was full of hope and energetic thinking to achieve higher and higher. I knew I had to go a long way, so I tracked back to focus on my studies needed to write my 9th standard final examinations. I studied hard and excelled in the examination again, topping the exams.

In 10th standard, I focused more on studying as I was in my final year and about to appear in the matriculation (Board examination) examination. I had already set the goal to become a research scientist. I spent more time studying. In between, I participated in a district-level debate competition organised by Sarva Shiksha Abhiyan Mission on 'Child Labour'- participants came from colleges/universities, mostly studying B.A, M.A and engineering students. I had strong reasons to oppose child labour practices in various activities-domestic works, constructions and so on. I was so inspired by Dr Kalam's speech during the NCSC-2008-youth has enormous potential to ignite their minds to realise the 'India Vision 2020'.

The evaluator teams were so satisfied with my speech that they placed me for the first prize certificate along with the trophy. We went back to school after the event, and the director of our school praised us for the performance. During the same year, I was awarded the 'State Child Scientist Award' by the Assam Science Technology and

Environmental Council, Govt. of Assam and the 'Certificate of Excellence' by the Bodoland Territorial Council (BTC) on 26th January, Republic Day. This moment instills in me so much joy, encouraging me to do something different...! I finally took my board exam at my best and got first division, and was praised for having the highest marks in the centre. After the announcement of my matriculation result, many organisations invited me, along with my parents for a prize ceremony; the happiest moment was seeing my parents' happiness while receiving 'Aronai' offered by the organisers- 'Aronai' a Bodo, traditional attire used for welcoming the guests.

I had to make the decision what I wanted to pursue at college. It was tough for me as I had no idea which streams I had to select to realise my dream. I chose the science stream and also took Bodo as a subject for an elective. I found difficulty following the subjects except Bodo (MIL)- but I was determined to pursue science, so I worked hard to catch up with my fellow students. Later, I started liking solving problems. Time passed too fast; it was soon the time of my final Higher secondary examination- I had prepared well in all the subjects, the results were announced. I knew when I got a call from a college friend as he saw my name in a chart- that I had secured a first-division result. In between, I got an invitation from a 'Garla Bata Trust' to accept the award called Garla Bata Talent Award. I accepted the award and became the first from a Bodo community to receive this honour (Award). This award was given for my outstanding performance in national-level competitions and for securing first place in matriculation.

After higher secondary, I opted for engineering. I took an engineering entrance examination, but I could not make it at first, so I went to the city to prepare for the next attempt. I prepared well and attempted both national and state levels, as well as some private colleges. I passed all entrance examinations but could not make it to the 'national importance' colleges. At the state level, I was on a waiting list; but in the meantime, I was selected for an undergraduate course at a university. I decided to attend counselling there and was admitted to the Bachelor of Technology (B.Tech). The moments during the B.Tech were unforgettable- I adapted myself well to the multicultural people and learnt shared values and languages along with advanced engineering concepts in the classes. Learning Hindi from my B.Tech fellow from Northern India will never be forgotten!

I had in mind I would go abroad for higher studies- I tried scoring good marks along with building a good profile for my curriculum vitae in the third year of my B. Tech itself-I had a clear objective of going to Europe for my pursuit: Renewable energy integration into the electrical grid. I was in the final year of B.Tech; we were at the peak of placement sessions, and most of my friends were getting multiple offers from companies; I concentrated mostly on getting good recommendations from professors from my department.

Unfortunately, I missed my little brother; my brother was a good mechanic and genius in repairing any technical stuff-so the insurgents targeted him to be on their side who had just taken his matriculation examination and had expired in an encounter operation. Hearing the news, I was astonished by this fact - I did not know the evolving situation. My parents tried to resist him joining the insurgency outfit, but he was afraid of disobeying the decision of the group. He was still under 18 years old and unable to make any decisions, but he was forced to do their work. He could have been a good human being today, doing something impactful-but we lost him early due to outfits misleading the local youth. I consoled my mother to take care of her emotions and talked to her every day most of the time. Mother told me she fed my brother even when he was hiding in the jungle when he was in trouble after being forced to join the outfit. Finally, I graduated with a B.Tech tag as the first engineer from a village in 2017; my brother missed this happy moment. I had many things to teach and learn...but not everything could be controlled.

Still, I had a long way to go...almost all my friends in the village were married and had their children. But I was still deciding to further my education... Staying in the village environment... I could not have done all this. It was my father when he got drunk on Sundays and had his loud voice to remind us that he wanted us to get educated, and his plans to send us to Japan to be scientists that began all this. Alongside Mother who saved us from communal riots - I felt what my parents desired for me after my brother died. Mother told me not to go home after the incident, as I may have been targeted by police for possible connections. The situation was in total unrest until 2020. After graduation, I dropped my application for my master's in Sweden because they were researching more on renewable energy or sustainable energy. I had my father's words in mind, but now I had my own decision to pursue studying abroad too.

I got an offer letter from several good universities but failed to attend due to financial constraints on the first go around. I took a drop for one year; in the meantime, I appeared for a scholarship interview in the same year;

the Ministry of Tribal Affairs, Govt. of India, conducted the interview by offering a National Overseas Scholarship for studying abroad. I tried hard for the opportunity and made it on the first attempt. My parents, especially my father, were so happy to hear about my selection. Till the scholarship process was over from the government side, I returned to my alma mater schools, where I matriculated. I re-applied for the Master's- and finally got the offer while teaching as a teacher at school. While teaching mathematics, I enjoyed teaching students an easy way to learn it.

I had regular travel to the ministry in Delhi to speed up the verification process- as I was responsible for teaching, I adopted a smart approach to teaching the students. I was afraid of experimentation as I followed the strict question pattern of the matriculation exam. I left them in between till I completed almost all of the syllabus. I had confidence in myself that my students would excel in their exams. I already had a Schengen Visa at hand by July 2019, and I also got an approved scholarship from the ministry by August 2019. I decided to take my Father along with my uncle to Delhi to see me off to Sweden.

I saw such happiness on my Father's face while onboard a flight for the first time. Now, my father might realise his words to my mother when drunk were becoming true! I finally departed from Delhi airport alone to a new place. Until then, I had a good command of the English language…I learned a language and improved on it. Finally, I arrived at Landvetter airport at night; I took a bus from the airport to Korsvägen, Gothenburg central. I am very thankful to my ever-lasting-friend for taking me to his room for the night to stay. The next day he guided me to my apartment and college. The place was really new for me. I have never seen such a clean and green-organized city. I saw people of any age cycling on the street! People here jogging at night and it made me realise the horrible situation I faced during childhood in my village. We still did not have electricity in the village till 2019. I feel extremely happy to start my new journey here. I made a video call to my mother with a new Swedish SIM card. It was a completely new experience talking on a video call with my mother. She was happy to see me at the place which I tried hard to realise my dreams...at the same time she worried about the new place. I assured my mother I was in good shape here… don't worry, Aai (Mother)!

I got busy with my classes; we had regular exams within two months that didn't follow a semester system; rather, they followed the quarter system. I adapted myself to the new culture and discipline. I remember, during the class, I raised my hand, calling out Sir to the professor, and asking questions on things I didn't understand. My fellow European students looked at me with confusion, I knew that here we could call any professors by their first name.

As the days passed, I also got to know more about European culture and my international friends' back-grounds. We had diversity classes, excluding elective subjects, which allowed us to communicate with international students and learn more about different cultures. I roamed different places with friends during weekends-amazing places to refresh the soul after hectic compact schedules! Many of my European friends spoke English like me- so I asked about the medium of instruction in their schools, and they responded they preferred to learn in their own mother tongue...in Deutch, Svenska etc. I then realised that my decision to study in my mother language was a bold decision which gave me confidence now that I heard about my fellow friends' backgrounds! I got my scholarship from the Indian Embassy in Sweden; I am very much thankful for all the support while pursuing my education.

At the end of 2019, the news of COVID-19 broke out in Italy for the first time, and the situation went uncontrolled and spread into Sweden too. Our classes were taken online, but we still had practical work in a physical mode. By 2020, COVID-19 had spread in the city; we had strict guidelines from the municipality to obey the rules of social distancing. In India, COVID-19 swept badly-taking lakhs of people's lives. I had regular talks with my mother about the situation - I was so nervous at that time. Never distant from home in such an extreme situation- this was even more severe than I could have imagined. My mother advised me not to come home, and I knew that if I came, I couldn't finish my education. As I have seen difficult times and faced challenging situations, I was determined to finish my course. Thankfully, even with the odds in life, through utmost care in this foreign country and my day and night struggles, I presented my Master's thesis-which was the last part of my Master's course.

After post-graduation, I came back to India. Once I arrived in India, things had already changed in my village in Assam. We have peace now in the region and in our village. The outfits with whom my brother was associated came to the peace process. Parents of our village wanted their children to be educated...no more child marriages. We had light even during the dark moon-what a transformation in such a short span of time. The Sunday is not the same Sunday now; father transforms for our education. I cried with utmost pride seeing all the positive change.

The lesson I learnt from my past is that, no matter what the situation, if someone is determined to achieve, anything is possible. I am happy to be the first Bodo from a community to have such a scholarship studying with 'Bodo medium'. I have proved that a person who has doubts about studying in another language cannot excel in education. We should not learn to blame the situation; rather, we must learn from it and move forward with bigger steps so that once we return, we achieve everything has been left out.... that is the power of education in social transformation.

Suzette Bishop

Suzette Bishop lives in Texas with her husband and two cats. Her books include She Took Off Her Wings and Shoes, Horse-Minded, Hive-Mind, Cold Knife Surgery, and most recently, a chapbook, Jaguar's Book of the Dead. Her poems and essays have appeared in many literary magazines and anthologies and received an Honorable Mention in the Pen 2 Paper Contest and first place in the Spoon River Poetry Review Contest.

It Took the Two of Us to Not Have Children

"No, they aren't planning to have kids. In fact, that's part of what attracted them to each other in the first place. Neither one wants to have children." I wasn't disappointed to hear this when I asked whether a relative and his spouse were planning to have children. It had been exactly the same for me and my husband. In fact, I was thrilled to hear they were following their own feelings and beliefs, confidently sharing their decision with family members.

What shocked me was how matter-of-fact this family member sounded telling me about the couple's decision. After years of feeling judged as lacking, inferior, and selfish by this very person and other family members, it was odd, perhaps telling about the sea change happening with a new generation and about a greater respect, at least in my family, for the decision when it was the husband who was the blood relative explaining the rationale. The emphasis on their choice to be childfree being a mature decision between two partners was also refreshing but starkly different from the critical approach I experienced. I was often treated as if it was my decision alone, my husband never mentioned it, my mother even telling me recently it was her greatest disappointment that I didn't have children.

Before that moment, my mother had always told me it was my decision and that she was ok with it, especially since she already had grandchildren through my older sibling. I should do what makes me happy, she always told me, particularly as time passed, making it clear my husband and I wouldn't be having children. While growing up, I never remember her urging me to have children or telling me it was my duty. Where did this one-hundred-and-eighty-degree shift in my mother's perspective come from? I don't think she was just being polite earlier when she said she supported the decision. She sounded sincere, and she's never been good at hiding how she feels.

That shift pointed to the women with children in my family who drifted away from me but toward each other. All were practicing Catholics as well, motherhood a sacred vocation. Had they been chipping away at my mother's faith in me in her last years, criticizing my not going to church *and* not having children, not being worthy? Unfortunately, I can't come up with any other explanation for my mother's sudden shift on this subject and her words towards the end of her life, which were deeply hurtful. If I'm right, it says volumes about how these women, perhaps their spouses as well, believed I was doing something taboo, radically deviant, deserving of being scolded even by my mother.

Still, I refrained from telling my mother that watching her struggles with motherhood had a lot to do with my not having children. While motherhood was sacred and given in the 1950's, in reality, my parents seemed overwhelmed, not always on board with childcare. In photos, my mom certainly looks joyful holding my sister and I in her arms. The photos don't show her frustration and burnout bubbling to the surface, however, even screaming at me sometimes, descending into frightening rants, nor the time she left for a week, nor our visit to her in a mental hospital. While not in the photo albums, those images stay with me, too.

My parents decided to stop having children after my sister, a bit unusual for the 1950's to only have one child. It speaks to the strain my mother felt. But, oops, I came along, and it was a minefield. The marriage was in deep trouble, my mom had had a breakdown, my sister, gifted but hyper, had already worn her down. A drought and dried-up well made being the perfect mother and housewife impossible (this was before disposable diapers, mind you). My parents had followed the script of what was expected, but life hardly complied. I'm very grateful I was born and my parents tried to provide a stable home despite the turmoil, but the lesson I learned was to have children only if you really wanted to have children, not just because it was expected (and that the rhythm method of contraception wasn't very reliable, thus, my unplanned appearance).

I tested out my feelings about having children. Post-divorce and with the loss of a stable home life, I started baby-sitting at thirteen to earn money, the main way available to me at the time. I loved some of the children I babysat. I loved holding babies, playing board games, tucking them in. Less fun were the temper tantrums and the constant vigilance to make sure no one harmed themselves, no one swallowed something they weren't supposed to, no one tripped and hit their head, everyone stayed entertained despite short attention spans. Their parents looked haggard, desperate for the break I provided, even hiring me when they were broke. One couple dropped me off, racing away quickly, never paying me. Sometimes there were signs of abuse, one mother eventually giving up her two children.

I went on to work at a summer camp during college; I worked at a daycare center and shelter for youth, later. I've taught college for over thirty years. All of these experiences required me to nurture, to be patient, to play, to slip in words of encouragement or counsel or to just listen compassionately. Hopefully, something good stuck and was carried forward. I loved doing those things, being there for children and young adults, but I also loved coming home to quiet, my own space, my writing and studying, my time, and handing the children back to their parents. I needed breaks and regeneration, especially if I was going into a helping field like teaching, especially without the extended family to help *me* out, something my parents lacked, too.

Even if the family support had been there, college teaching usually requires moving to where the jobs are, which means instability, isolation like my parents faced following my father's career wherever it took them, far from an extended family support system, the village that helps to raise a child. It was just them doing all the house and childcare work on their own. It would have been the same for us. While greatly admiring those who still parent under these less-than-ideal conditions or worse, I didn't feel I could. I knew firsthand the devastating impact that had on the child from my mother's time-outs and my father's neglect after my parents divorced. He paid child support, helped out with college tuition, but he wasn't really there anymore.

My husband's childhood was similar. Sadly, my husband's mother died of cancer when he was ten. This meant becoming a latch-key child while his father worked all hours, processed grief, leaving my husband responsible for his younger brother—taking care of him, even making him dinner despite his own loss, worrying about their safety when left alone. My husband is gentle and funny with friends' kids and with our nephews when they were children. He's been told by most of his past girlfriends what a wonderful father he would be, and they would be right. But a previous relationship ended abruptly when he realized he didn't want children while his girlfriend did and assumed he did, too. He'd had enough of bearing a heavy responsibility for another life too young, a child responsible for a younger child. He'd done the work under impossible conditions. He brought this up early in our relationship, not wanting to find out we felt differently late into the relationship like before.

And like me, my husband gives a lot to teaching, helping others. Having to be on his own at eighteen, serving in the army for a few years, he also still acutely feels the stress of juggling finances, something else we both had to do too young. He was forty while I was thirty when we married, and we both had more to complete for our doctoral degrees. I would have had to get started on a family fairly soon before our degrees, job security, student loans, and livable conditions were sorted out. We lived like students in a one-bedroom apartment sparsely furnished with hand-me-downs from friends, a mattress on the floor. I was still searching for steady employment. Poorly paid adjunct teaching and freelance copy-editing, the jobs I landed and loved, barely helped to pay the bills. Furniture? Not affordable.

My husband, who was landing more interviews than I was and actual full-time academic job offers, accepted a second job at a small liberal arts college. While it came with a salary increase, other perks, and hints about hiring me, too, this turned out to be a mistake. Unlike the larger university where he was previously employed, colleagues and administrators were puzzled that we didn't settle immediately into starting a family with me staying home. Most of the professors were male and married, their wives staying home to have children, even home-schooling them because they felt the school district was inadequate.

Instead, I wanted and needed to work. While I admired the dedication and labor division of these arrangements, I couldn't help but guess some of the couples who lived in nice houses with furniture must also have had family money allowing them to live well on one lowly professor salary. We didn't. We were still in an apartment, two-bedroom by now, with mostly the same furniture. This is where I worked at a shelter for youth and eventually was hired by the same college to adjunct. By this time, I was also driving an hour out of town to see a therapist because of my grave sense of isolation and alienation. She said the place I described to her sounded like the 1950's not the 1990's. We never fit in, in part because we didn't have children.

Once my husband returned to teaching at a larger university again, I was relieved to be at a workplace and among an academic community where it was considered normal for women to work outside the home. I did still encounter a few colleagues and administrators, sometimes students, who treated me strangely because I didn't choose to have children. The city we moved to was larger, and I was mostly left alone off-campus, too.

The medical community in this city, however, is where I encountered puzzled, sometimes bewildered responses to being childfree. One time when getting my annual mammogram, the technician stopped taking notes and looked up at me after she asked how many children I had and I said none. "Why not?" she demanded. Gynecologists tended to be primarily obstetricians, women not seeming to visit for health reasons and post-menopause. One doctor tried to convince me to get a hysterectomy when I mentioned I didn't plan to have children. Keeping my uterus and not having children stymied her. Others looked grim about my risk of endometrial cancer because of the lack of pregnancies.

Yes, pregnancy gives you a healthy break from estrogen for nine months, but they acted alarmist, equating not getting pregnant with choosing to jump off a cliff. Certain death would follow. Once while examining me, one gynecologist commented, "Actually, given the procedures you've had for cervical cancer, I don't think your cervix would have held a baby, anyway," as if answering me saying something like, "I don't know if I made the right decision not to have babies." Besides rarely chatting in the middle of a gynecological exam, I never said that, didn't feel that regret, didn't want his reassurance about my decision. He was the one to say this in his own head, the one needing the reassurance about mine and my husband's decision. I kept switching gynecologists hoping to find one who wouldn't treat me like a zebra or a uterus, not offering lucrative opportunities beyond annual exams.

Writing this essay is the first time I have added my voice openly to any supportive discussion of being childfree. Honestly, it's only with my husband that I've felt I can be open and not judged. Afterall, he understands and makes this decision with me. I hope it will be easier for my young relative and his partner. A family member who once judged me harshly explained their rationale for being childfree as the most natural and right decision made thoughtfully as a couple, just as it should be understood. That's a start. And my wishes for their happiness? I just practiced a kind of parenting, significant in its own right.

Kayla Pica Williams

Kayla Pica Williams is a fourth year in her English with a creative writing emphasis PhD at ISU. She obtained her masters from CalArts and has published several short pieces in Stirling Lit, Club Plum, Unlikely Stories, and Rosette Maleficarum as well as a novella in Big Fiction Magazine. She is a second-generation Peruvian American who enjoys long walks with her King Charles and calls her mom daily.

The First Thing I've Ever Written in First Person

(I)

Alongside a picture of Bart from Simpsons and a mutation of Finn from Futurama; I pull the black pen over the greenish paint of the bathroom wall. I am normally intimidated by the thought of permanence. I never properly know what to say. It was placed across from the only toilet in the building that was meant specifically for CalArts MFA creative writers. Every girl who used the bathroom and every guy who took a shssit would see it. No one could miss this.

Do you ever want to slam your head against the wall until it cracks open?

I leave and there's no one waiting. The hallway lit by impure, too-bright overhead lights, is as thin and empty as it's always been. Breaking a rule makes my stomach tingle, being honest makes my hand shake. I want to puke and run back with a knife to scratch at the wall until no one can see the awkwardness of my y's.

No one would know though.

This isn't like high school, where you see your classmate's handwriting everyday on assignments you work on together. Or even like the end of my undergrad. Four years spent reading comments on pieces and you begin to learn how to read the awkward curves of the various i's and k's. They bring up a face in the back of your mind.

In graduate school, less than three weeks in, students and teachers would sit and shit and see nothing but *y's* and *w's* imprinted at eye level. But maybe one would be holding their workshop piece collection, with mine on top, and recognize the *a* of cracks coincided with the *a* in my name. Then they would come and find me and ask. Or maybe no one would recognize the handwriting but they would realize someone was in trouble.

What if readers think I mean slam my head until the wall cracks open?

Finn popped into my head, his multitude of tentacles nearly encroaching on Bart's territory.

What if they think it's just another piece of art?

(II)

Can you tell me something happy?

Typing is easier. The letters line up perfectly. There is no reason to erase and rewrite the same phrase because it would always turn out exactly the same. Even if I had the knowledge of the under workings of technology, could reach in and pave my own handprint, it would still be shifted back into proper position. All y's with a nice end curve.

My best MFA friend at the time was once a teacher and it shows in his preparedness to lecture, as well as his eagerness at times to do so. I ask him a lot of foolish questions — why are there two pieces in the google drive? Which author is that? What DOES fugue mean? — but he never talks down to me. Never even questions why I wouldn't know these things, even when I should. So typing another question is easy. Asking for something happy is not anything that will make a lasting impression with him. Just another question.

Hmm a tell or like a gif.

We continue talking. I receive a gif and funny story about a swing set. He tells me that I am a good person, likely because he knows I don't genuinely believe it. When he asks if I'm okay I throw out the expected answer that passes through people's minds quickly.

I'm fine.

I've gotten into an annoying habit (to him) of

repeatedly asking one of my other MFA friends if he is okay. A portion of it is that I cannot read him, something I'd like to believe I can see a little more clearly than others. The *s a d* spells clearly across faces in a neat penmanship that borders on cursive but is somehow more legible. So I ask him because that is what I would want someone to do for me. The other portion of it is that I feel he is someone who would mean it when he asked me back.

You know those days when you can't get out of bed without having a mental breakdown?

I throw out the line in a way that is not entirely too serious. Circled in blue as it comes out across the white backdrop of an iPhone. I don't tell him that I haven't eaten anything all day or that I'm almost out of my meds. It's edging there, closer, and that causes me to panic, has me wondering if he can see the smears of writing on the back of my hands and realizes how ugly they look.

You should still go to the party though.

My words change the topic effectively and he doesn't respond. There is relief in dismissing it, in knowing that he won't think about it again.

(III)

My mother prefers phone calls over texts. She is familiar with the way my *a's* and *s's* curve on the page, has seen them since I've grown up. As a child I used to run to her with crayon versions of them in stories I had written about butterflies hatching in class. She saw them progress past the shaky curve around into a solid half circle that forms assuredly.

How are you doing? Really?

Since the discovery of technology and my moving out of the house, she has not seen my handwriting. From her distance across the country she cannot see the notes that I have written on the back of my hand. There is no way for her to check my refrigerator and realize it is empty. My grocery list, three weeks old, written in small print and pinned with a magnet that says "art" to the door to where my frozen chicken should be.

There is no finality to her question. She will ask again. Tomorrow it will be written out in straight letters over text. The day after it will be said again over the phone. I can change my answer and there is assurance in that. It does not have to be all encompassing, has no sense of permanence.

I'm okay.

I do not add the qualifier: *enough.*

(IV)

Hey girl - have you read my piece yet?

My friend in the BFA acting program doesn't respond to the text I've sent her repeatedly. I know what she will say either way. She is busy, she has acting classes and multiple jobs and just got back from a wedding out of state. No matter that she said she would read it weeks ago or that she would read it on the plane.

I want to be mad at her. I had listened to her crying about her break up and then her joy a few weeks later at her new relationship. We had talked numerous times over the phone, me swallowing, her lamenting. I wanted her to answer one of the times that I called.

But how can I?

I had gotten closer to the truth with her than I had

with anyone else. Had managed to let the "not feeling okay" slip past the iron gate that was my lips. But that was not telling her. That was not making her understand. There is no law that says she has to understand what I am trying to tell her. I could drag her across campus, to a building she never went to, point to my awkward *y's* and misspaced question mark on the wall, already there for two-months-and-who-knows-exactly-how long. It was just ink.

I could scratch it into my stomach to give her something to see. My H's are quite pretty, easy to carve in three simple strikes over and over until the skin is red and raw. I rarely drew blood and they always healed. When they didn't, they were pock marks across my stomach that would forever look like slightly discolored freckles. They were just scars. It all felt easier and less permanent than letting it pass my lips in a voice that would likely crack and be too quiet, would need to be repeated.

Help me.

It was never supposed to happen again.

(V)

It was the one thing I never felt the urge to rewrite.

Journals from when I was a child were thrown out or ripped apart because I didn't like my handwriting. Flowers, pinks, purples, all tossed in as ashes with the food rubbish and paper waste. I could likely fill a bookshelf with the amount of pages I had deemed unworthy due to my terrible scrawl and my all-consuming need to find perfection. Words upon words have been discarded again and again. But I only wrote one draft.

I'm sorry Mom and Dad.

It's too hard.

I can't anymore.

Please forgive me.

I love you both so much.

I'm so tired.

I'm not strong enough for this.

It would be the most permanent thing I had intended to write. The last thing I had ever meant to say. Someone was meant to find it and give it to the parents across the country. I look back on the sloppy i's that are not fully capital and whose top and bottom are misaligned. How the words are off center and do not create equal white space on either side of the page. In a non-manic state, I cringe at its inability to stand up to the task I had assigned it. My hand twitches on the side of the page on instinct but I never rip it out.

No matter how many there are.

(VI)

Do you want to go to Kogi with us?

The question comes through with the exact same s's and a's I use in my own texting. There is no difference between the two of us in the digital world of facebook messenger. He cannot see the awkward way my *y* treads the line between cursive and print. No a's with the hook on the side of an *o* versus the hook resting on the top.

I wonder if it is this lack of knowledge that makes the

writing burn in my throat like acid. Every time I see them I want to explain how much their friendship means to me. That I was in class contemplating which way to kill myself – where to buy the meds, what road to step into, where to jump from – before they invited me out. Included me. Said I was a part of the gang. I did and still do want to cry.

Voicing it seems easier now, six months after the last time I was pinned with a number and the doctor's *bipolar* stained papers with my name on it [shorter than *chronic depression* and carried much more weight than *borderline personality disorder*, but there were still not enoughs's ore's for *multiple suicide attempts*]. The papers were stowed in my "important papers" accordion file on the top of my bookshelf, along with the files from five of my eight other hospital stays.

The first time I had swallowed pills they had just been small red Motrin tablets that went down easily even without water, could not have killed me despite what I wanted. I did not know. How suicide sits in your body, weighs down the back of your mind. How in giving up for one moment, one time, I was starting a cycle that would haunt every decision I would make. How it would bleed through the s's and *a*'s of *classes start today* written on the back of my hand. Would taint the *i*'s and the *r*'s of *sign up for martial arts*. So that every time I made a new friend, I felt they had no idea who I was until I showed them the way my *y*'s curve at the end of the multitude of *sorry*'s I have written.

I have tried to kill myself.

Repeatedly.

That is all I can think about as I shit and consider responding to the note that has been written in black ink and uneven handwriting, underneath my original message on the bathroom wall.

The wall or my head?

My mental health journey began when I was 15, this piece was first written when I was 22.

Now I am 28.

My mental illness is 13 years old.

My illness is a middle schooler. She can walk herself to school, because it's not too far, and skips along the sidewalk as she does. My illness is a tween. Boys do not have cooties but lips, scratching against her skin unpleasantly – for now. My illness is a preteen. She has tried on trainer bras, has felt her chest in the shower, wondering about the lumps her nurse mother told her about. My illness is a child. She cannot drive or drink, but she argues she is old enough to make her own decisions despite the fact that she knows nothing. My illness may be a woman. She may need pads, tampons, carry them in her purse, hope no one notices her bleed.

My illness may be tall. She takes after her father, has outgrown me, though there's still room to grow. My illness may need glasses. Her eyes were once strong, now weak, she's old enough to need to see the board. My illness may pick out her own clothes. She likes blues and purples, showing off her shoulders, and covering her arms. My illness has a lot of friends. She brings them over, they trample my house, and I'm left to clean up the mess. My illness may cry alone. Somewhere deep inside her room, where I cannot reach her. She covers her eyes with spoons to stop the swelling. She hides her notebook in a locked jewelry box. My illness may be old enough to cut herself, but she doesn't. Not anymore.

The thing about my illness is she is still changing. After my last hospital visit at 25, we found a new therapist who makes us confront our trauma. Discusses how the average coping mechanisms do not work for me. Teaches me that the 'love' I felt from the men who abused me is not what true love is meant to look like. The only time I truly cried as an adult was with her. I wept like a child. In front of another living, breathing, human being. There was not something I had done after I had been emotionally abused by a man who said he loved me.

I was diagnosed with inattentive attention hyperactivity disorder. I resisted, fervently. I had flipped through diagnoses as quickly as one could flip through the DSM. Borderline personality disorder. Depression. Bipolar. They slipped over me like a blanket. I snuggled into one, learned its crevices, warmed it with my heat. Then – *rip*. I am left cold, open, raw, vulnerable. At twenty-eight, I thought myself immune to the breeze.

I felt myself freeze.

The questions pour out of my psychiatrist as easily as if she were pouring lemonade. Quick, effortless, repetitive, endless. It must taste sweet on her tongue. The more she asks, the more I swallow, as it circles my mouth I grow adjusted to the acidity and come to revel in my thirst being quenched. Strawberry lemonade. It clicked. A pen in its cap. A belt in its buckle. A key in its lock. A cap on its jar.

A gun - cocked.

My therapist told me I do not have to defend them.

My parents, my teachers, my therapists, the adults who deemed me progressive because they did not see my struggle. *The first thing out of your mouth is that it's not their fault. That can be true,* and *you can still be mad at them.*

I think back. My inability to start cleaning, feeling the yelling in my bones. My procrastination with important projects, feeling the yelling in my skin. Speaking loudly and randomly, feeling the yelling in the backs of my eyes. Overfocusing, being unable to focus, feeling the yelling in my throat. Undiagnosed ADHD, feeling the yelling in my soul.

I cannot stand yelling anymore.

I cried like a kid with a busted knee, in therapy.

Not long after my therapist would point out the symptoms of autism that I had. I took to this diagnosis more easily, lived with it, breathed with it. After three months with both diagnoses, I felt more assured in myself. I could explain why I thought the way I did, I could explain things that were difficult for me, I could explain a lot of things I had once never understood about myself. The suicidal ideation? That was the Rejection Sensitivity Dysphoria (RSD). There was a reason on the page, in my reading, the reason for all the helplessness and despair I endured in a three letter syndrome.

I still live with the knowledge that I nearly took my own life sixteen times in less than ten years. When I tried to get life insurance – because someone who didn't know my history told me I would be fine – I was denied as too risky. Too hard. Too difficult. I cried when the 16.50 dollars I had sent them as a downpayment came back in the mail. I had been so happy to be such an adult.

Since my mental illness was born – she has tried to die 16 times, been hospitalized 10 times, had over a dozen different therapists, even more different doctors, had at least 10 different medications, missed over a year's worth of classes (starting from high school and going through grad school). Since my mental illness was born I graduated high school and undergrad with honors. I moved across the country twice in pursuit of my education. I got my Masters in my dream field, now I'm one year away from having a PhD.

My mental illness and I have come to terms. We're still growing and learning. We're still changing. But I can hold her in my arms and rub her back when she is scared. I can cradle her against my chest when she cries. I can tell her everything is going to be alright.

I can tell her everything is going to be alright and actually mean it this time.

Debasree Basu

Debasree Basu's Doctoral degree from Jawaharlal Nehru University, New Delhi is on her thesis titled, A Psychoanalytic Approach to the Gothic in the American Hard-Boiled Detective Fiction: A Study of Raymond Chandler's Philip Marlowe Novels which later culminated into a book. During the course of her doctoral research, Dr Basu visited Mansfield College, University of Oxford to present a paper on her thesis. She has taught at Departments of English at Kamala Nehru College (University of Delhi) and Amity University, Noida. Her areas of interest include studies on crime and detection, gender and popular culture. Her research interests have resulted in several published papers and conference proceedings. She is happily single and childfree and continues to facilitate students globally in the areas of creative writing, public speaking, and soft skill training.

Some(body)'s Story

Iam an urban, educated, unmarried, childfree woman who chose to leave her moderately well-paying job in the academic sector and returned to relocate to her hometown during the Pandemic to become the primary caregiver of her senior citizen parents.

Of all the "feats" that I have managed to amass in my odd 40 years of mortal life, the one that I have not been much appreciated about is the fact that I did not particularly feel obliged to tick the marriage checkbox on the list of my essentials. As far as my memory goes, the pre-teen self of mine, had miraculously deduced that the roles of wife and mother aren't exactly my cup of milk (err...just stating my preference, hence the deviation). Anyway, the fact remains that I am very much single and more so interested in keeping the status quo that way.

When I reflect upon it, I realise that consciously I was never invested in any relationship because neither I had the time nor, more importantly, the inclination to be honest. I am self-absorbed, blatantly dismissive of other people's opinion when it comes to exercising my subjective choices. However, does that mean that I have not had to experience veiled taunts, jibes, sneers ever? The answer is NO. Instances of behind the back gossip, rumoured link ups with co- workers have been quite a few. Non-existent romantic relationships have been fabricated; my sexual orientation has been debated upon. The list is endless.

In my professional capacity as an educator of liberal arts, I have been admired and respected by my students for my independent perspectives. Surprisingly, while teaching gender sensitive, volatile texts to a mixed gender class, I have been subtlety told to "tone down" my apparent "aggressive" and "radical" stances lest I provoke the students to be "non-conformists". I have learnt and relearned a lot from my students, and I would like to believe that our exchanges were academically stimulating and productive with the space to share our varied experiences.

Nevertheless, I have never felt any maternal instinct towards my students. They will always be my students and co-learners, never my children. I AM CHILDFREE-consciously, intentionally, deliberately in every way and I'd like to keep it that way. I am not responsible towards their upbringing but am to a certain extent, responsible for facilitating their value system which eventually they might choose to follow or otherwise. I consider them as individuals who are bitterly and 'betterly' exposed to their surroundings and do not exactly need our guidance all the way.

The fact that the nomenclature "childfree" as opposed to "childless" is in vogue, shows the trajectory that has been undertaken and covered. We have come so long so as to debilitate the archaic impositions of stereotyping a woman as a 'life-giver'. I am a caregiver and I do not consider myself incomplete for not having experienced the cultural and consumerism glorified status of motherhood. I was not comfortable taking responsibility for a child either via adoption, nor was I ready to undergo the period of gestation.

During the invigilation duties or while charting the timetable for classes at my erstwhile workplace, I used to be given morning duties and morning classes solely because I had no family residing with me, specifically husband and child. Therefore, it was taken for granted that I would 'manage' to report on time. I had to travel for almost 3 hrs daily round-trip commute but there was never consideration shown. At an individual level, I had to be quite vocal about it to ensure some changes.

I distinctly remember, quite a few years back during the pre-Pandemic era, I had chanced upon a family gathering. By virtue of living away from family, saved myself the obligation of socialising with my extended family. My cousin had asked me to hold her 8-month-old who was quite curious to figure me out. I refused and was probably a bit direct about it. My disinterest sparked quite a debate which needless to say, ruined the much desired family reunion.

It is quite clear to me that my propensity towards being a mother was never existent. The emotional effort of raising a human in a world like the one we are living in, the financial investment, the reduction in my access to solitude and spontaneous opportunities would all have been compromised- and I was never OKAY with it. The more and more honest and introspective I have been about how I would prefer to exist in the world, parenthood has been less and less relevant to me.

One of the reasons why I resigned from my job was that I realised that I had reached a dead-end and in no way was the job catering to my personal growth and development. Like Sisyphus, I was just making the futile attempt of rolling the burden all the way up, only to see it come crashing down. I could indulge in such decision as I have intentionally deviated from financial liabilities. No one, but myself, is dependent upon my earnings and I earn enough for myself.

Guilt is a potent tool that induces remorse which has

been often generously used by people around to trick us into doing something which we would preferably not do. I am stunned to see how much some people are invested in denigrating women who are childfree by choice. A choice that is none of their business. Are the glorified mothers really upset about how much freedom I have, or are they upset that they haven't been able to take it away from me yet? I often, at my workplace, have been subjected to tasks apparently because I do not have "distractions". As if my efficiency, my credentials did not matter much. Not that I owe an explanation to anyone, but a society that idealises married women and worships motherhood, being single and childfree is quite out of the box. It is almost as if I am free, then I am morally wrong.

I wholly support anyone who wants to be a parent, I've just never felt the ovarian ache my friends gush about when encountered with the tiny fingers of a baby. It's not that I hate kids. My social network profile is often flooded with photographs of their kids birthed by my "mother counterparts". At times, around 20 to 30 pics of the child with very slight variations in gestures, smile, etc. I really feel sorry for those chubby souls!

I do, however, covet for a life which is free of responsibility, which gives me the opportunity to opt for new mistakes like licence to cause accidents, I mean driving. I am bad at it you see! I have lately joined a community of single women from diverse walks of life where monthly meet ups are held to showcase the talent, skills and enterprises of achievers who celebrate life. Many of them are childfree and find it extremely fascinating to get an insight into the varied threads of stories woven into a web of connectivity.

My freedom is extremely precious and intoxicating which is non-negotiable. But it is not good enough for many. I suppose, it will never be good enough if you exercise your choice.

It's weirdly surprising when people tell me that I'll change my mind about marriage. In my case, it is mostly marriage because, well...you get the chronology right!! The subtext of "You'll change your mind" dates to the idea that marriage followed by motherhood is the normative stance and anything otherwise is deviant. Why and how should I change my mind? I have monthly cycles, which are related to fertility but not to marriage/child lust. And there's a "clock" counting down to my infertility. But there's no spontaneous, natural internal change that makes me suddenly crave for marriage and want a baby.

People want to pass on their genes; the end of your family's bloodline seems unbearably sad – but that's not particularly rational, at least not for me. I do not think my bloodline includes the DNA for altruism. I doubt whether my blood holds the cure to cancer; it is just a thread in a regular embroidered pattern. There's also an instinct to pass on what you know. I do it sometimes – through my lectures, my writings, not that they matter much but it's enough for me. Since my faith in self-reliance has not shaken, I have no reason to believe that I won't continue the way I have been till now.

I am looking forward to an inevitable parent free life as well, and the eventuality of it does not bother me or for that matter, does not scare me either. I am very comfortable with the knowledge that I will probably have no one within my immediate social circuit. People often question my indifference and say that I will tone down with age and regret or repent upon my decision. I have questioned myself as well. But the bottom line is, I cannot trade away my years of freedom with the premonition of what's in store for me in my old age.

On good days, my singledom feels like a loyal ally who allows me to design my space the way I want it to, to be selfish, to embrace a role than most women in my country can enjoy. On hard days, my singledom becomes my nemesis, a ruthless interrogator who asks uncomfortable questions, reminding me that I have not chosen a fitting trajectory and that there will be consequences. But it does not surface doubts. I am alone, not lonely and I am not in denial of my socio-cultural position.

So, just bring it on life! Just bring it on!!

Sureshika Piyasena

Dr. Sureshika Piyasena graduated from Miranda House, University of Delhi and read for her PhD in English at Jawaharlal Nehru University, New Delhi, India. Her debut collection of poems titled Little Lost Loves was published in May 2021 which is a chapbook on the theme of miscarriages and infant loss. Her second collection of poems is titled Palimpsest.

She has taught English Language and Literature at the University of Sri Jayewardenepura in Sri Lanka, City University of Hong Kong, and The Hong Kong Polytechnic University. Her areas of research interest are in Feminist theory, Comparative Literature, and Gender studies.

Alone

I was on all fours on a government hospital bed in a foreign country, just trying to breathe in between contractions.

It's a terrible feeling to have no control over your own body. It's not fun when your body doesn't allow you to breathe and there's another being inside you. You have to be in labour to truly understand why it's called labour. I was determined to have a vaginal birth so that I wouldn't have to go through a C-section, as I knew there was no one to look after me. I pushed so hard my anus got damaged.

People ask me what my birth story was. Especially because I was away from home living in a foreign country. They ask me how long I was in labour for and how I got to the hospital etc. Very often I lie because the truth is so harrowing and shameful. The shame is not mine, but I didn't want the world to know that I was treated badly by a person I fought with everyone to marry. I didn't want pity.

We met when I was a student in Delhi. We dated for two and a half years and then got married in Sri Lanka despite much objection from my family. He was four years younger than me, a Christian while I was a Buddhist. He was an outdoor educator and rock climber while I was an academic. He gave up his career in the army to marry me as the army would not have granted him permission to marry a foreigner. Back then I thought it was love that made him quit the army for me, but I didn't know he had abandonment issues at the time because of his father's suicide.

My parents paid for our wedding reception but only his best friend attended the wedding from his side. His family in India said that they don't have passports. He didn't want them to be there either. I found that terribly strange. Even though I was fighting with my siblings and parents I wanted them to be there when I was getting married. I did two jobs to be able to pay for our wedding rings. We both found jobs and lived on rent on the outskirts of Colombo.

I had left my family and friends in Sri Lanka and moved to Hong Kong because my husband got a job in HK. I was teaching at a University at the time and I loved my job. I thought we would have a better life as our life in Sri Lanka was very basic. My relationship with my mother and my sisters had soured because I fought with them to marry him. Little did I know…

We were given a studio apartment by the company that he worked for in HK. It was near the beach and was beautiful. I tried to make it as homely as possible and to be grateful for what we had got. But he was always at work and I was so lonely. Even when he was at home, he was always watching something on his laptop. I was desperate to find a job. I applied to all the universities in HK and managed to find a teaching assistant job. I had the wrong name and the wrong skin colour to be teaching English. It was so difficult to find work even with a PhD. At one point I was working in a restaurant. I'd rather chop vegetables than stay home. I felt that if I stayed home, I might be sent back to Colombo in a coffin. If I killed myself, then my family would have to collect my body. That would be very inconvenient for them and I knew they would curse me. When you live by your own rules, people wait for you to fail, to say I told you so and feel good about themselves. People don't like women who live by their own terms.

Life in HK was so lonely. He would not tell me even when he was leaving the house or where he was going. I used to come out of the kitchen and realise he was gone. He never told me what his workday was like or whether he would be coming home for lunch. Either he didn't turn up for lunch or would come home and ask for food. When I told him that he needed to communicate more he said that

I don't need to know where he is. He would watch movies on his own on his laptop and didn't even ask me if I wanted to watch. He would watch movies on the bed despite me telling him that the noise disturbed my sleep. I also noticed that his stories were not consistent. I was so lonely and suicidal but desperate to make my marriage work especially since I had gone against my parents' wishes.

In the ward the nurses were talking to each other in Cantonese and I wanted to know what they were saying. I was worried for my baby and the pain was intense. They tried to make me sit on an exercise ball but I just couldn't. I could feel her head in my pelvic bone. Then lots of chatter in Cantonese and I was rushed to the labour room from the ward. When I was wheeled out of the ward, I desperately looked for my husband, in the corridor leading to the door of the ward, but he wasn't there. In the labour room the nurse gave me a phone to call him but he didn't pick up. I called 14 times in between contractions. No answer. The nurse asked me if there was anyone else I could call. I managed to say no. There was no one else. I gave her back the phone. I thought to hell with him and decided to give birth on my own. Anyway, I had made up my mind to do this on my own many months ago. Later he told me that he had gone to the pool to practice kayaking because the nurse said that it is not possible to determine when I would be giving birth.

The pain was intense. I looked over my belly and there was no one. I called out to the nurse. For someone who is very particular about who is near me, calling out to a stranger was a first. I'd rather have a stranger who speaks basic English than no one at all. No one talks about how much effort it takes to push a baby out. The word 'labour' is appropriate but definitely not the phrase "was born" for a vaginal birth. You have to GIVE birth.

He turned up finally. It's like my daughter waited for him. Probably a foreshadowing of how she has to wait for him for the rest of her life just for a call, or a reply to her text.

I needed an episiotomy. I didn't even feel the cut. My body had given up. It was sheer willpower. I finally pushed her out after 18 hours of labour. When she was kept on my chest she looked straight into my eyes. It was amazing. There is life before this and after. I used to fear nothing but now there was so much fear for this being who was mine. Even as a child I was not afraid of the dark or of imaginary monsters. Maybe that's why I didn't spot a monster when I saw one. Extreme bravery can lead you to monsters under the bed. Sometimes they get into your bed too.

Nine months before this when I showed him the pregnancy test, he said that it was negative although there were two stripes on it which showed that I was pregnant and I had to convince him that it was positive. He completely ignored the fact that I was pregnant and didn't prepare for the child at all. I bought everything and prepared the cot while he kept telling me I was getting too much stuff. I was only buying second-hand stuff and collecting things which were given away for free. People give away a lot of baby stuff for free in HK because they have no space to store it because apartments are very small.

He tried to leave me alone at home very close to my due date and go to a conference on an island that didn't have phone reception. His boss told him not to go as we were in an isolated place, far from the hospital. It was only then that he decided to stay home. When I was in labour at home, he was watching youtube videos with his ear phones on and said that he couldn't see me in pain and completely ignored me. My contractions began at 1.00 am and by 6.00 am I told him we needed to go to the hospital. He called a taxi and we went to the hospital. He walked ahead of me and went into the emergency section of the hospital without going to the maternity ward. I realized he didn't even know where to take me. I guess he saw pregnancy as an 'emergency.'

After our daughter was born he was very supportive for a while and helped me with looking after her but it depended on his mood. If we had an argument, then even if the child was howling in the cot, he would not pick her up. He would very often say that children are a nuisance and that they ruin marriages and lives. Once when my daughter and I were both sick, he went to town to get dinner and didn't come back home. When I called he was having beer with a friend and said he forgot that we were waiting for him. When my daughter was one and a half years old I decided to get out of this marriage as he was extremely moody and unreliable and treated her as if she was a nuisance. However, he lost his job and I had a job at that time so I still stuck around as I felt sorry for him and my daughter was so small; I desperately wanted my marriage to work out.

In August 2017 I had a miscarriage and he was not supportive at all. When I went for the scan, the doctor said there was no heartbeat. I remember getting into the bus to come back home to my daughter like a zombie. I was numb. I went in for a womb wash. Just before I was taken into the theatre I went to the toilet and a huge clot came out. The commode was completely red with blood. I had never seen so much blood in my life. I wanted to put my hand in and take the little piece of mass that had fallen into it. I made up my mind not to and flushed and walked out. That was the most difficult flushing I have ever done.

The next year I got pregnant, and I was thrilled, but he was adamant that I have an abortion. He told me it's not the right time and we can try in a couple of years. He kept telling me that he doesn't want to have this child now and was very angry that I had got a cot which someone was giving away for free. I had another miscarriage. I bled for weeks. I didn't go to the hospital for a womb wash because he wasn't even able to put our daughter to sleep. I knew she would not sleep without me. And maybe I needed her more than anything else. While one was dying inside me, I held on to the only one I had.

Our relationship deteriorated rapidly after this. I convinced him to go for therapy. I had lost all respect for him at this point. I didn't want him to come near me. Then he realized that I would probably leave him and he started pestering me to have another child with him. I didn't let him come near me. I knew this was a trap. He started gas lighting me saying that I'm not trying to save our marriage.

After our counselling sessions I realized that his issues stem from the disruptive violent childhood that he had. As a child he was thrashed by both his parents. He has a burn mark on his leg and used to have a broken tooth: both a result of his father's violence towards him. When he was 12 or 13, his father has committed suicide when he was at home and he had also been sexually abused as a child by another boy in his neighbourhood, which he says his mother knew about but ignored. She ignored everything and just kept asking him to pray. A professor of psychology that he spoke to, told him that he creates his own reality due to childhood trauma. I wanted to protect myself and my 4-year-old daughter so I borrowed money from a friend and left Hong Kong despite the pandemic and came back to Sri Lanka in November 2020 at a time where there were no flights in the midst of covid.

We had a ten-hour layover in Dubai and we had to go straight into quarantine in Colombo. I was nervous about how my daughter would react to being locked in a room for two weeks. I packed new toys in our suitcase to give her each day. This meant I had to leave behind my precious books. I had given up on life itself at this point. I was in survival mode. I hadn't said anything to my family because I didn't want to stress them out. It was my incredible friends who supported me every step of the way.

I set up the house all by myself and tried to get our life back on track. Enrolled my daughter in a school and I found a job. I couldn't afford a car so I started cycling with a seat at the back of the cycle for my daughter. When my husband realized I wasn't coming back, he started threatening me. The irony was that he kept threatening to call my mother and tell her things about me. So I decided to tell her why I came back. I told her how he asked me to have an abortion, how he was abusive and uncaring. She just sat and listened with a smirk on her face and then after I left, she called a close friend of mine to check if what I was telling her was true.

He wanted to take away whatever family support that I was getting. A few weeks after this he got someone to call my mother and tell her that I was having an affair with one of my friends and that's why our marriage didn't work out. Of course my family believed him. My friend was petrified and he stopped talking to me. I lost all my support systems. It was only my school and Uni friends who were there for me. My mother called me and blasted me saying I had brought shame on the family and that she didn't believe a word I said. She forgot to cut the line and I was heartbroken to hear her discussing me with my sister and they both agreed that I am a liar. I was heartbroken, overworked and stretched in every way. I just couldn't function. I couldn't sleep. I realized I needed help. I reached out to a therapist as I knew I had to be mentally sound to raise my child.

Therapy helped but the pain is still there. Some wounds don't heal.

When I came back to Sri Lanka, there were many anonymous people who messaged me asking me if I am still with my husband, as he is living with someone else. I just ignored them and kept going, trying to raise my child. There were many questions from my daughter as to why her father doesn't call her. I messaged him and told him to speak to her. They had a video call and they spoke. A month after that he asked if he could speak to her. Then about two months later I asked him to speak to her as she started crying at night saying only that she doesn't have a father. I took her back to Hong Kong but he didn't want to see her. He lied to us and told us that he is not in HK.

Then someone messaged me saying that she really needs to speak to me about my husband. I mustered up all the courage I had and replied. She told me that she was the girl who was living with him all this time and that he had dumped her and was living with another woman now. She wanted to know the truth about him. He had told her that I am a monster and that I ran away with his money.

How do I explain to a seven year old that her father

is delusional, emotionally damaged and is suffering from childhood trauma? My daughter says she can teach him how to be a parent. She believes she can teach him to love. I have to muster up all the courage I have to get through the day. A woman can do anything, especially if it is for her child.

Maria D'Arcy

*Maria D'Arcy, is
a multi-talented
storyteller, dancer and
author who lives in
Paris and is very much a
woman about town with
her extravagant hats and stylish clothes.*

*Her enterprising spirit snowballed into a
one-woman-show, a mix of Celtic literature
and oriental dance.*

*D'Arcy's purpose in life is three-fold: to
entertain and contribute to society. She
considers her novel as her legacy, a story
which evokes tolerance and empathy between
different creeds while adding a huge dash of
romance and spirituality. Her third arch is to
help the very shy gain confidence in English
conversation, theatre, and dance.*

Child-free and Worry-less

It was in a bustling Dublin bar, getting merry with friends,
on my 34th birthday it dawned on me I need not be ruled

and squashed by the ominous warning of the biological clock tick-tocking away…

The dread of leaving it too late disintegrated. My mum who worked in a maternity hospital would tell me of all the complications of her day, of screaming mothers giving birth and at the age of 35, an institution where the authorities labeled a pregnant woman as gone-by-best date. With my fresh decision to break from expectations I became as light as a summer breeze and realised I didn't want the domestic humdrum of family life, a narrow life of chores that was the sole thing my little mum knew. I was liberated from the chains of cultural conditioning and Catholic upbringing, released from the concept that our purpose on earth was to procreate. Instead, I decided to create.

At the time I was working in a primary school as a teacher and habitually wished I could turn on a voice recording of me saying to the disruptive kids to avoid the stress of being unkind,

"Stop that, sit down, be quiet and no you can't."

Motivating and disciplining children is a difficult balance to obtain especially if you attempt to do a concert, a play or painting hour. Certainly the children could be cute but would squabble over a pencil, a banana or my attention. I opted to transfer my attention to the Arts.

Dance classes in belly dance, Balinese and burlesque led to me feeling feminine and empowered. The more beautiful my reflection in the mirror due to the sequenced costume and lavish cosmetics, the more charismatic my show was. The art of seduction became easy. I learned to walk tall, evolving from a plain-Jane to being a serial kisser.

All the same, next on my agenda was to establish a

long-term relationship I was hooked on. Relationships need to be honed and surveyed constantly lest they descend into hell. It was, in fact, hellish after I married Adam or to be exact three years later. He had a paranoid sense of unfairness and exploded into a two-year tantrum if he deemed my plate of dinner bigger than his or that I had put his sugar in my tea. I bought all the essentials for running a home while he bought himself the enhancements. I left him to his sweets and got a divorce. He wished to claim it as an annulment in the eyes of the Catholic church since I had informed him I didn't want children but he had signed the marriage contract and knowingly consummated the marriage.

Strangely, I felt even more liberated from domestic life, had more the right to be me, to be free, to travel, to explore. During my two-month summer vacations from teaching I went to Canada, the USA, to China and Thailand, to Australia and Vietnam and, of course, around the old continent of Europe. Travelling alone or in duo with a partner who pays his way is much more affordable than family prices.

An ad in a local magazine called out to me: "Come to our café-philo get-together and discuss values, purpose and the meaning of life."

At first I was nervous or insecure, not sure my contribution would be as clever or articulate as the others' who had studied famous philosophers, though gradually when I did speak my viewpoint was assimilated as sincere and refreshing. It is an uphill struggle to change the world and its staid values but it is quite easy to influence or enhance the daily life of people around you. A smile at an old woman will make her day and I discovered that dressing flamboyantly tickles many-a-person.

They feel uninhibited just looking at you, perhaps wishing they could dare to be so original. The café-philo circle was stimulating, far-reaching and fun. They made me see the bigger picture, the universal dimension of being alive with quotes from Plato, Marx and Sartre because by this stage I was leaving Dublin and set up home in Paris. I grew from reading traditional W.B. Yeats to trailblazing Simone de Beauvoir. Hail to Simone, our trendsetter, our avant-gardist, whose campaign was to recognise women's equality, sexuality and right not to be a mother.

"I am too intelligent, too demanding, too resourceful for anyone to be able to take charge of me,"

she stated. Born in 1908, she was a pioneer of living a fulfilled and adventurous life without being weighed down by children, conventions or patriarchal society.

In Dublin it was teachers, neighbours, and peers who were my friends. On arriving in France I soon discovered French people were not so welcoming, therefore to build up a social life I had to take initiative, reach out and I chose la crème de la crème: Isabelle an intellectual song-writer, single and child-free but with a rock 'n' roll boyfriend, and since we both liked extravagant hats and suggestive lyrics we mounted a show entitled "Naughty Dames of Paris", an exuberant song-n-dance performance.

Indeed all the women I have befriended are not burdened down by children though have enduring relationships with men. Michelle is an international humanitarian worker and seeks to save people in disaster zones. Anne is an executive of Eurostar but anticipates a bad future ahead. She is thrilled not to be passing on a planet of climate change catastrophes to a progeny of her making.

Meanwhile I get immense job-satisfaction working as a coach to help French people get over the barrier that they need to be eloquent before they say their first sentence in English. Often they think they are too old to learn but it's not true. Receptivity to a new mentality and determination to succeed are the stepping-stones to paving the way to success.

Moreover I met a man, an American, Daniel, whose first wife left him because he didn't want to settle into suburbia and have children. He is a photographer and I like to be photographed. Together we dress up, go out, and behave like teenagers, sipping wine, getting merry, singing, dancing and amusing others in Montmartre. Without children to regard you as old you stay forever young.

Paulo Kellerman

*Paulo Kellerman is
a Portuguese writer.
He is the author of
six plays, two operas
and a short film. He
has published twenty-one books. He has
conceived, coordinated or participated in
projects with dozens of creators from a wide
range of artistic fields. He is responsible
for the Fotografar Palavras project, which
since 2016 has involved around 300 creators
(photographers and writers) from 32
countries. He is co-founder of the publishing
house Minimalista.*

Paper Elephants

I - Throwing paper airplanes at the moon

The first close contact I had with death happened when I was a teenager, when my grandfather died. He was a very active and dynamic man, still young, and with whom I had a very close relationship; he died unexpectedly, after a hospital complication, without any time for psychological preparations or goodbyes. My reaction wasn't brave: I refused any funeral event, or even to say goodbye to him.

My parents' house was right opposite the church, and through my bedroom window I could have watched the people going in and out of the church; the arrival of the hearse; my grandmother's endless weeping; the silent people staring at the ground; but I didn't. Hidden in my refuge, I refused to look out the window and witness the evidence of reality; I listened to music, in a naive attempt to feign some normality; but the sound of music was overlaid with melancholy and the slightly macabre melody of the church bell repeatedly ringing, announcing death.

A few years later, my grandmother died. Although my relationship with her was less intimate than the closeness I had with my grandfather, my reaction to her death was different. I was present at every moment, including at the funeral. I placed myself on the other side of the window: from the entrance of the church I repeatedly looked at my parents' house, studying the window of the room that was still mine even though I no longer lived there. I remembered the younger version of me hiding behind that window, running away from my grandfather's death. I felt no shame or embarrassment, no regret; only longing.

The day after my grandmother's funeral, I wrote a text. I believe that writing it represented for me an attempt to pay homage to my grandmother and also a private farewell, a moment from the crowds in the church and cemetery. In this text, written in the form of a story, I recounted my last visit to her, in the company of my daughter, the only great-granddaughter she ever met; I described the funeral in detail; and I asked some questions, not needed and generic, about death, time and memory. This text ended up in my third book; and as it is constructed as if it were a story, no reader will take it for what it really is: a personal and objective, factual testimony, without any of the fictional elements that characterize all the other stories in that book.

This text ends as follows: "I don't know what I'm writing all this for. My grandmother couldn't read."

These two sentences, written almost twenty years ago, sum up some of the concerns and perplexities that have always accompanied me as a writer. What is writing for? What is the function of literature? Why do I write? What's the point? In the specific case of this text, I believe I wanted to deal with events, resolving them in me through writing; and to preserve memories. Just that. Or all of that.

Perhaps writing is, after all, a naive attempt to deal with the most profound and mysterious of all subjects: death. Naive and perhaps inconsequential, but heartfelt and passionate.

(Like a dreamy child throwing paper airplanes at the moon, with the secret hope that when they get there, someone will catch them and throw them back.)

In the voracity of everyday life and the unstoppable advance of time, it's important to create moments of pause; that's what literature is for (for those who write and for those who read): it offers a chance to pause. It's like looking out of a window and contemplating something new, or the same landscape as always but from a different perspective; and then returning to the voracity of everyday life and reintegrating the unstoppable advance of time. Writing that particular text allowed me to create a window that I can return to again and again; publishing it in a book is an invitation for each reader to look through that window and see their own grandmother.

I wrote a text for my grandmother, but I only wrote

it after her death, making it impossible for her to read it. However, if it had been written before, she wouldn't have been able to read it either; she was illiterate. It seems both strange and beautiful - literary, as if it were a story - that I, the grandson of an illiterate person, have published twenty-something books.

Meanwhile, the text for my grandfather is yet to be written.

II - I never played soccer again

Being a popular teenager in the 1980s meant being a good footballer. For a boy not being able to participate in the permanent informal games happening in every free moment of school life, and to play a useful role in those games, was a condemnation to a certain ostracism. I was a bad soccer player. This meant that in order to be part of a team (i.e. spend hours running around waiting for someone to pass the ball; and when someone did pass the ball, not knowing quite well what to do with it) I had to pay my way in; sometimes by offering my classmates small cakes ("bolas de Berlim"); sometimes by doing various school activities for them, such as homework.

The arduous task of trying to be popular (or at least not completely invisible) was tiring, distressing and inconsequential; from frustration to frustration, I lost interest in trying, resigning myself to a certain invisibility but saving money on "bolas de Berlim". At the same time, something unexpected started to happen: some teachers began to present my texts to the class. They were answers to normal school tasks, but written by me in an abnormal way; I did it with some creativity and, above all, with humor. Some teachers appreciated this humor and decided to read the texts to the whole class, perhaps as an act of general relaxation but also as a practical demonstration of how creative and original one could be, even when answering worn-out and unenthusiastic questions about history or geography.

This brought me, completely unexpectedly, the desired popularity. It also allowed me to realize that different paths could be followed to reach the same goal; soccer wasn't an inevitability, and realizing this was a relief: and perhaps acting somewhat radically, I banned it completely from my life. Not out of spite or even revenge, but because soccer had never really interested me. It was just something so omnipresent that I didn't even question it. This conscious withdrawal also brought with it some learning, because you don't reject something so popular and dominant with impunity. It was possibly the first time I consciously realized that refusing to do something that not only isn't questioned by the majority, but seems to be seen as an identity mark of that very majority, has consequences. Not being part of the majority can be quite lonely; but also deeply liberating.

But that wasn't the most valuable learning that the teachers' readings to the class gave me. There were twenty or thirty teenagers sitting in the small classrooms on the third floor, and in front of them there was a teacher who looked at them and read them something written by me; among those twenty or thirty, I was just another member of the group; a spectator. The teacher would read and the twenty or thirty would laugh. Real, genuine laughter. And those laughs fascinated me because they seemed magical. I wasn't the one causing them, with my behavior or some funny or involuntarily laughable action. I stood there hidden, invisible, without any intervention; just another member of the group. A spectator of the consequences of something I had created at another moment. That's what fascinated me: realizing that it wasn't me who was causing a reaction in my colleagues; but my words, the way I had used them.

That was when I began to grasp the real power of the written word and its potential as a tool; to perceive the impact of literature, even though I hadn't still fully understood the meaning of this concept, literature.

I thought:

This is what I want to do forever.

I thought:

I want to work with words so that they (and not I) create an impact on others. Away from me, in a classroom, across the street, in a distant city, somewhere on the other side of the world: create an impact, cause a reaction; even on those who know nothing about me, nor want to know; on those who have never seen or will see me; even if I can never witness such reaction.

I thought:

I just have to believe it can happen, that it's a possibility. That somewhere there will be a reaction.

(Like a dreamy child throwing paper airplanes at the moon, with the secret hope that they'll get there and someone will catch them; it's all it takes, that there's a possibility that they'll be caught).

That's what I wished for in the small classrooms on the third floor. That's what I've been doing.

III - I'm a story

Over a period of three years I was involved in the

creation of an original contemporary opera. Involving a professional team of dozens of people, including composers, singers, directors, technicians and a sixty-piece orchestra, I was responsible for writing the libretto. The result of these three years of work was presented in the most prestigious auditorium of the country, with a capacity of twelve hundred seats, in two sold-out sessions.

Although the challenge of designing an opera was fascinating in itself, this particular creation had its own characteristics that made it not only a challenging artistic project but also a production with a human and social reach, with a potential for transformation in its participants that elevated it beyond the usual artistic dimensions.

In addition to the entire professional team, dozens of young inmates were included in the creative process (and played a leading role). With a prison as its main partner, the overall aim of the project was to involve these young people in a large-scale professional production, offering them new experiences and tools. By using art and artistic expression (both classical and unconventional) as an element of self-worth and positive affirmation in society, it was possible to deconstruct prejudices and reconcile apparently separate worlds. To build bridges and cross them. It was possible to thrill and question, bring perspectives closer together. It was possible to challenge each of the different people involved in the creation, but also the audience who watched it afterwards, to try to look at the world through the eyes of others.

I had work sessions with dozens of young prisoners. My aim was for the story told by the opera to be personal enough but also comprehensive enough to be able to emotionally involve each of its participants, containing individual and collective elements of identification that would allow each person involved to say, unquestionably, "I am present, I feel represented". I listened to each of the individual stories, realizing that everyone wanted the opera to portray their own personal story. And the opera could indeed have been based on each of the stories I heard. We could have had sixty operas, not just one.

The story each person tells about their life, the individual narrative they create from the events they experience, is a fundamental identity mark in their relationship with others (and with themselves). People mentally improve their own stories (a subtle blend of reality and fiction, of experience and dreams, of honesty and manipulation), and then share them, hoping that they will function as a presentation, a kind of business card; in the same way that they listen and relate to the individual stories that others tell. Organization in society is based on a permanent sharing of stories, a dialogue between stories. In this sense, everyone is a writer: we all compose narratives that have an internal logic, an addressee, a specific intention; and one of the primary narratives that we all compose is the individual story through which we want to be identified. The story we tell when someone asks: who are you?

We are all stories.

That's what I began to intuit when I heard the teachers in the third floor classrooms reading my texts: not just the power of the word, but the importance of the story. The stories told in the corridors of a high school can be as harmless as desperate ways of seeking attention, understanding, empathy, acceptance, validation and affirmation. The same happens in a prison. The same happens in groups of friends, in families. The same happens on social media. The same happens when a writer publishes a book.

I listened to more than sixty prisoners. I may not remember all their names; I may not remember all their faces; I may not remember the way each one looked or shook hands, how they laughed, how they got emotional when they talked about their mothers. But I remember their stories. That's what I keep, that's what stays with me: the stories they told about themselves and the way I related to those stories, the impact they had and the questions they raised in me. It was the stories that remained.

We listened to all the stories and learned from them. We identified something of ourselves in each other's narratives. We harmonized. We discussed it. We chose. We decided. And then we created something together: a new story incorporating elements, details and subtleties from each of the stories on which it was based. We built a puzzle in which each individual story was a piece, but which together told a more complete story.

(Like a dreamy child throwing paper airplanes at the moon, with the secret hope that they'll get there and someone will catch them; and to make sure that the planes can actually reach the moon, he asks his friends for help so that together they can build the best plane possible; a plane with the best chance of achieving its goal).

And in the end, we cried together.

IV - The stories we wear

The stories we tell work like clothes.

They protect or disguise our nakedness, drawing attention to a particular aspect or trying to divert the focus from another; they hide. We put them on to be seen in a certain way, to convey a specific idea, a concrete sensation; they are a manipulation.

But we can also tell stories that accomplish the opposite function: they undress us. They are stories that reveal and expose us. We undress them in order to be seen in a certain way, to convey a specific idea, a concrete sensation; they are manipulative.

And there are stories that achieve both objectives simultaneously. They hide, but they also reveal. They reveal while concealing.

I came face to face with this duplicity (which is difficult to detect and decode) in a project to write a book of testimonies. The aim of the book was to tell the story of a battalion of Portuguese commandos who fought in the colonial war in Africa in the early 1970s. This story was to be told through two different but complementary approaches: on one hand, from an objective and factual perspective (which would be handled by a journalist); on the other hand, from a more subjective and literary perspective, anchored in the emotions and feelings of those involved (which would be written by me). In order to accomplish this, it was necessary to carry out dozens of individual interviews with members of the battalion, but also with their families and with people from outside the group who had experienced or witnessed the same events. It was necessary to listen to their stories.

We heard individual stories and collective stories. The first were based on a personal interpretation of the reality observed and experienced, filtered through each person's convictions and emotions. The seconds were told as individual stories, but they were so similar to each other, regardless of who was telling them, that they seemed to be almost exact copies of the same original story, a master story; they were collective stories in the sense that they had been adopted by the group who seemed to follow a script, but these were told as if they were personal and unique. The former revealed, the latter concealed.

Telling a story of excessive bravery can hide fear; telling a story of excessive indifference can hide guilt; telling a story of excessive detachment can hide cowardice; telling a story that is too colorful can disguise a gray reality; telling a story that is too gray can disguise a black reality. Or it could be that the story told doesn't intend to hide anything; the bravery could have been real, the indifference could have been real, the detachment could have been real, the colorful could have been real, the gray could have been real.

The man who speaks with ease about the atrocities he committed against those he considered his enemies is the same man who speaks with disconcerting tenderness about the dog that died in his arms. He calls the dead enemy insulting names and weeps when he remembers the dog. How can such an immense contradiction be reconciled?

It's important to listen to each story without evaluating or judging it; without attaching labels to it, without putting it in identifying boxes; sometimes you might not even understand it. We simply have to listen. When we look at the sea, we don't evaluate or judge it; we don't need to understand it, we just need to look at it. It's important to listen to the sea of stories that come to us, to each island that each of us is. It's important to know that it's this sea that unites us with the other islands.

(Like a dreamy child throwing paper airplanes at

the moon, with the secret hope that they'll get there and someone will catch them; and then one day he stops and sits down to wait while looking at the moon, because he suddenly remembers how extraordinary it would be if paper airplanes would arrive from there).

V - Contamination

In the middle of summer 2016, with too much free time to fill and a certain need to entertain my laziness, I challenged a dozen friends to a project I called Fotografar Palavras (Photographing Words). The idea was simple: bring together artists from two fields (writing and photography) and challenge them to create collaboratively. Taking part meant possessing two characteristics: curiosity and generosity. The curiosity to look at the other person's work and be affected by it; the generosity to allow the other person to look at their own work and recreate it; the curiosity and generosity to see the other person's recreation. The project grew and became what it is today: a platform that has already involved more than three hundred artists from thirty-two countries in the creation of almost four thousand four hundred original contents; almost four thousand four hundred recreations.

The synchronization between ideas, enthusiasms, complicities and stories is the basis of the project. And it's this synchronization that I'm looking for more and more; in the work I do for the theater, for example, where the word takes on a voice, a body, movement; or in the books themselves (of those I've published, nine have been shared with other people - illustrators, photographers, writers); in the projects I've developed with musicians, painters, architects, photographers, other writers.

I'm fascinated by hearing other people's stories. I'm

fascinated by telling my own stories. And I'm fascinated by mixing my stories with the stories I hear or see or read, creating and telling stories together with others.

I'm fascinated by building together.

(Like a dreamy child throwing paper airplanes at the moon, with the secret hope that they'll get there and someone will catch them; and one day he stops throwing airplanes and calls his friends; he points to the moon and asks: what if we went there to see what we can find?)

VI - Story maps

Artistic creation is an attempt on the part of the creator to look outside themselves and discover themselves within, to grasp the outside from the filter within; it is an investigation, a testing of possibilities and scenarios; a daydream. It is therefore an individual and intimate process. But nothing prevents this process from communicating with others, equally individual and intimate; there's nothing preventing a dialog arising, an integration.

As if artistic creations were, after all, the construction of an individual map. Each story we live represents another dot on our map; and each story we hear is also a dot. References, signposts, warnings. Over time, lines, patterns, and marks begin to appear. Over time, we learn to locate and guide ourselves better on our map. Over time, we look at the map and find destinations.

Shared artistic creation is an attempt to establish a common map. Looking at the same reality from different points of view, comparing views and letting them contaminate each other; like changing glasses with the other. Each story lived or heard together represents another dot on the common map. And just like the individual map, each common map that is built allows everyone to locate and guide themselves in reality. It's not a replacement, but a complement.

(Like a dreamy child throwing paper airplanes at the moon, with the secret hope that they'll get there and someone will catch them; and one day he stops throwing airplanes and calls his friends; he points to the moon and asks: what if we went there to see what we can find? But first we need maps, don't we?)

VII - Paper elephants

We are storytellers. We tell stories to others and to ourselves; real stories, invented stories, invented stories that we think are real. We turn stories into memories. We appropriate other people's stories and make them our own. We assume ourselves to be the protagonists of infinite stories and also of the main story, which we call life. We relate to our own stories and to those of others. If someone tells us a story about a child who has lost their parents, we get emotional; even though we don't know the parents or the child; even though it may not even be true. It's the story that we relate to, it's the story that affects and influences us, that provokes a reaction.

And just like the stories we tell, and which mirror us, our identities are fluid and changing, evolving; sometimes contradictory. Indefinable. It's difficult to delimit the boundaries and limits of a story, to make it definitive or static; and if that happens, the story is always subject to different interpretations, different analysis and contradictory reactions. Just like individual identities. Just like people.

As a writer, I believe that there are no boundaries or

limits that can contain a story; the possibilities are endless. The same goes for people and their lives (which are mirrors of their stories, and vice versa): anything is possible.

(Like a dreamy child throwing paper airplanes at the moon, with the secret hope that they'll get there and someone will catch them; and suddenly asking himself: why airplanes? What if I threw paper boats? Or paper elephants?)

VIII - Once upon a time

This is the story of the writer who, after the death of his illiterate grandmother, wrote her a text.

(The author would like to thank Elsa Arrais, Sandra Fine, and Dr. Khusi Pattanayak).

Frances Sanchez Merson

Frances Sanchez Merson, a native Texan from El Paso, lives in the Texas Hill Country with her husband, two dogs and a cat. She's a vegan who enjoys running and wine. Her other pastimes include spending time with her friends and family and discussing Texas & Mexican-American history at great lengths.

A Seat for Everyone

When I think about Mexican culture/families the first image that comes to mind is a large family table. A long brown table with anywhere from six to eight to ten chairs outlining the smorgasbord of food. All stereotypes aside: food, family, and faith are what I know to be the pillars of Mexican culture. You grow up praying, fulfilling your commandments as a child (if you're Catholic), marrying a man in a strictly heterosexual society, and filling your world with children.

If I had to draw the family table in my kitchen it would

look a wee bit different. My husband and I sometimes eat standing up on our kitchen island. Food is still a very big deal even though it is just the two of us. Since the Mexicans I grew up with never measured, I am not good at making any Mexican dish into a "smaller portion." I only know how to enchiladas in trays of 24 at a time. I only know how to make gorditas in batches of 10 or 12. It's a lot of food for me and my husband but making my grandma's recipes from scratch brings me great joy. When I think about all the things that have brought me joy throughout my life…it was everything but birthing children.

There are four chairs at my rectangular wooden table with a bench for extra seats. Seats are usually occupied by one of my three nephews or my niece during the weeks that she spends with us in the summer. There is a large kitchen island with 5 stools. Whenever I make enchiladas it looks like a scene from Dexter, with red spots of chile here and all over the backsplash. I never thought that I would enjoy cooking so much.

Unlike other Mexican kids I knew, I didn't spend my childhood in the kitchen with my abuela or tias. Mainly, because we had a very small kitchen and we are not a big family. I often joke about us being fertile-light. I only have one tia and only had one set of grandparents from my mother's side. My sister, Sophia, got to learn to make tamales before I ever did. I didn't know my biological dad but my mom did find a wonderful man when I was 12 and he's been the father in my life. They married when I was in high school.

I remember how much my grandmother enjoyed cooking. She would cook for our church's festivals and fundraisers. She made all of our holiday meals. We all loved seeing her in the kitchen. Without them knowing it, my grandparents were rebels in their own way. My grandmother did all the cooking and my grandfather did the dishes. Very uncommon considering they were depression-era babies.

I spent my childhood figuring out where I fit in the world. Growing up on the border in El Paso, in a barrio known as the Segundo Barrio– home to immigrants and citizens. The Segundo Barrio is one of the oldest neighborhoods in El Paso and is part of the last 200 acres of land given to the United States from Mexico in 1963 via the Chamizal Convention Treaty. It is an area rich in history and culture from two countries.

It was common to have families with mixed citizenship status. Unfortunately, during my childhood living in the barrio, I was surrounded by gun violence and teenage pregnancy. I never thought about marriage or being a parent, I was too busy wanting to look like Kelly Kapowski on Saved by the Bell. But I was too curvy and my ethnic hair was too wavy. Haha! I appreciate those waves more now! Once in high school, I started figuring out how to get into a good college. I wanted a different life that did not include living in El Paso. I wanted to see the world beyond the border and I never thought about being a mother or a wife. I felt this way all while dealing with an almost non-existent period. I can count on two hands many periods I had, up until that point. A foreshadowing of what was to come in my late twenties.

As a first-generation college graduate, you often don't realize how many hurdles you have to jump through and how many paths you have to continuously walk solo. I realized my life's choices were going to create gaps or divisions between me and my parents and my family. It meant I had to figure it all out on my own. My mom had me when she was about 22 years old. I graduated college when I was 22. My dream was to become a journalist and lend a voice to the voiceless and tell the stories that no one thought was important. Since I had started blazing my own trail, like many first-generation grads, my biggest concern was making my family proud and finding a career that would allow me to care for my parents when they were older. Again, never thought about having children or marriage.

Having such a narrow focus on my career, and trying to figure out my place in this world–I often turned to cook. I remember learning how to make everything from sopapillas to barbeque sauce in my mother's kitchen after college. I had a somewhat normal-ish social life in my 20s but dating was hard. The few guys I casually dated never turned into relationships because "How many children do you want to have?" was always the second question and my answer was always "0." The guys I dated then were so concerned with having children, it was an overwhelming question and in the pit of my stomach, I always knew I did not want to have any children. It was hard to say out loud but I didn't feel any shame saying I didn't want children because honestly, I felt too young to make such a huge decision. I was barely employed and was living at home. Marriage and children were nowhere on my short-term goals list.

One goal I did achieve was working for what was my then-dream company, CNN. I spent the majority of my twenties in DC while attending graduate school and well, "the rent was too damn high!" Like seriously though, I was paying way too much money for a broom closet and I had just started dating a guy outside my race. I had no time to seriously think about having children because I could barely afford to pay my rent and travel to Texas to spend holidays with my family.

My parents, sister, uncles, and my one cousin— see, I told you—we were, dare I say a fertile-light Mexican family. I only cared about spending time with them. This was right about the time that my closest friends started to marry off and for a brief moment, I thought, " Omg, my gosh am I going to be left behind?" Are we old enough to get married? Marriage and the age to get married are based on where you live and how you are socialized. I realize that now. The pressure we put on ourselves to achieve "X goal" by the time we reach "X age," is not healthy. We determine when and what bullet points belong on our timelines.

Marriage was something I never seriously considered for myself. I looked at my partner at the time and thought, "Could we make it work?" It didn't feel right and children still were nowhere in my mind. To backtrack for a minute, when I was 23, I got on birth control because I wasn't having a period. I wasn't pregnant because I wasn't having sex. For years, we've been telling women that they have to have periods right? So I panicked. I had a few periods in college that were painful and made me bedridden. Then in my 20s, Planned Parenthood told me it could be the early signs of Endometriosis but they weren't sure.

I did the whole thing where I cycled (period pun intended) through various types of birth control pills and some worked and some didn't. Thanks to Obamacare, I was able to stay on my parent's insurance for a year to help pay for my prescriptions. Then I had the bright idea to apply to Georgetown University for grad school and get on their health insurance plan. Completely forgot about all the Catholic rules that would be imposed on me as an unmarried woman trying to use birth control to perform a basic function…like giving me a normal, pain-free period. Not possible. Trying to convince doctors at a catholic institution that I needed an in-depth look at my ovaries was a no-go.

Again, at no point throughout this painful process did I think about birthing a baby. More power to the women who want to swap pain for more pain (i.e. childbirth). Missing periods and fearing when I would get a period left me paranoid and just feeling unwell all the time. But whenever I was homesick or stressed I still used cooking to relieve that stress even in the crappiest of crappy apartments. I would find time to make one of my grandmother's recipes. It usually required me to cart around frozen containers of my mom's red chile for enchiladas in a checked bag between visits or a bag of dried chiles so I could practice making it from scratch. I didn't expand my repertoire to include rice or beans because, you know, "the rent was too damn high!" Having enough funds for rent and tortillas was my usual goal.

When I did think about the future I envisioned having my parents sitting at my own dining room table serving them a giant tray of enchiladas, watching them dip a tortilla chip into a batch of my homemade salsa or guacamole. And thanking my mom for finally gifting me my grandmother's olla for frijoles. Picturing this table included a chair for each of my family members, and myself. No kid's table. It wasn't until I was 28 did I have to have a serious conversation with myself about children. At that point, my periods were so painful. My employers were skeptical when I needed to miss back-to-back days of work because I couldn't get out of bed. Even when I had female bosses, I still didn't feel right having to explain how bad my periods were for me. Those ladies would say, "I know, my cramps are bad too." Are they? Because you never miss work. I am not minimizing anyone's period pain. I felt ashamed and embarrassed having to re-explain my complicated undefined period pain.

I remember being 27 and going to the OBGYN for my annual exam, right as the exam was nearly over–as I was sitting up. The doctor says, "You are 27, next year, we plan for a baby." Looking so confused, cold, and extremely uncomfortable as I adjusted myself on the table to turn to stare at this man, I said without missing a beat, "Who's baby?" Yes, I was in a relationship but in no way did I think we were the childbearing type.

He was relying on his parents to make all his decisions for him and I was just trying to pay rent and work my way up in network news. I had already lost my financial aid and couldn't finish my master's because I couldn't afford to pay for my final class out of pocket. I had just moved into a slightly more expensive apartment and my ex–couldn't decide if he was going to law school. Honestly, when were children ever going to be the topic of conversation with these other more important matters?

Remember how I said there would be plenty of paths I'd have to walk alone as a first-generation college graduate? Well, this was one of them. Especially since my sister was about to have her first child. A beautiful baby girl named Laila. An amazing soul that filled my heart with a deep, profound love and the need to protect her at all costs. At no point did my body say, "Hey, I think we need to make her a cousin."

It was the exact opposite. I said to myself, I want to be the cool auntie, not the one who buys you booze when you are underage but the one that might let you sneak out to meet a boy because unbeknownst to you or him, your former NSA-employed uncle will ALREADY be tracking him anyway. Hahaha! Life has a funny way of pointing you in the right direction. Laila was born about three years before my hysterectomy and before any of my closest friends had started having kids.

You know that biological clock that is supposed to start ticking at some point in your 20s well mine never did. And from everything I knew about me and my body, it was never meant to…at 28, I had had it with painful debilitating periods and repeat work absences. I was emotionally and physically drained paying for birth control which was doing nothing for me.

I was at a turning point in my life, my relationship was pretty much over and my periods had sucked up every ounce of energy I had left. I was in so much pain. I didn't think about childbirth because my vagina and my pelvis were over it all. There was no way I could think about anything else. Except for being an auntie to Laila.

The first time I held my niece, Laila, I could picture her sitting at the table in my kitchen helping me make enchiladas. I could picture my sister across the table with her phone and laptop working while Laila and I cooked. Ironically, she's never asked for a cousin. I've always told her that I was put on this earth to be her auntie. Her birth only further confirmed one of the many roles I was destined to fill in my lifetime. I would know deep, unconditional love and the worry that comes with carrying for someone else even though I didn't birth them. My love for Laila solidified many things and it was time. Time to put this pain to rest and live my life as the cool aunt.

I'll never forget the hell my health insurance put me through trying to get my hysterectomy approved. It was my second year working for a humanitarian nonprofit in DC and I was missing work because I either had a bad period (every three months with my birth control) or I had debilitating PMS pains. Either way, it was too much to keep explaining to my boss who was a man, and bonus ...was one of my best friend's dad. Talk about awkward... and yes, I know HIPAA. But at some point, you run out of ways to say, I can't get out of bed because my cramps have me bedridden and I'm afraid to move because I've already stained the sheets once and don't want to wash them again. Does blood ever wash out? This might be a question for Martha Stewart.

My OBGYN recommended a hysterectomy even though he was uncomfortable with the idea of giving a 31-year-old unmarried woman no chance at procreating. You read that right, I was 31. So many years had passed since I was initially diagnosed with Endometriosis. My life had taken so many turns up until this point. I had just gotten out of a long-term relationship and needed to focus on my health.

My health insurance finally approved my hysterectomy two weeks before the scheduled surgery date. Nothing like dragging it out till the last minute. And if you ask me, it was probably their way of seeing if I would change my mind. The insurance agent on the phone, not my doctor, said, "I heard that pregnancy can sometimes cure endometriosis." Not a chance I was willing to take and according to my doctor being pregnant and carrying a pregnancy to term were two things he didn't think I could do. Why was I going to put myself through that emotional trauma? I just wanted a life without pain. When I looked down at my chair at my dining room table I wanted to see crumbs, not blood.

What I remember the most about the day I got a hysterectomy, is my mom kissing my forehead as she and my dad walked out of the prep room. They wheeled me away when we suddenly stopped in front of the OR's double doors. The nurse says, "I'm sorry Ms. Sanchez but legally I am required to ask you this again. Are you sure you want to go through with this because it cannot be reversed?" Without any hesitation, I said yes.

Because of this procedure, I've been pain-free for seven years. No, no menopause yet. It ended up being what I like to consider a life-saving and life-altering decision. The procedure revealed I had Adenomyosis, a condition in which endometrial tissue exists within and grows into the uterine wall and is common in women who are between the ages of 40 and 50 years old. No, it was not life-threatening but felt like it at times. Do I have any regrets? No.

My recovery was rough but it seems that anything you do with your reproductive organs takes weeks for your hormones to stabilize. I was ready for a pain-free life and I've become a marathoner since then. What I was not ready for was the ongoing questions and stares and overly critical society that is very pro-procreation. Making friends has always been hard but moving to a small town in Texas where everyone has kids makes it harder. When COVID hit, we left the Maryland suburbs for the Texas Hill Country. We traded in our train passes for a new Ford Bronco and a new construction in a newly developed neighborhood right outside San Antonio.

From what I gathered, we are probably (at least it feels this way at times) the only ones without kids on our street and most of my local friends are empty nesters or have grown children. It is women in my age group who have a hard time befriending people like me. So no, it has been the best experience in that regard. I am blessed to live just about an hour and a half away from two of my best friends. I get to be the cool auntie to more kids than I ever could have imagined.

My husband and I are overjoyed and completely fulfilled being fur parents to two dogs and a sassy cat. In the last two years, we've seen my parents and nephews, and niece just about every two months. Way more than we ever did living in the Maryland suburbs. More importantly, we are blessed and we are loved, living our life on our terms. Now, I get to have my nephews, niece, sister, brother-in-law, two dogs, and a cat gathered around my kitchen island while we make my grandma's enchiladas. A seat for everyone we love the most.

Jalpa Sukhanandi

Jalpa Sukhanandi is a development professional with 16+ years of qualitative experience in the social-development sector. She completed a Master's degree in Development and Human Rights at Swansea University in 2013. Jalpa has versatile experience in project development, program monitoring and evaluation, designing and implementing a multi-sectoral program, and its implementation. Currently, Jalpa serves as the Deputy Manager for Coromandel International Limited, where she has developed projects focused on improving education, health, environmental sustainability, and community development in Gujarat as part of the corporate social responsibility strategy for the organization.

From Dream to Degree -
My Quest for Education

The time and year, 2004, when I was in my fourth year of B.Sc. in Fisheries Science graduation program, it was a primarily male-dominated, less popular, and least preferred program for girls in the Saurastra region (one of the culturally rich, feudal, and patriarchal-dominated areas of Gujarat) in those early days. Ours was the 10th batch, and in this decade, only 4 girls passed out from our college and started jobs, but none of them pursued further study in this field.

Scientist Dr. Shobha was a visiting faculty member from CMFRI -Veraval (Central Marine Fisheries Research Institute), originally from Kerala, and an extremely knowledgeable, charismatic teacher who had sown seeds of thought in my mind to pursue higher studies in the same field to become a scientist. A doable task, but there are other challenges along the way. The first challenge was to get admission with a very high rank so that I could secure a scholarship, as finance was the biggest challenge. Convincing my parents to allow me to do my higher education in another state was the second challenge, as they were very protective and had a strong opinion. Except for Gujarat, none of the other states are safe for girls, and I was aware that convincing them was a next-to-impossible task!

This is 2023; for almost 17 years, I have been living on my own as an independent me in a different city. Hold down, take a breath, command your thoughts, and don't make a wild guess. I didn't fight or take extremely strong steps to be where I am now, but I navigated ways to deal with the situation, explored new options, and developed courage to counter hurdles and overcome adversity. Keep yourself awake and open while reading me; the narratives may provide you with a different kind of exposure or story, you may find many people have reacted in a certain way as they have carried their traditional baggage, however, changes have been observed over time amongst them. So do not make the mistake of portraying someone as a villain or hero in this write-up. Everyone played their role, contributing to my growth and journey. Though this is not a lesson book, you will get three takeaways from this experience: Be consistent with your efforts, accept the situation and people the way they are, and have faith in humanity!

Regarding counseling parents

Allow me to share how I partially overcame my second challenge. We were six people—my parents and four siblings—living in a one-room kitchen house. Our house is in the city area, so most of our relatives, friends, and known people usually visit us. One day, one of my professors, Dr. Prakash Badikar, and a few college friends were in the market and suddenly visited my house. I had introduced my teacher to my mother (she had formal education till 7th only, but was welcoming and had a command of hospitality), and they started chatting. I was one of the good students, performing well in my academics. My mom was doing all kinds of reviews about my progress, checking when the new recruitment would happen in the government department so that her daughter would get a job.

While having this conversation, my tutor suggested that your daughter go for higher education, as nobody knows when government departments announce vacancies and process for recruitment. While listening to this, my mother immediately called my father, who used to sit at one of his friends' shops in the evening just to give them company. Within 5 to 7 minutes, he reached our home. He greeted my tutor; my mother had briefed him on what had been discussed and informed him that the tutor was suggesting higher study. My father nodded his head and said, "We will see." Let her complete graduation first. My tutor felt a bit uneasy. Maybe he got the unspoken message that my parents are not convinced yet. He started sharing my academic performance, attitudes towards study, and how their daughter is behind the professors in learning and improving her English as well. He firmly told my parents, "Jalpa is not only your daughter; she is mine as well, and if she wants to study, I will take full responsibility." A determined word from my teacher melted my mother's heart. Dr. Prakash and other students returned to their place with a request to think about his offer.

It sounds a little strange—why should someone else take responsibility for a person? In a small and remote area, this is normal. Girls in Saurastra regions are not very privileged; with a conservative society and limited information, it is difficult to even enroll in non-traditional courses. A thumb rule for girls in this area was to complete their 12th class enroll in a traditional gender-oriented course, i.e., PTC (a teacher's certificate course) or nursing, do their job, get married, have kids, and follow all customs silently. Coeducation after a certain age was not encouraged among the girls. There were a few incidents where a few youngsters eloped from the coeducation school; one of the shameful situations for parents, especially girls' parents, was that if girls were studying in coeducation, they would have affairs and elope, restricting their mobility and education.

I remember one of my classmates in 12th class making this mistake, and as a repercussion, other girls in the town suffered many restrictions. A lesson I learned: your every action has implications for others, especially when you are a girl, so behave responsibly! In such a situation, it can be understood that if some other person takes responsibility for their daughter, they can trust their daughter, have some courage to come out of conservative notions, challenge the status quo, and allow the kids, especially daughters to achieve their goal. My parents do not hold any formal education degrees, but when they receive good feedback about their kids, they open their minds, allow them to follow their dreams, and make new moves. Finally, my tutor's counseling worked, and I was allowed to pursue my higher studies.

An award and responsibility: the scholarship

For a girl like me from the lower middle class, scholarships are a boom. While writing this, I am recalling those days when Maa Saraswati and Maa Laxmi both joined hands to create a deserving future for me and my family. In my school days, followed by 10th class students had to opt their academic stream, i.e. science (in India Science stream means natural science), commerce, or the arts. I got a reasonably good score in 10th board, decided to select science, which my parents have supported, and took admission to Govt. Boys' High School.

Yes, I studied at Boys High School, as it was the only school in my town (at that time) that had a science stream and was a government school with no fees for girls. For the 12th board exam, I enrolled in a few subject-specific private tuition classes but later dropped them as we couldn't afford the fees. The 11th and 12th standard periods were somehow miserable. My only uncle was diagnosed with cancer and later died within 6 months of the disease diagnosis; three deaths in my mother's close family, the situation where my parents', especially my mother's, time and care diverted towards managing people and family rituals. Since my mother was not available at home, being an elderly girl, I needed to take care of the house, nevertheless, my younger sister was a great support. In all adverse circumstances, I appeared in the board exam and passed it in one attempt, which was an enormous achievement for me and my family.

A girl opting for science and cracking the exam in the first attempt was probably the first case in my family. Now the first task was to select a degree course, for which my parents and I have started exploring information and filled out a few admission applications for diploma and degree courses. As aforementioned, our house was in the middle of the town; one of our known aunties and her friends visited us; and my mother shared my progress and search for proper academic selection.

My aunt's friend shared her graduation and employed daughter's progress. Her daughter took admission to a fisheries science college that was based only in my town. She applied for a graduate scholarship (for girls) and received scholarship support from the government every year, which helped her finish her graduation. After completing her graduation with 2-3-year Govt. had declared recruitment in the Fisheries department and now she is having govt. job. With this information, my graduation course selection was finalized by my mother. Ironically, we belong to a very traditional Sadhu family, a strict vegetarian family, and now the girl from this family is going to school where she has to work with fish, marine, and inland resources. It was very strange, but this was destiny!

Thus, I started my graduation program in fisheries science. On the day of orientation, a few professors asked us why you chose this course. Response from few students were - it was a good course; they desired to go for some special and professional course, and so on. When it came to me, my answer was very practical and straightforward without any filter in front of all the students: I wanted to join some professional courses that have options for scholarship support to continue my study and are based in my hometown, so there are no extra living expenses and financial burden on my family.

This course is a perfect match for my career aspirations and financial support, so I enrolled in it. Later, a few of my classmates were making jokes on me and bullying me, saying this girl has joined the course for SCHOLARSHIP. Initially, I got hurt, but gradually I started ignoring them. I understood that I was awarded a scholarship based on my performance, and it's not a charity. It's a reward for my hard work. Let me share one instance that may provide some insight on how scholarship went beyond my study aid.

During my third year of graduation, a strike happened in the factory where my father was working. The union and factory management were extremely stubborn with their demands, neither of them coming up with a common solution. This strike lasted for more than 60 days. The factory workers did not get their monthly salary as they were on strike; it was a tough time for many workers, who are the only earners in the family. Being mill laborers, they were hardly receiving a salary of Rs. 4000 to Rs. 6000 after all deductions. They have to cover all their family's expenses with a limited salary, such as rent, food, and school fees. The women in these families were stressed and suffered the most as they had to manage the children and the household without a salary. However, they never showed their stress and pain to their kids or other family members.

What courageous ladies! Luckily, I got my third-year scholarship of Rs. 3000 during this period. As I had paid my semester fees and purchased my books, I didn't need any money. That time, this amount was also huge for me, and I used to hand it over to my mother. This time, my mother took some money for household expenses, and the rest she distributed to other workers' families. The amount was very small, but it has fed at least four families' stomachs for a few days. Thus, scholarship support also feeds families at very critical times. My mother is always an inspiration to me. She could have kept the entire scholarship with her, but she thought about others and supported them. From my mother, I learned an important lesson: "Be generous, happy, and satisfied with whatever you have."

Last semester, my graduation was full of intensive internship programs. We had a study tour for 21 days, an internship at an aquaculture farm for 15+ days, and spent 2 months at a fish processing plant, as well as working on small projects with the fisherfolk community. The fundamental idea behind having a 6-month fieldwork was to equip us with practical and hands-on experience. Meanwhile, we have started appearing for interviews in processing industries so that we have a job after our graduation. I remember one of my classmates and I going to one of the processing plants for an interview. We have interacted with Mr. Thomas (originally from Kerala), the general manager of the company. His advice to us was not to look for a job but to go for a master's, as it would add value and have good market demand. I was a bit of an ambitious girl, and words from Mr. Thomas had sparked my higher education dream.

The medium of instruction for my primary to secondary school was in my first language, i.e., Gujarati, while my graduation was in English. Initially, I couldn't grasp everything, but later I started improving my command of the English language. My professor, Mr. C. R. Trivedi used to be a very strict teacher who personally took an interest in improving my English and built confidence in me. Mr. Thomas's input, disciplinary support from C. R. Trivedi, and moral support from Badikar Sir had pushed me to think about higher education. Though I was doing preparation for the master's entrance test, C. R. Trivedi asked me to prepare for the CAT and other competitive exams as well. I obeyed his advice and started preparing. I appeared for the Fisheries Masters entrance test but didn't achieve the cutoff marks for getting scholarship support. Without a scholarship, I can't do my master's. It took some time for me to come out of this situation.

Newspaper reading was a good habit I had developed, which later helped open new doors for my study. I read an article in the newspaper: a private institution offers a one-year diploma in NGO management with guaranteed job placement and scholarships for deserving candidates. Taking this article in my hand, I ran towards C. R. Trivedi's office. He suggested that I apply for the course and start working on entrance exam preparation. Since Badikar sir has already done my parents' counseling, they were okay with my higher study preparation.

Graduation with scholarship support. Now it was time for higher education. I applied for the course, paid the entrance exam fee, and started preparation. The exam date has been announced. The exam center was in Ahmedabad (400 km) from my hometown, Veraval. My father asked one of his cousins to accompany me, as he used to travel to all these big cities and has a lot of travel-related information. We took the night bus, reached our destination, and appeared for an exam. My uncle and I were impressed with the institution's infrastructure, facilities, and people.

The EDII - Entrepreneurship Development Institute of India campus won the Aga Khan Award for Architecture in 1992. Visiting such an institution felt like a dream, and being accepted was unimaginable. My focus was on the exam, so I ignored my surroundings until I completed it. To a great extent, I did fairly well in the examination, which has given me confidence that I should wait for an interview call. My uncle told me, "Beta Jalpa, the majority of the applicants who appeared for the exam came in their private cars; this is the institution where elite families can afford to send their kids to study; studying in such an expensive institution is out of budget for us, who can't even afford to cycle." Somehow, I didn't take his word very seriously. My goal was to perform well in exams, prepare for interviews, and do my best to get scholarship support.

A few days later, I received an interview call from EDI India. This time my father joined me; we traveled to Ahmedabad, and I was there to appear in an interview along with more than 200 other candidates. Candidates were chatting with each other in English, dressed in blazers and formal suits. I was very simple in my Indian outfit, sitting silently and waiting for my turn. Around 2 p.m., a person called my name, directed me towards the meeting room, and I followed him. After knocking on the door, I entered the room and observed that six panel members were sitting on the other side. I greeted them, took a seat, and introduced myself.

One by one, each panel member asked various questions, a few on my family background, my study of the fisheries and agriculture sectors, my economic status, and how I knew about this course. Initially, I started replaying in English, but when I felt I was not clearly communicating my answer, I politely asked permission to answer in Hindi, and the panel was kind enough. They were basically checking how much I am clear on a few fundamental principles, the subject, and my career goal. Since I applied for a scholarship as well, they were doing an extra assessment. I impressed the panel members with my answer and strong determination for my career. Once they finished their round of questions, they asked me if I had any questions for them. I thanked them for a good round of interviews with a question asking their name, introduction, and how they know about fisheries science, as it is not a very popular or known subject in public. They started introducing themselves and replied, like how you chat with us, we chat with others and get a little bit of information on various subjects.

I need to acknowledge that they were all very humble. The panel that interviewed me included a banker (from SIDBI Bank), two faculty members (experts in the development sector), and a representative of NABARD Bank - India's largest agricultural sector bank. Sometimes I pat my back, saying, "Jalpa, you have impressed these people!" I left the room with a message from them: "People on the deserving scholarship list will be announced after 4 p.m.; wait some time, and if your name is there, the second round of interviews will be tomorrow." Outside the interview room, other candidates and my father were wondering why my interview took so long. While moving down the ladder based on my experience and performance in the interview, I was sure that I had to stay there for the second round of interviews. We waited for the interview result and saw my name on the scholarship interview list.

The second round was quite tough and competitive. Career goals, aspiration, and a strong determination to work on social change were the key assessment criteria. Based on my knowledge and exposure, I tried to convince them. Later, I got to know that I was one of the strong candidates but did not have any working experience, while other candidates were experienced people from the social sector. Nevertheless, I was still hopeful for my selection. The course coordinator shared that they would inform us of the result in a month. We started returning in a state transport bus in heavy rain, and water was leaking from various holes. Luckily, the bus was not full, and I was changing seats to protect myself from getting wet.

We had a discussion within the family about my study plan. The course fees were Rs. 65,000 (at that time), and the on-campus hostel facility cost Rs. 50,000. I shared that if I get a full course fee scholarship, then I will join the course and find accommodation in a nearby village to manage the living costs. My family was not okay with this option, as they were always concerned about the safety and security of their daughter.

A few days later, I received a call from EDI India saying I had been selected and needed to join the institute on September 17. The course director was on the call and asked me to share my email ID, which I didn't have at the time; he suggested sharing my fax number to send the letter. I provided the fax number of one of the PCOs. They have provided 85% of the scholarship, which included full course fees and partial accommodation services. My parents need to manage the rest of the amount in two installments. My mother packed the necessary items, my father booked the tickets, informed his cousin (who accompanied me during my exam) about my achievement, and we started traveling at night. My parents and I reached the institution a day before the joining day to see all the arrangements. The campus and hostel had security facilities, which was one of the essential and relieving aspects for my parents, and they started their journey towards my hometown.

The next day onwards, I started my study and gradually got some praising words on my performance during the interview from the faculty and panel members who later visited the institution. Mr. Nabaru Sengupta, our course director and panel member in the interview, shared in one of the classes, "We have given the opportunity to each candidate to ask anything they want to ask us (the panel member), but only this girl was brave enough to ask a question to us. The person from NABARD was also impressed and told us she is a strong and deserving student for a scholarship immediately when she left the interview."

For the second installment payment, my mother took too much pain and spent many nights sorting chickpeas and other grains—home-based grocery sorting and cleaning work she took from a local wholesale vendor to manage our expenses. Her hard work paid off. I studied hard, completed my course, secured a job, and gifted a sari on Diwali from my salary, and as usual, she affectionately screamed at us, saying, "Why are you making unnecessary expenses?" That's how the mother behaves!

Working in the development sector for 7+ years has developed my core strength in community development and empowerment. Self-reflection in my work to date has triggered my greed for specialized courses. From local to state-level competition, and from there to international competition, was my next target. Later, I was awarded the very prestigious Commonwealth Scholarship Award from the Commonwealth Scholarship Commission of the United Kingdom. That's another interesting journey that can be shared later.

Ronnie Jameson

Ronnie Jameson is a former (retired) publisher who ended up running a large firm with a staff of 1200 whilst possessing less than a high-school diploma, for which she is not-at-all-secretly very proud. She's a motherless, fatherless, sisterless woman who has traveled the world, raised many cats, and is happily married to a man who loves her despite her tendency to wake up grumpy really late. She loves her daughter who died before she reached 2 years of age more than she can put into words, and hopes the love she has left in this world, helps others to feel less alone.

Isobel

I had a child at the age of 40 with a man I hardly knew whilst on a vacation in Italy. I named her Isobel and she died aged 14 months at home.

Leading up to this event, many things occurred that could have derailed me and almost did. I am not a religious person so I can't account for why I'm still standing. Pain has a tendency to bowl you over, destroy you, but I see it like a phoenix rising out of the ashes, whatever is left, can rebuild, until it can't.

It was never my intention to defy definition but when I look back on my life, from a 65-year-olds perspective I can see that I did.

Losing Isobel was the most painful thing that ever happened to me but it wasn't the first bad thing that happened. Life is a tapestry of experience much like weaving a carpet, we can look back on things and wonder; 'how did I cope with that?' But incredibly we just do and we keep moving forward, even when it seems impossible. The trick is not to become cruel or bitter in that process, no matter how bad things are, it isn't a reason to hurt or be bitter toward others. We're all in this together, and the world is a better place if we are kind.

I was born in Germany in the 1950s. My parents immigrated to Australia when I was a small child with my sister and I. At the age of ten I was in the city with my parents and my sister and my mum was crossing the road with my sister to get some groceries. Somehow a car knocked them down and they both died within a week after being rushed to hospital. My father and I actually witnessed it. I can't remember it well, it's like a bad dream that I have tried to forget, even though I think it's very important to remember it. Perhaps trauma shouldn't be recalled, I don't know, but after that life became very hard.

My father had a mental breakdown and he was taken to a sanatorium. My grandparents were dead, there was no one to live with, and having lost both parents and my sister I was put in the foster care system. Predictably it was awful. I was shunted around from home to home before finally being placed more permanently with a 'nice' family who were extremely religious and shamed me for almost everything daily.

At the age of 16 I met a boy; I think that's pretty commonplace when you have been deprived of normalcy. I was a good student, but I wanted a family more than I wanted anything else. He and I were planning on getting married, but my foster family forbade it and said if I went through with it, I would be cut off. I intended to go through with it despite them and moved out and lived with the boy who was 19 and already working. On the eve of our wedding, he was killed riding his motorbike. I was only 17 by that time and felt like I was a widow. It was surreal and horrific but you're amazingly resistant at that age. His best friend was due to go to India for a pilgrimage around the holy sites. I only knew I did not want to stay in Australia where all I experienced was judgment. My foster family had completely cut me off so using the money I had in savings from my weekend jobs, I went with my dead fiancées best friend to India.

Bear in mind India in the 1960s was THE place everyone who was not from India wanted to go. I suppose we weren't very original, following The Beatles and others to find ourselves. Ironically, I did find myself. In the beauty and mysticism and intelligence of India, I felt more of a connection than I ever had in Australia, especially back then when Australia was like a poor version of England, from twenty years earlier. We traveled and traveled, amazingly not running out of money, and in this traveling, I found some of the grief of losing my fiancé and my parents, began to be replaced with a hope that despite such tragedies early in my life, I could still thrive.

At one point I got very sick. I couldn't keep anything down. I was literally wasting away. Some nuns in a convent took me in and I was nursed for six months, nearly starving to death and dying, but somehow eventually recovering. The sickness was a form of cleansing. I went to the brink and I came back from it. I didn't really understand death but I knew I wanted to survive. I felt lost and I had no real education or money or support, what was I going to do next? My fiancé's best friend was going on to Germany and suggested I go with and see if I could find the rest of my German family. When I was well enough that's exactly what I did.

We landed in Berlin where the cold, rain, gray skies seemed the antithesis of India. I instantly regretted being there and hated it. But when we drove out in the countryside I saw a beautiful side to Germany, despite the horrible post-war buildings and division between East and West. I found some cousins who amazingly were very supportive and asked me to stay on. A lucky thing considering I had run out of all my money and didn't know what I would do next. I completely overstayed my welcome the way young people do and I also met a man, which might seem premature considering losing my fiancé but a year in a teen's life is forever, and I was desperate for a family and belonging.

The man was a trainee musician, he played in the philharmonic and was desperately talented. I think now he was probably neurodivergent but we didn't know that at the time. We got married and I moved in with him and began living as a German wife. It was an odd life, I was so young, barely 18 but already I had experienced so much. I felt lost, numb, empty and at the same time hopeful things could change. I believed if you just loved someone everything would resolve, but of course that was very naïve. He was traveling all the time, whilst away he had multiple affairs and this before cell phones, so we were not even in touch very frequently. I began to resent being trapped in a small flat in a bad part of town always waiting for him to return.

In time he was transferred to a philharmonic in the UK. I was glad to move because it afforded me more working options as my German was not good. In the UK I spoke the same language and the economy was better. Soon I was working as an assistant to a publisher which didn't pay well but was immensely fulfilling. I didn't even have my high school diploma so it was a real boon to be employed in such a good starting position. I worked really hard to show my gratitude and threw myself into my career because my husband was away all the time. I met some great friends who were all really creative and began to live the life I hoped I would live all those years ago in Australia.

My father died in the sanatorium having never recovered from the trauma of losing my mum and my sister. He also had a pre-existing mental illness but I truly think it was heartbreak that finally killed him. I felt numb when I found out, but at the same time I had never been allowed by my foster family to visit him and it was like I had lost both parents the day my mother and sister died. I didn't drive because of it; I was too afraid and that was probably the biggest fear I had. I saw life as being something that could be snatched away so easily, and it took a lot of therapy to stop letting my fears take me over. At times I felt agoraphobic or just plain terrified of living, because I always assumed if I was happy, life would laugh and snatch the happiness away. It was like a dysfunctional superstition but a very real one.

I had been very influenced by my time in India and I began following a Swami in the UK who had a big group of followers. It was a common thing to do in the 60s and 70s and I really fell in with the theories and life practice of these followers. It gave me comfort, even if others thought I was some type of cultist, because they talked about how hard life could be and how we could survive it anyway, through realizing it was hard but not giving up. I was superstitious. I would end up in a sanatorium like my father or die young like my mum so this helped anchor me to the everyday. I met a man in the group and we grew close, especially as my husband was traveling all the time. Eventually I got divorced from my husband and moved in with this man. It was in a way a bad match as we were both broken people trying to find some sound land, but I also see how it was a way for me to leave an unhappy marriage I got into on a rebound from losing my fiancé. It didn't last and I spent several years living alone. By this time, I had a really good job despite my lack of education and I felt really proud of how far I had come. It is not possible these days to build a career as easily if you are not educated but it was back then and I took full advantage of that.

On a trip to Italy, I had a very short holiday romance, and consequently got pregnant. I had always wanted children but my husband did not and so it didn't happen and then I assumed wrongly I was too old to have children. I gave birth to a healthy baby girl. She was and is the love of my life. The time we had together was the best in my life. I cannot regret having her because I would not know today what real love is, or have the memories of our time together. I do regret that she died, it goes without saying, but I try every day to remember that at least we had 14 months together. She died of cot-death, nowadays known as SID, just one day not waking up. I was destroyed and again, I credit my therapist for helping me get out of the worst of it. When she died few people knew much about SID, there were no support-groups, no internet groups, I was alone in my loss and I believe this is true for most of us.

I have not been the same since. Who could be? But that said, I carried on, because I learned from an early age, we really don't have any choice but to carry on or let it break us. I did not want to end up like my father. Yes, I wondered why me, I mean how many bad things needed to happen? And why? But I don't believe in curses and I do not believe in a traditional 'God' so I don't think we are being punished for anything, I think it's just like nature, if a cat has babies and they are eaten, it's just nature. Nature can be cruel. We try to overcome nature, dominate it, but I learned in India when I was very young by seeing the extreme poverty and death rates that we cannot escape it. Why some people have it 'easier' I don't know. I don't subscribe to the 'God only gives you what you can handle' theory at all, I think what I have endured is worse than anyone should handle.

What helped as well was going to group therapy. I went to that alongside my Swami group and between them both, they helped me out of the worst of the grief. I actually ended up meeting a boyfriend through this and we got together. He had a young ten-year-old daughter. It was very hard for me because I loved her almost instantly but it was like a constant reminder of losing my daughter. I think I tried to make up for that by informally adopting this daughter, but it didn't really work because she wasn't mine and I knew it and sometimes I would be cruel to her because of it. I regret that but I also understand we aren't bad people when we do that, we are grieving and unable to know how to deal with it healthily. I kept defying definition over-and-over with being uneducated and yet able to succeed in my career, by being broken but being able to keep going, but sometimes I just wanted life to be easier.

Her father and I didn't work out, mostly because he did not understand how the loss of my daughter impacted my everyday life. I think men have a hard time with emotions and grief and they can be really insensitive even if they don't mean to be. I broke up with him and kept in touch with his daughter for a long while but eventually it just hurt and we agreed it was best to let it go. I know I hurt her, as she was seeking a mother, but I couldn't be a mother anymore to anyone. I had to be selfish and do what was right for me. Amazingly and unpredictably, I was invited back to Australia by a cousin whom I had gotten to know and I decided almost on a whim to go, having not lived in Australia for 2 decades by that point. When I got back the most unusual thing happened; I felt at home. This place I had run from seemed like the very place I wanted to now belong to. I ended up meeting an amazing man and after about a year of a long-distance relationship he asked me to move back to Australia permanently and I did. Moving was not easy. I was still in touch with my ex's daughter and leaving her felt like a betrayal, but she was very mature for her age and understood my happiness was important and I couldn't give her what she wanted. She told me to go and find joy at last, which coming from a young girl really moved me and I never forgot that. I moved to Australia and it reminds me of that saying; wherever you go there you are, I was home.

That was a long time ago and since then I have had another career, been married for 2 decades, regained my

Australian accent and have two godchildren and 4 cats. I think I defy definition because most people going through what I have gone through would have given up or gone mad. I don't blame them either, or judge them if they had. I almost did it myself. I don't know what stopped me other than a series of events that led to where I am today, a place of peace and happiness. I talk to Isobel in my head every single day. Her absence in my life will always be devastating. I have lived in spite of this and will continue to, as long as I can.

Some people say I am strong, but I'm not really. I am no stronger than my father who died in the sanatorium. I just keep going and that's my way, and I don't condemn him for his way, because life is hard for a lot of us and we just have to do what we do, we can't be someone else. I credit therapy and my Swami and I credit my trip to India where I spent a year learning the value of a radically different culture and the mercy and kindness of its people. I am not a big fan of Western culture because it's all about 'me me me' and I think the key to happiness is not to be self obsessed or materialist. I also believe in kindness and mercy, without which I would not be alive today. I try to give back as much as I can.

Yes, there are times I feel very sad. I have thought of taking my life quite a few times throughout the years especially when I lost my fiancé and Isobel and even when I was a child and I lost my mum and sister. I wonder how my life would have been if I had not lost them. I am staggered by the amount of loss. But in that loss, I do not stay. I can't dwell on what may be, because it isn't and never will be. I can only try to fix what is now and what I can actually do something about. I don't think it's a case of being strong so much as being honest and just giving it my best. I am not a perfect person, I struggle like everyone else, I just think what doesn't break you – you can learn from and grow from and whilst you may grow with broken pieces, nevertheless you will grow if you let yourself.

I didn't really mean to defy definition but in many ways, I know my life has. I have one regret; that I did not treat the young daughter of my boyfriend well, and she was hurt by that. I think ironically this occurred because she reminded me of myself. I think sometimes when we hurt people, we do so unintentionally because they trigger something in us, that reminds us of a deep pain and we lash out or reject them. I believe I did the latter for that exact reason. I wrote to her some years later when she was grown and apologized and explained. She didn't need to forgive me; I may not have been able to do the same in her place. But she did forgive me and she said she really understood as she had been abandoned by her mother and knew what emotions it provoked and how it could twist you. We are in touch today and that brings me gladness that I didn't completely ruin that relationship which is precious to me now.

In my life so far, I have learned how challenging it is for any of us to succeed when hard times happen. I don't subscribe to the American idea that 'only the tough survive' because I think the meek inherit the earth, in that when we let go of our egos and stop competing and hiding our vulnerabilities, that's when we really are alive and can be present and helpful for others. It is my mantra and I return to India every five years or so, to prostrate myself at the feet of a temple that taught my Swami (who has now passed away) and I remind myself of my place in this world (an ant) and my insignificance and I am purified by the death of my ego and all the Western ways of being. I still do not really believe in a conventional God nor in perfection, but I do hope I will see my daughter again, wherever she is, and I hope she will be proud of her mother, who tried. Because that's what I have done. I have tried.

Susan M. Conway

Susan M. Conway pushes boundaries in her writing, fearlessly tackling a range of controversial subjects. Through her storytelling, she aims to challenge societal taboos, provoke empathy and foster a greater understanding of the diverse human experience. Beyond her writing, Conway is an advocate for social change and equality. Her work has been published in several Indie Blu(e) Publishing anthologies including Darker Objects and We Will Not Be Silenced. She actively supports organizations and individuals that promote the rights and being of marginalized communities. Conway continues to challenge readers, confront societal norms and shed light on the often-silenced stories of those on the fringes of society. You can find her on Facebook @AuthorSusanConway.

Empty Spaces

There are for some of us, empty spaces created in humans since realizing God left these lands a long time ago. Creating empty spaces rather than trying to fill them, seems the reverse of logic but what if it's not? Defying definition involves asking questions and refuting long-held beliefs that no longer work. Reclaiming yourself isn't easy but it's imperative if you want to be real to yourself and your children. This is about breaking free of some of those social mores. Keep an open mind. I'm not asking you to agree, I'm asking you to be open to other perspectives and possibilities. Let's consider things we don't usually consider, in our examination of how to tear down and rebuild common perceptions and misconceptions.

Let's Learn- Nihilism:

From Latin nihil 'nothing' is a family of views within philosophy that rejects generally accepted or fundamental aspects of human existence, such as knowledge, morality, or meaning. The term was popularized by Ivan Turgenev and more specifically by his character Bazarov in the novel Fathers and Sons.

There have been different nihilist positions, including that human values are baseless, that life is meaningless, that knowledge is impossible, or that some set of entities does not exist or is meaningless or pointless.

Scholars of nihilism may regard it as merely a label that has been applied to various separate philosophies, or as a distinct historical concept arising out of nominalism, skepticism, and philosophical pessimism, as well as possibly out of Christianity itself.

Contemporary understanding of the idea stems largely from the Nietzschean 'crisis of nihilism', from which derive the two central concepts: the destruction of higher values and the opposition to the affirmation of life.

Earlier forms of nihilism, however, may be more selective in negating specific hegemonies of social, moral, political and aesthetic thought.

Let's Learn-Defining the Generations:

The Greatest Generation: Born 1901-1927

The Silent Generation: Born 1928-1945

The Baby Boomer Generation: Born 1946-1964

Generation X: Born 1965-1980

Millennials: Born 1981-1996

Generation Z: Born 1996-2012

Gen Alpha: Born 2013 – 2025

And now, the meat and potatoes.

I hear it all around me.

I see it with my own two eyes and have drowned in this deepening trench a time or five myself.

I see it in my 19-year-old son's eyes.

I watch him struggle and I know what I am looking at, because this was my journey too, as a former Christian.

There is a void where indoctrination used to be. And this void, a festering wound only growing deeper and sicker, and more feverish, and more bruised, until we learn how to reconnect with the Self that was pristine, the self that was the silent observer of this life that your mind shapes by thought and experience and stories… that thing-that quiet settled thing-that reverent knower of what has been, IS, and will be before the mind can even register it-the limitless primordial immortal.

Minds and mouths filled with the living water and it's murdering them.

There isn't a day that goes by where it doesn't feel like their own hands aren't around their own throats because of this one question whose mere presence is the bane of their existence:

With WHAT do we fill this nothingness?

Here is another for good measure...

How is it that you are eating of and drinking of the body of Christ yet you are still so thirsty and starving?

I didn't raise my son in a Christian household.

He wasn't raised in a home with religion at all.

He was not forbidden to read, or research, or study, or seek out multiple sources of information, or ask questions. He was encouraged to do all of those things.

He was given the space, the opportunity, all of the green lights, and the enthusiastic support of myself to make his own determinations and curate his own paths and belief systems.

He was curious about my path as a Witch. I answered his questions honestly and taught him some of The Olde Ways if he asked me to. Never did I try to convert him to follow in my footsteps-as I am still finding my own footing in this ever-shifting world, and because he is a human being first and foremost who deserves to experience all that living life in the body he inhabits currently has to offer.

I can only offer him guidance and wisdom. It is not my responsibility, not my duty, not my intention to ever mold and shape someone into anything. I will protect you; I will love you, listen to you, support you, hold your hand through the good times and through the worst. I will offer wisdom if asked, I will be a constant beacon of support and encouragement. Most of all, I will be honored if given the opportunity to see my young men grow into the fullest, most authentic brilliant fully expressive versions of themselves possible.

It is not my responsibility, as a mother, to ensure my children believe as I believe and do as I do and speak as I speak. It is not my responsibility as a human to do this to anyone who crosses paths with me on this journey. I have taken it on as my duty as a mother and as a fellow human being to unbecome from what I couldn't control as a child so that I can become the most authentic fully expressed version of myself that I could possibly be so that when others who are on the same journey have questions, I will be able to offer some perspective. My goal is to become love embodied. My goal is to leave a legacy of love when I transition from this body to whatever form this energy becomes next.

As a girl who was indoctrinated with Christianity and have denounced it fully since my late teens, I know the void that leaving your religion leaves. It is the same void that is left after leaving an abusive partner or relationship. It is the same void that is left behind when a loved one passes away. It is deep, it seems bottomless at times, and you feel lost. It feels like you have been ousted from the only home you've ever known.

As a species, humans are worshippers. We seek to give praise and worship to something. It is practically encoded in our DNA. So, when the light comes on, and we begin to realize that what we have been devoted to is taking from us and not nourishing us, when we realize, we are going to have to make that difficult decision to let go, we will be grieving the death of that. The death of religion, the death of what is no longer serving us, the shedding of old skin.

A lot of us Millennials have stepped away from organized religion as we are learning how to have a deeper and more loving and reverent relationship with ourselves. We are also feeling the pain and seeing the devastation indoctrination has wreaked on who we are as individuals and the entire world. We see what colonialism/mission work has done to Natives globally. And, most millennials do not want this to continue. So, we are doing the deconstructing and it's messy-but we are also moms and dads… We are moms and dads that don't want our Gen Z kiddos to make the same mistakes our parents and their parents and so forth did.

Millennials have decided that we don't want to continue to hand down piles of ruin and trauma to our kids. We have decided that if it isn't going to be us that do something then who is it going to be? Enter Gen Z… They are old enough to begin making their own decisions and are finding their places in this world. Yet they are struggling. I see it in my sons' eyes and hear it in his speech and ideologies (which are still forming-give them time, they're still kids…) I see it in his lack of desire to be a real go-getter at the moment. Millennials are not indoctrinating their kids. We are giving them the space and freedom to decide for themselves. And as a worshiping people-remember, it is virtually encoded in our DNA to be a worshiping communal people, they do not know how to handle the void they feel in the absence of religion. I was there too. I didn't know what I would fill that nothingness with.

Enter Nihilism. Nothing exists, it's all a simulation, we're all just meat suits wandering around until we die, our existence is pointless, and the big one…. I didn't ask to, nor did I consent to, being brought into this world. You made that decision for me. Now, I just have to exist until it's my time.

That is a fair and valid point, Gen Z. You're correct. I don't know if I should apologize, but I do know I'll hold space for you.

Enter Elder Gen Z Kiddos…

The Honey Badgers

These children are out here protesting, doing sit-ins in the schools, marching, organizing, rallying, and do not have any fear. I am here for it. This is the generation that has filled the void with purpose.

We must hold our Gen Z'ers tighter as they are the product of a generation that cast themselves into darkness, had the venom of rejection and shame spat into their eyes, sat squarely in the fires of transformation and burned away all the bullshit so that we would no longer continue the cycles of toxicity and abuse our parents and generations before them exacted upon us and one another. We deconstructed and are learning how to lay the foundation for a generation who doesn't know how to exist without trauma and abuse because it is so far reaching it is in the bone and the blood.

We can hold them tight, we can protect them, even from themselves at times, we can guide them and live our lives as breathing examples of how to do life in a deep and reverent loving relationship with the self and with the community. They need the extra love and foundation, the extra help, the extra encouragement, they are struggling because the Millennials have destabilized and begun the dismantling process. Please keep the faith, love Gen Z harder, hold them tighter, offer ideas and support them as they work to find purpose in a destabilizing deconstructing non-religious world.

Years previously this would be seen as defying definition, as definition was closely aligned with religion and indoctrination and following without questioning, the footsteps of your elders. It is a very positive thing that we break from this tradition of suppression and consider the value of letting our children grow without putting our own notions of 'right' and 'wrong' on their shoulders. They dismantle what came before them, because that's human nature, if given the chance. That defies the definitions that came before them, and gives us all a chance to find new ones that are more honest.

Epilogue

Dr. Khusi Pattanayak

Defy Definitions: Celebrating Extraordinary Journeys of Underrepresented Lives was born out of the need to document stories and share stories of those eccentrics, odd balls, misfits, whom we encounter on a regular basis – in the neighbourhood, on the way to office, in the barber shop, during family get togethers – and wonder why are *they* like this!? And sometimes we, the questioner, receive the familiar cold, perplexed, bewildered look which translates as why are *you* like this!?

Ah, the irony!

The grand narrative of social expectations expects that one *must* voluntarily accept the unwritten cultural norms as all abiding because this fosters a sense of connection and understanding within the community and does not disturb the established social harmony. Yet there are individuals who refuse to abide by these rules; such willing acceptance is not spontaneous for them. This refusal to adhere to preestablished values and attitudes always pose a threat to the power structure because non-conformist behaviour unsettles those who benefit from the existing order. That is why, to retain their influence and control over society and to legitimise their ideology those in authority eulogise the normative behaviour as they question, ridicule, and look down upon those who hold an unorthodox view of life.

Eventually the freethinkers, despite their contribution to the society, are slowly and strategically pushed to the fringes of non-acceptance and gradually their presence is erased from the general discourse. They are identified as deviants and rebels who are on a mission to challenge the status quo for selfish reasons or for no reason at all - a very manipulated narrative that discourages others to consider themselves as catalyst of change that may pave foundation for societal shifts.

Furthermore, in any society the Every (wo)man, more often than not, remains an unsung hero as his/her/their story is not considered worthy enough to be remembered as their battles are belittled by the macrocosm of conformity and formalism. With the passage of time, these unique stories get obliterated as they are not endorsed or recorded by the dominant histories for they focus on the lives of ordinary people and do not belong to those who are at the apex of social hierarchy. As we grow, both intellectually and biologically, we learn to appreciate the power of collective narrative that mirrors the complexities and nuances of living within a certain socio-political context and value the need for shared humanity that unites us all, breaking down stereotypes and prejudices.

This anthology in a way is an ode to all those free spirits who have conquered their own battles; have remained unheard, unseen, and unforgiven by the society for being who they are while inspiring many with their dissenting approach.

The first essay in the anthology is Ann Doyon's

How Do You Kill a Culture? The paper raises pertinent questions those which have been deliberately dodged and ignored for decades. She wonders how, eugenics, an inhumane and barbaric form of social experiment could be appropriated in a just society that only leaves behind lost identities, inherited trauma, and broken families. Family and its paradigm are at the heart of Didi Artier's Why I'm Childfree at 53. From the vantage point of experience Artier highlights how being from a progressive society may not always mean easy acceptance for someone who is lesbian as well as childfree.

Acceptance issue reprises itself in Devereaux Frazier's I Could Tell a Lie. The essay elaborates the plights of a black man living with certain mental health condition which gets detected much later while its symptoms manifested earlier leading to collapse of self-esteem and brought in existential crisis as he found it difficult to fit into social groups. Fitting in, though of a different kind than Frazier's, forms the crux of Rebecca Huston's narrative. In her Freak, Huston informs how time and again she is rejected by the society because she did not confirm to their myopic parameters of preferences.

This limitation of choices permeates across social strata and geographical boundaries as is evident from Nimisha Bowry Dhawan's Childfree by Choice. Dhawan insists it takes immense courage to live a life that does not subscribe to generally accepted worldview and her decision to remain childfree is based on practical rational realities and is not a cowardice choice. Courage and determination defines Dr. Belinda Román's Breaking Borders. Dr. Román's position as a member of an underrepresented community taught her early in life that to earn a respectable position within the socio-political order one must be well educated. Her tale of overcoming sexism and prejudice to earn a PhD shatters numerous glass ceilings while making a case for the need for inclusion and diversity.

Inspiring journey continues as Selsene Crosier takes us through her life in My Mother My Hero. Crosier recapitulates how her otherwise voiceless mother fought against sadistic patriarchal cultural practice of female genital mutilation to give her a new lease of life. While on the other hand, memories of unfortunate motherhood made Adrija Chatterjee take certain life-altering decisions. In her Childfree by Choice, Chatterjee elucidates the repercussions of a regressive childhood; how it can have lifelong impact on an individual and why she and her husband mutually agreed it was best to not be responsible for a human life.

Human life and its unpredictability entwine in Dr. Rondalyn Whitney's Lies in the Afterlife. Having experienced death and loss from close quarters and realising the way lies and narrative function, the author through her essay reminds the readers of the absurdities of living. Even Nina Chari in No Regrets: The Barren Spinster Chronicles highlights this absurdity of living and wonders why a random stranger should have an opinion about someone else's womb! She goes on to explain that in a conservative society, even family and friends don't make it any easier for a childfree woman; they are always ready to serve the debate of no 'family' versus lack of professional advancement.

But professional advancement for a nonconformist is not easy. Elizabeth Jaeger discusses these perils in her Fired. Jaeger was fired from her position of employment in an unjust manner but she did not let this setback bother

her and continued encouraging others to embrace their true self. While acceptance of self is difficult, it is equally difficult to accept one's own surroundings at their face value. Goutam Saha points out in The Diary of a Doubtful Agnostic that questioning sacrosanct presences is an otherwise conservative society or household is always filled with unforeseen challenges.

Social challenges are visible in other forms too, for instance if a lady decides to stay childfree the society considers it to be a wasted life. Vanessa Rowan Whitfield in Moon Music explains how her decision to remain childfree gave license to society to infantilise and denigrate her. Denigration, sometimes due to ignorance, brings despair. This is evident when one reads Pallavi Deka's Dawning a Special Life. In her piece, Deka chronicles the struggles of a professionally competent mother who tries her best to raise a neurodivergent child in an uninformed sleepy town where even the best is not considered enough by the society.

Adversity becomes part and parcel of Jennifer L. Gibaldi's life as she writes in Beating the Odds. As Gibaldi tries to anchor her tempestuous existence and conquer personal and professional battles, she turns herself into an epitome of endurance and perseverance. Following Gibaldi, we have B.A. Brittingham's Oeuvre that breaks the structural tradition of the anthology with her poem - essay. Brittingham's verse composition underscoring her decision to remain childfree not only captivates the intellect with her reasons but also acts as an interlude for the book.

But intellect and reason does not hold water when caste and melanin get intertwined in social discourse. Dr. Paromita Mukherjee in her Saga of Colour writes about her ordeal of growing up in an environment that could not accept her wholeheartedly because she did not possess a certain skin tone. Sincere acceptance is equally difficult when one decides to not 'start a family,' a euphemism for not having children. Nancy Dunlop in Dear Child I Never Had addresses this by underscoring how a childfree lady is automatically designated an inferior status both in professional and personal front and why she can never be anyone's favourite.

Such misguided notions are not always conceptual, sometimes they are visual too. Kimberly Burnham in Mistaken for a Man takes the readers on a life odyssey where Burnham's androgynous appearance has confused, bemused, and offended many. Identity crisis forms the nucleus of Iris Ng's writing. In her Through a Coloured Lens: Overcoming Racism and Building a New Life for the Sake of Our Children she mentions, being a third culture kid, it was not easy for her to survive a system that viewed the world through a jaundiced eye.

It was not easy even for Aishwariya Laxmi to resist the pressure of her surroundings and chose a childfree life. In her Childfree in Chennai, the essayist makes a case for childfree individuals and wonders how fair is it to expect an individual battling physical, emotional, and psychological issues be responsible for a human form. Life wasn't fair to Khwrwmdao Basumatry either who engaged himself in serious academic pursuit to fulfil his father's wish. His Cultivating Dreams: Paving the Path to Pursuing Abroad is a story about realising the significance of education and the role it plays in building a mature society.

A matured society by the virtue of its progressive nature should accept the fact that every individual is different and no one should be labelled as 'radically deviant' for adopting an alternative view point. Suzette Bishop in It Took the Two of Us to Not Have Children reminds us precisely of this and insist that one should procreate because one wants to and not because society expects us to do so. The all-pervasive societal rejection is recounted by Kayla Pica Williams in The First Thing I've Ever Written in First Person – a poignant tale that delves into child abuse and mental health struggles.

Debasree Basu's Some (body)'s Story is reflective of the ways in which society persistently uses guilt as a weapon to emotionally manipulate independent women to 'settle down,' a very civilised way of suggesting someone get married and bear offsprings. While marriage and children are integral to any civilization, they are not particularly revered and celebrated unless they fulfil certain criteria; else they are condemned and criticised. Dr. Sureshika Piyasena's Alone is a testament to such social hypocrisy and describes how she refused to surrender to an abusive marriage.

Maria D'Arcy too fought her way to find her own happiness. In Child-free and Worry-less she informs the readers how she found support in most unexpected places that helped her overcome her personal crisis. Stories of transcending obstacles and walking through the untrodden path to create something more meaningful is intrinsically woven into Paulo Kellerman's Paper Elephants.

Frances Sanchez Merson in A Seat for Everyone recounts her determination to move out of a violent environment to explore the world which eventually brought her peace, despite all the highs and lows. Embracing the ebb and flow of life, Jalpa Sukhanandi never let her circumstances distract her from pursuing knowledge. Her essay, From Dream to Degree - My Quest for Education, emphasises the need for girl-child's education and stresses that a tiny shift in mindset can bring about an ocean of change.

As a venerable, who led a radical life, Ronnie Jameson in Isobel advices everyone to hold an empathetic view of life because 'we are all in this together'. And Susan M. Conway in Empty Spaces rightly points out that at this juncture of history we are witnessing not just individuals but an entire generation who are defying definitions in various forms and holding protests and educating the populace on issues that concern the humankind.

When I embarked on the *Defy Definitions* journey, little did I realise, just like our protagonists, I too would have a difficult path to tread.

Once I was clear on why the idea needs to be developed - to bring to light the missing alternative narratives in the ever-evolving discourse landscape - and had put a plan in place, I shared the concept with Ms. Candice Louisa Daquin, a dear friend, and an industry expert. She instantly gave her consent to be part of the project and since then has held the proverbial fort each time the weather was rough; a generous gesture, that a 'thank you' cannot compensate.

Our initial focus area of being childfree by choice came across numerous disapproving, sceptic, and contemptuous responses; only few favourable ones. On the other hand, we received many queries about considering to include submissions on other forms of social transgression. After much contemplation, we agreed to diversify and include other lived-experiences. This time we met with more enthusiastic response. But along with eagerness we were bombarded with concerning queries. Moreover, invitation to friends and acquaintance for a personal essay were politely turned down, because they did not know 'what to write,' or their struggles felt 'too privileged,' or they did not feel like sharing their struggle 'at this juncture;' as others decided to opt for a diplomatic silence. While some decided not to submit their article or withdrew their piece after second thoughts; some were not interested in sharing their photos while some had reservations about revealing their location or identity.

We were certain from the outset that we did not want any anonymous piece for the anthology as it would have defeated the purpose of the collection – to recognise the struggle of the individual; to provide a name and face to those who have remained on the margins of acceptance; and to build a supportive and non-judgmental community. Moreover, if an author decided to remain hidden under the cloak of invisibility, that meant s/he was still in the process of accepting himself/herself as s/he is within the given context, or the identity reveal might cause more harm than good to the individual; either way it did not feel appropriate to include such pieces and we were honest about it (our original call for submission was clear on that aspect).

But this process of acceptance and rejection (from both ends) made two things very clear – it takes extreme courage to tell one's own story to an unfamiliar world without worrying about the consequences; it is difficult to narrate one's own story from his or her own perspective in his/her own voice because it requires a lot of introspection and contemplation, and the war-torn opportunity- deprived capitalist-society hardly allows us any time for such self-observation.

The sole purpose of sharing the intricacies of this creative process is to reiterate the idea that no journey, from inception to completion, is seamless; to demystify the idea of a perfect reality; and that we all face challenges in each phase of life, undergo a transformative evolution before reaching our final form – either through acceptance or denial, or by aping the dominant power or by choosing to raise our own voice however meek it might be.

Barring the necessary editorial intervention, we have not meddled with the distinct authorial voices as that would have compromised the natural flow of the writing; plurality of experience; and heterogeneity of perspective. Afterall, there is no 'right' way of telling one's own story like there is no defined way of living one's own life. Thus, leaving enough room for the readers to bring their own interpretation of the first-person narrative essays.

Aakriti Kuntal's digital artwork Chords and Wings that graces the cover of *Defy Definitions* wonderfully captures the essence of the anthology. Explaining the philosophy behind the artwork, Kuntal mentions:

The movements of birds are sewn along a natural coherent energy. There isn't always a binding force. However, when one glances at the paths of the flights of birds one is quite simply engulfed by the extraordinary geometric displays. Alone, and in groups, birds come to defy expectations. They touch the nimble sky and sketch portions of absolute ecstasy for the eye to see. These coherent movements are quite akin to the thoughts and feelings in the human— when following a path, a direction, a motive, they display remarkable characteristics. Unique visions can be achieved and just like the birds appear as if they are musical notes on a sheet, so are the human's thoughts.

Defy Definitions, we realise, is unevenly balanced especially when viewed from a gendered lens. Not that we intended. But that is how it eventually was.

I hope the experiences that the anthology homes will inspire the readers to undertake a journey of self-discovery that is marked by courage, empathy, and imagination.

And before I close the pages of this anthology, I would like to extend my thanks to the fearless authors whose life stories have left an indelible mark on me; to the custodians of wisdom whose DNA I carry, Giribala and Kailash; to the goodwill strategist, Ratikanta; to the synergizer Candice; and to the dynamic cover artist Aakriti. My deepest gratitude to Mr. Satya Pattanaik and Black Eagle Books for their unwavering faith in our project and giving life to *Defy Definitions: Celebrating Extraordinary Journeys of Underrepresented Lives*.

Aakriti Kuntal

A akriti Kuntal is a poet, writer and visual artist whose work has been published in *The Night Heron Barks*, *Silver Birch Press*, *Selcouth Station*, and *Poetry at Sangam* among others. She was awarded the Reuel International Prize 2017, shortlisted for the RL Poetry Award 2018, and nominated for the Best of the Net.

She can be reached at: aakriti.kuntal@gmail.com

Instagram: aakriti_kuntal

Dr. Khusi Pattanayak

Dr. Khusi Pattanayak wanted to study at Hogwarts, but she did not receive her letter. So she decided to be a woman of letters & completed her PhD in English literature. She has swashbuckled both academia and corporate world in her 13+ years of professional experience. As a Corporate Communication expert, she has transformed words into profits and strategies into success stories; a true-blue Holmes & Poirot baby she neither overlooks an oxford comma nor a decimal point. Dr. Pattanayak writes in and translates from Odia, English, Hindi, and Bengali languages. She has collaborated as author, translator, and editor in various international projects. Books and chapters written by her are taught in several Indian universities; her columns on cinema and culture are simultaneously serious and sassy. As a visual artist she has had the honour of designing cover pages of Amazon bestsellers and has been included in prestigious art collaborations. She is also a featured model.

Dr. Pattanayak is a minimalist who believes in sustainable living & flaunting salt-pepper hair.

You can reach her through
Facebook@drkhusipattanayak or
Instagram@drkhusipattanayak or
mail her at pkhusi@rediffmail.com

Candice Louisa Daquin

Candice Louisa Daquin is of Sephardi French/Egyptian descent. Born in Europe, Daquin worked in publishing for The American Embassy before immigrating to America to study and become a Psychotherapist, where she has continued writing and editing whilst practicing as a therapist. Daquin has worked at Jewish Community Centers and Rape Crisis Centers both in Texas and Ontario, Canada. Her area of specialization is adults sexually abused as children. Prior to publishing her own poetry collections, Daquin regularly wrote for the poetry periodical Rattle and The Northern Poetry Review. Daquin is currently Senior Editor at Indie Blu(e) Publishing, a feminist micro-press and Editorial Partner with Raw Earth Ink. She edits for Parcham Literary Magazine, Tint Journal and The Pine Cone Review.

Daquin's poetic work takes its form from the confessional women poets of the 19th and 20th century as well as queer authors writing from the 1950's onward. Her career(s) teaching critical thinking and practicing as a psychotherapist have heavily influenced her work, with explored key themes including, sexual-dysfunction, sexual-abuse, parental-relationships, mental illness and queer-identity. Daquin's work is also significantly imprinted by Audre Lorde, Françoise Sagan, Angela Carter, activist

Egyptian physician Nawal El Saadawi, Navdanya seed bank creator/campaigner Vandana Shiva, Pablo Neruda, Israeli PM Golda Mier, Toni Morrison and feminist philosophers bell hooks, Hélène Cixous and Luce Irigaray.

Daquin is co-editor of the award-winning anthologies *SMITTEN This Is What Love Looks Like: Poetry by Women for Women*, *The Kali Project: Invoking the Goddess Within / Indian Women's Voices*, *The New Condemned: Contemporary Albanian Poetry in English*, *Love Letters to Ukraine from Uyava – Любовні листи до України від Уяви*, *We Will Not Be Silenced: The Lived Experience of Sexual Harassment and Sexual Assault Told Powerfully Through Poetry, Prose, Essay, and Art*. Her latest personal collection is *Tainted by the Same Counterfeit* (Finishing Line Press, 2022).

Black Eagle Books

www.blackeaglebooks.org
info@blackeaglebooks.org

Black Eagle Books, an independent publisher, was founded as a nonprofit organization in April, 2019. It is our mission to connect and engage the Indian diaspora and the world at large with the best of works of world literature published on a collaborative platform, with special emphasis on foregrounding Contemporary Classics and New Writing.